BOOKS AS BODIES AND AS SACRED BEINGS

Comparative Research on Iconic and Performative Texts

Series Editor

James W. Watts, Syracuse University.

While humanistic scholarship has focused on the semantic meaning of written, printed, and electronic texts, it has neglected how people perform texts mentally, orally and theatrically and manipulate the material text through aesthetic engagement, ritual display, and physical decoration. This series encourages the twenty-first-century trend of studying the performative and iconic uses of material texts, especially as encouraged by the activities of the Society for Comparative Research on Iconic and Performative Texts (SCRIPT).

Published

How and Why Books Matter: Essays on the Social Function of Iconic Texts

James W. Watts

Iconic Books and Texts

Edited by James W. Watts

Miniature Books: The Format and Function of Tiny Religious Texts

Edited by Kristina Myrvold and Dorina Miller Parmenter

Reframing Authority: The Role of Media and Materiality

Edited by Laura Feldt and Christian Høgel

Sensing Sacred Texts

Edited by James W Watts

Books as Bodies and as Sacred Beings

Edited by

James W. Watts and Yohan Yoo

SHEFFIELD UK   BRISTOL CT

Published by Equinox Publishing Ltd.

UK: Office 415, The Workstation, 15 Paternoster Row, Sheffield, S1 2BX
USA: ISD, 70 Enterprise Drive, Bristol, CT 06010

www.equinoxpub.com

First published in Volume 10.1–2 of the journal Postscripts.
© Equinox Publishing Ltd 2019.
© James W Watts, Yohan Yoo and contributors 2021.

All rights reserved. No part of this publication may be reproduced or transmitted in any form or by any means, electronic or mechanical, including photocopying, recording or any information storage or retrieval system, without prior permission in writing from the publishers.

British Library Cataloguing-in-Publication Data

A catalogue record for this book is available from the British Library.
ISBN-13   978 1 78179 884 3 (hardback)
           978 1 78179 885 0 (paperback)
           978 1 78179 886 7 (ePDF)

Library of Congress Cataloging-in-Publication Data

Names: Watts, James W. (James Washington), 1960- editor. | Yoo, Yohan, editor.
Title: Books as bodies and as sacred beings / edited by James W. Watts and Yohan Yoo.
Description: Sheffield, UK ; Bristol, CT : Equinox Publishing Ltd, 2020. |
Series: Comparative research on iconic and performative texts | Includes bibliographical references and index. | Summary: "In this volume, an international team of scholars addresses the theme of books as sacred beings—Provided by publisher.
Identifiers: LCCN 2020005935 (print) | LCCN 2020005936 (ebook) |
ISBN 9781781798843 (hardback) | ISBN 9781781798850 (paperback) |
    ISBN 9781781798867 (ebook)
Subjects: LCSH: Books and reading--Religious aspects. | Sacred texts—History and criticism.
Classification: LCC BL65.B66 B66 2020 (print) | LCC BL65.B66 (ebook) |
    DDC 208/.2—dc23
LC record available at https://lccn.loc.gov/2020005935
LC ebook record available at https://lccn.loc.gov/2020005936

Edited and Typeset by Queenston Publishing, Hamilton Canada.

Contents

	List of Figures	vii
1.	Introduction James W. Watts	1
2.	Performing Scriptures: Ritualizing Written Texts in *Seolwi-seolgyeong*, the Korean Shamanistic Recitation of Scriptures Yohan Yoo	9
3.	Embodying the Qur'an Katharina Wilkens	25
4.	Scriptures, Materiality, and the Digital Turn: The Iconicity of Sacred Texts in a Liminal Age Bradford A. Anderson	37
5.	Being the Bible: Sacred Bodies and Iconic Books in Bring Your Bible to School Day Dorina Miller Parmenter	51
6.	Body Building in the Hindu Tantric Tradition: The Advantages and Confusions of Scriptural Entextualization in the Worship of the Goddess Kālī Rachel Fell McDermott	67
7.	Saints' Lives as Performance Art Virginia Burrus	83

Contents

8. Aspiring Narratives of Previous Births in Written and Visual Media from Ancient Gandhāra ... 97
   JASON NEELIS

9. Daoist Writs and Scriptures as Sacred Beings ... 115
   JIHYUN KIM

10. Books as Sacred Beings ... 137
    JAMES W. WATTS

   INDICES

   AUTHOR INDEX ... 151

   SUBJECT INDEX ... 155

List of Figures

2.1	*Seolwi*, making or installing paper figures and banners.	11
2.2	A *gyeonggaek* reciting scriptures while remaining seated in a local festival.	13
2.3	*Seolwis* reflecting the contents of scriptures.	21
6.1	Diagram of the cakras in the subtle body. Kangra, Himachal Pradesh, c. 1820.	71
6.2	Ramprasad Sen (c. 1718–1775), singing to the goddess Kālī. Popular drawing, Kolkata.	71
7.1	Teresa Murak. Seed. 1976.	86
7.2	Gina Pane. Action posthume de l'action Death Control, 1974.	87
7.3	Hannah Wilke. S.O.S. - Starification Object Series. 1974–1982.	89
7.4	Hannah Wilke. "Intra-Venus Series Number 4, July 26 and February 19, 1992–1993."	90
7.5	A) The stylite-tower of Umm er-Rassas near Dibhan on the Kings' Road, Jordan. B) Luis Bunuel. "Simon del Desierto." 1965. C) St. Simeon the Stylite on his column. Mosaic in St Mark's Basilica, Venice, Italy.	92
7.6	Six Stylite Saints. Icon, date unknown. By permission of Saint Catherine's Monastery, Sinai, Egypt.	94
7.7	Pilgrim token of Saint Simeon the Younger (front and back), late sixth to early seventh century.	94
9.1	Spontaneously Formed Jade Characters (DZ97).	121
9.2	A Seal on the *Complete Works of the Patriarch Lu*.	129

— 1 —

Introduction

JAMES W. WATTS

The theme of books as bodies and as sacred beings has long played a role in my thinking about iconic and performative texts. Meerten ter Borg's essay, "Canon and Social Control" (1998), first stimulated me to think about this topic. Ter Borg pointed out that scriptural canons function as authorities less for people's beliefs than for their social identities. People feel like the scripture belongs to them, and that they belong to it. This identification and devotion gives the scripture, in ter Borg's words, a "quasi-personal charisma." George Heyman (2006 [2008], 221)[1] built on ter Borg's ideas to describe the historical relationship between changes to Roman Catholic scriptures and canon law. He concluded that "the canonical quality of law and scripture is a belief in the numinous, quasi-personal mediations of the divine in both." When I began to theorize the social effects of ritualizing scriptures, I divided scripture rituals between three different dimensions of texts: the semantic dimension of interpretation, the expressive or performative[2] dimension of reading, memorizing, singing and acting out texts, and the iconic dimension of a book's material form and visual appearance. The theories of ter Borg and Heyman led me to identify the "quasi-personal charisma" of sacred texts as the rhetorical ethos generated by ritualizing especially their iconic dimension (Watts 2006 [2008], 151–152).

---

1. References to *Postscripts* are dated as follows: cover date [publication date].
2. Though I have called this dimensions "performative" in many of my previous publications, that term creates confusion with performing rituals, which can involve all three textual dimension. "Performative" also evokes a broader range of theoretical implications (see Velten 2012) and applications (see Burrus in this volume). Therefore, I suggest calling it the "expressive dimension" instead to focus attention more narrowly on how people express the contents of texts mentally, orally, visually and dramatically.

James W. Watts is Professor in the Department of Religion at Syracuse University in Syracuse, New York, and a co-founder and Secretary-Treasurer of the Society for Comparative Research on Iconic and Performative Texts (SCRIPT)

Introduction

Confirmation of this thesis appeared in a collection of essays edited by Kristina Myrvold on disposal rituals for sacred texts in different religions and cultures. These essays repeatedly documented the human tendency to create disposal rituals for sacred texts that are modeled on funerals for humans. The most vivid example was provided by Myrvold herself. In 1988, a businessman in the Punjab created a crematorium where worn-out copies of the Sikh scripture, the Guru Granth Sahib, can be ritually disposed of in a respectful and devout manner. The grounds of the crematorium includes space furnished with beds where the books can lie in state. Then they are burned on "the respected pyre" in "a fire sacrifice" (Myrvold 2010, 135). The popularity of this practice soon led to building several more Sikh crematoria for books around India. They are willing to dispose respectfully of the scriptures of other religious traditions as well. Other essays in the volume show that Jews and Hindus have often disposed of worn-out sacred texts by imitating the funerary rituals of their traditions (Schleicher 2010, 21–24; Broo 2010, 96–102). The ancient Buddhist practice of inserting sutras in stupas imitated doing the same thing with the Buddha's bodily relics (Moerman 2010, 71). Even Christians, who have not institutionalized any rituals of book disposal, sometimes ritualize the disposal of bibles by imitating funerary burials or cremations (Parmenter 2010, 59–66). These examples show a widespread tendency to treat sacred books not only like beings and persons, but specifically like human bodies as well.

The tendency to regard iconic sacred texts as personal beings goes beyond disposal rituals. In India, it has led to granting a book legal rights comparable to those of humans or gods. In 2000, the Sikh's Guru Granth Sahib was granted the legal right to own real property. The Indian High Court classified the Guru Granth as a "juristic person," a status for corporations and other non-human legal actors that had previously been granted to images of gods ensconced in temples (Myrvold 2007, 151). Though recognizing that Sikhs regard their scripture quite differently than Hindus regard divine images, the court argued that, for legal purposes, ritual installation of the Guru Granth in its gurudwara functions similarly to divine images installed in their temples. It specifically distinguished the Guru Granth in this regard from other scriptures, such as the Bhagavad Gita, the Bible, and the Qur'an (Rao 2000; Kapoor 2010).

This limited legal analogy between deities and one book of scripture reflects much more extensive analogies promulgated by the religions themselves. William Graham (2010 [2012], 16) noted that "There is an observable tendency in every tradition for a scriptural text to partake of the transcendent reality it is perceived to reveal, represent, or mediate." Mystical traditions especially tend to equate deity with divine scriptures. Jewish *kabbalah* describes the Torah as the body of God that is composed entirely of the divine name (Wolfson 2004, 223–224). Muslim theologians debate whether the Qur'an was created by Allah or was divinely preexistent (Suit 2010 [2012], 191). Christian theology describes both scripture and Jesus Christ as the "Word of God," and medieval Christian art could treat them interchangeably (Parmenter 2006 [2008], 168–172). According to the ancient Hindu Puranas, intoning a mantra expresses the essence of a deity in sound. A book that contains the mantra therefore also makes deity visible (Brown 1986, 81). Veneration of the Buddha's Dharma in its paradigmatic expression in the *Prajñaparamita* sutras led in medieval times to the sutra being depicted and venerated in the form of a goddess (Kinnard 1999, 114–175). Today, at least one Hindu community is extending similar veneration to the *Bhagavad Gita* (Joanne Punzo Waghorne, personal communication). Such rhetoric and ritual practices treat various scriptures as more than sacred objects. They turn books into divine beings and treat them like the sacred bodies of gods.

I was delighted, therefore, to accept Yohan Yoo's invitation to give the opening paper at a symposium at Seoul National University in October, 2017, on the topic, "Books as Sacred Beings," and then to help edit the conference papers for publication. Yoo brought together an international team of scholars to address the theme of the conference from an impressively diverse range of primary materials and perspectives. As a group, their papers melded to advance previous research in solidifying the conclusion that human cultures, especially religious groups, often ritualize bodies as sacred books and books as divine beings. These studies collected here not only increase the range of examples of this phenomenon. They also show the wide variety of ways in which the identity of books, bodies and beings gets ritualized and theorized. The title of this collection, *Books as Bodies and as Sacred Beings*, therefore extends the conference title to better reflect the range of topics engaged by its chapters. The sequence of chapters roughly reflects the title's thematic sequence: we start with sacred texts as material objects that human bodies manipulate and end with transcendent textual bodies. Of course, when describing how people use books in general and sacred texts in particular, the boundary between material imminence and spiritual transcendence turns out to be very thin indeed.

Rituals frequently manipulate material scriptures while also expressing their contents using words and images. It is less common for recitation rituals to also physically reproduce scriptures on the spot in writing and graphic displays. In the first essay, Yohan Yoo describes one set of rituals that does so: shamanistic rituals of scripture reading and reproduction in North and South Chungcheong Provinces, South Korea. In contrast to shamanistic practices in other parts of Korea, here their principle ritual activity involves seated recitation of scriptures while also writing key names and cutting out symbols derived from the scriptures on paper banners. Ritualizing the expressive and iconic dimensions of formerly Daoist and

Buddhist scriptures in this way is believed to invoke the gods' presence, drive away demons, and bring healing to the sponsors of the rituals.

While internalizing a sacred text is usually taken as a metaphor for learning and practicing its teaching, it can also by physically imbibed in various ways. Katharina Wilkens builds on her previous research on imbibing Qur'anic verses and ideologies of reading (2012 [2017]) to describe the aesthetic ideology that governs rituals of embodying and sounding the Qur'an as well as drinking its letters. The description of the Prophet Mohammed as "a walking Qur'an" epitomizes the goal of Qur'anic memorization to sanctify the student by embodying the scripture. Combining these examples with a review of recent academic theories about the aesthetics of religion, Wilkens lays out the case for distinguishing semantic from aesthetic ideologies of literacy in Islamic discourse as well as in academic studies of it.

In contrast to such rituals of physically imbibing texts, much discussion today about written textuality focuses on the transformative changes brought about by e-books and online texts. Though many people lament the loss of physical contact with material books, little of this discussion has actually focused on digitization's effects on iconic texts. That is the topic broached by Brad Anderson, who surveys popular as well as academic discussions of the digitization of religious scriptures. Despite much discussion of the ritual use or misuse of digitized texts, he finds that iconic ritualization of scriptures still tends to utilize, with very few exceptions, a material book rather than its digital equivalents. Contemporary investigations of materiality in religious practices underscore the agency of physical objects in ritual practice, and elsewhere. Ritualizing iconic books, therefore, draws attention to the limitations of digital formats.

Nowhere are the advantages of material books more apparent than when displaying them to make religious or political points. Dorina Miller Parmenter describes the development of a very recent Bible ritual in the United States: Bring Your Bible to School Day. This attempt to counter the appearance of secularization in American schools and culture has mobilized as many as 650,000 Christian school children to carry and display their bibles at their schools. Parmenter analyzes the rhetoric around this Evangelical movement on the basis of traditional Protestant doctrines of scripture dating back to the sixteenth century. She points out how processing bibles and the images of doing so in news media, advocate websites and social media engage both Lutheran and Calvinist theologies of scripture. In the end, it is not the bibles but the children carrying them whom the books index as "showing God" to their schoolmates and teachers.

Such an emphasis on people embodying sacred texts is common. Rachel Fell McDermott analyzes Bengali Tantric poetry dedicated to the goddess Kālī. Culling examples from her previous publications about this tradition, she shows how Bengali court poets in the eighteenth century popularized the esoteric Tantric traditions that had become associated with Kālī over the preceding millennium. These traditions emphasized entextualizing Tantric teachings through meditation so as to reproduce the macrocosm within the microcosm of one's own body. However, later Bengali poets reflect the rising popularity of *bhakti* traditions that simplify the tradition into pure devotion to the goddess herself, rather than trying to reproduce her journey within the body. McDermott thus charts the transition from esoteric to exoteric tradition that, for most people, changed their dedication to this Tantric deity from practices to be mastered into feelings of love and devotion.

Bodily practices with written sacred texts usually take place in religious cultures that encourage a wider variety of bodily disciplines for spiritual attainment, such as fasting and purification rituals. Some people become famous for going to ascetic extremes, and as a result attract admiring hagiographers who chronicle their lives. In an essay added to this collection after the Seoul conference, Virginia Burrus recounts some vivid early Christian examples. She compares their practices to those of modern performance artists who use their own bodies as the medium for their art. Burrus notes that how the bodily performances of saints and artists affect their audiences vividly and viscerally, but also how both depend on mediation to extend their performances: the ancient saints through the texts of their hagiographies, the modern artists through photography and video technology. More than other kinds of textual mediation, however, the bodily performance draws readers' and viewers attention away from its forms of mediation. Burrus argues that the saints' performances get mediated also by art in the form of iconography and by things in the form of relics. They thus exhibit three dimensions of performativity: textual, visual and thingly.

Narratives about venerated spiritual leaders also feature prominently in Buddhist traditions and art. It has long been known that Buddhist sutras have functioned as relics to embody the Dharma since at least the first centuries C. E. Jason Neelis focuses on narratives of the Buddha's past lives to show that these stories also transmit the Dharma both verbally and visually. He describes the religious lives of these narratives by tracing them in the iconographic programs of reliefs from ancient Gandhāra, some of the earliest extant examples of Buddhist art. Gandhārī scribes and artists appropriated these narratives by associating them with local people and shrines. As a result, people made pilgrimages to these places from as far away as East Asia in order to retrace the path by which the Buddha became enlightened across his many lives. Neelis argues that the goal of such pilgrims, and of the artists who marked their routes for them, was to come closer to enlightenment themselves by bodily following the spiritual path of the Dharma as described in these narratives.

Introduction

There is a mystical tendency in many religious traditions to consider their scriptures transcendent in one way or another. There are, for example, old Jewish and Muslim claims that the prototype of the Torah or Qur'an was written by God at the creation of the world and continues to reside in heaven. Jihyun Kim describes how Daoists made an even more fundamental claim. They regarded their scriptures as embodying *qi*, the fundamental energy of the cosmos. It produced scripts and scriptures even before the creation of the world, and the look and sound of sacred texts brought it into being. Daoist ritual uses of scripture therefore aimed to engage a transcendent and primordial state of being.

The tendency of books to be ascribed agency like people and deities leads me, in the last chapter, to explore why that is. Books manifest interiority like people: we speak of both as material containers for immaterial ideas. Books also generate common out-of-body experiences, they can be reproduced in multiple copies, and encountering them often changes us. Books are therefore material artifacts whose common use generates analogies that reinforce widespread hopes for bodily transcendence, resurrection or reincarnation, and theophany.

The Seoul conference in 2017, and therefore this volume of essays, was made possible by a generous grant from CORE (the Initiative for College of Humanities Research and Education of the Korean Ministry of Education) and the office of Research Affairs at Seoul National University, for which we are very grateful.

References[3]

Broo, Måns. 2010. "Rites of burial and immersion: Hindu ritual practices on disposing of sacred texts in Vrindavan." In *The Death of Sacred Texts: Ritual Disposal and Renovation of Texts in World Religions*, edited by K. Myrvold, 91–106. London: Ashgate.

Brown, C. Mackenzie. 1986. "Purāṇa as scripture: From sound to image of the Holy Word in the Hindu tradition." *History of Religions* 26: 68–86.

Graham, William A. 1987. *Beyond the Written Words: Oral Aspects of Scripture in the History of Religion*. Cambridge: Cambridge University Press.

Heyman, George. 2006 [2008]. "Canon law and the canon of scripture." *Postscripts* 2(2–3): 209–225.

Kapoor, Desh. "Lord Ram as juristic person and legal history of religious juristic persons." Pantheos, October 1, 2010. Online at http://www.patheos.com/blogs/drishtikone/2010/10/lord-ram-juristic-person-and-legal-history-religious-juristic-persons/ (accessed 9/21/2017)

Kinnard, Jacob N. 1999. *Imaging Wisdom: Seeing and Knowing in the Art of Indian Buddhism*. Surrey: Curzon.

---

3. References to *Postscripts* are dated as follows: cover date [publication date].

Moerman, D. Max. 2010. "The death of the dharma: Buddhist sutra burials in early medieval Japan." In *The Death of Sacred Texts: Ritual Disposal and Renovation of Texts in World Religions*, edited by K. Myrvold, 71–90. London: Ashgate.

Myrvold, Kristina. 2007. *Inside the Guru's Gate: Ritual Uses of Texts among the Sikhs in Varanasi*. Lund: Media-tryck.

Myrvold, Kristina. 2010. "Making the scripture a person: Reinventing death rituals of Guru Granth Sahib in Sikhism." In *The Death of Sacred Texts: Ritual Disposal and Renovation of Texts in World Religions*, edited by K. Myrvold, 125–146. London: Ashgate.

Parmenter, Dorina Miller. 2006 [2008]. "The Iconic Book: The image of the Bible in early Christian rituals." *Postscripts* 2(2–3): 160–189 = *Iconic Books and Texts*, edited by J. W. Watts (Sheffield: Equinox, 2013), 63–92.

Parmenter, Dorina Miller. 2010. "A fitting ceremony: Christian concerns for Bible disposal." In *The Death of Sacred Texts: Ritual Disposal and Renovation of Texts in World Religions*, edited by K. Myrvold, 55–70. London: Ashgate.

Rao, T. Padmanabha. "Guru Granth Sahib, a juristic person: SC." *The Hindu*, April 3, 2000. Online at http://www.thehindu.com/2000/04/03/stories/01030005.htm (accessed 9/21/2017).

Schleicher, Marianne. 2010. "Accounts of a dying scroll: On Jewish handling of sacred texts in need of restoration or disposal." In *The Death of Sacred Texts: Ritual Disposal and Renovation of Texts in World Religions*, edited by K. Myrvold, 11–30. London: Ashgate.

Suit, Natalia K. 2010 [2012]. "*Muṣḥaf* and the material boundaries of the Qur'an." *Postscripts* 6(2–3): 143–163 = *Iconic Books and Texts*, edited by J. W. Watts; (Sheffield: Equinox, 2013), 189–206.

Ter Borg, M. B. 1998. "Canon and social control." In *Canonization and Decanonization*, edited by A. Van der Kooij and J. van der Toorn, 411–423. Leiden: Brill.

Velten, Hans Rudolf. 2012. "Performativity and Performance." In *Travelling Concepts for the Study of Culture,* edited by Ansgar Nunning and Birgit Neumann, 249–266. Berlin: de Gruyter.

Watts, James W. 2006 [2008]. "The three dimensions of scriptures." *Postscripts* 2(2–3): 135–159 = *Iconic Books and Texts,* edited by J. W. Watts (Sheffield: Equinox, 2013), 9–32.

Wilkens, Katharina. 2012 [2017]. "Infusions and fumigations: Literacy ideologies and therapeutic aspects of the Qur'an." *Postscripts* 8(1–2): 115–136 = *Sensing Sacred Texts*, edited by J. W. Watts (Sheffield: Equinox, 2018), 115–136.

Wolfson, Elliot R. 2004. "Iconicity of the text: Reification of Torah and the idolatrous impulse of Zoharic Kabbalah." *Jewish Studies Quarterly* 11: 215–242.

— 2 —

Performing Scriptures:
Ritualizing Written Texts in *Seolwi-seolgyeong*, the Korean Shamanistic Recitation of Scriptures

Yohan Yoo

Performing scriptures by reciting, writing and materializing

Seolwi-seolgyeong is a shamanistic ritual that has been handed down around North and South Chungcheong Provinces, South Korea. *Seolwi-seolgyeong* has characteristics that distinguish it from other Korean shamanistic rituals. Above all, the main part of the whole ritual consists of the recitation of scriptures, in which shamans invoke the power of the gods appearing in scriptures. Shamans of Chungcheong area are commonly called "*gyeongjaeng-i*" or "*gyeonggaek*," which means "a person who deals with scriptures," and their activity in rituals is called "*dokgyeong*," which literally means "reading scriptures." From these names that emphasize scriptures, we can see that the recitation of scriptures has been recognized as the most important part of this ritual. While shamans in most other areas of Korea perform their rituals standing and enacting the stories of gods, the *gyeonggaek*s in the relatively long *seolwi-seolgyeong* rituals of the Chungcheong area remain seated and recite scriptures while beating a drum (*buk* or a double-headed drum called *janggu*) and a gong (*jing*). In addition, unlike shamans of most other areas in Korea, the shamans in the *seolwi-seolgyeong* ritual do not serve the gods lavish meals. Instead, the recitation itself is the main offering, and this is how one pleases the gods, though sometimes a very simple meal is also offered. *Gyeonggaek*s also strongly rebuke and subdue evil spirits through the power of scriptures, while in most other shamanistic rituals evil spirits are either propitiated or not directly dealt

---

Yohan Yoo is Professor and Chair of the Department of Religious Studies in the College of Humanities at Seoul National University, Korea

with at all. The *seolwi-seolgyeong* ritual is distinctive in that the *gyeonggaek* shaman is able to wield tremendous power in invoking gods and subduing evil spirits without ever having to leave his or her seat.

In this article, I demonstrate how the sacred power of scriptures is maximized and how their sacred status is secured in *seolwi-seolgyeong* by articulating a comprehensive way of performing scriptures.[1] Above all, in *seolwi-seolgyeong*, the gods' presence is made possible by performing scriptures in several ways: scriptures are recited, written, and materialized. Just like Judeo-Christian and Islamic traditions (Peters 2007, 140), scriptures are recited and what is recited is accepted as the divine beings' own words in *seolwi-seolgyeong*. It is clear that the sacred power of scriptures is mobilized primarily by being recited. But writing and materializing scriptures are also involved. "*Seolwi*," the first half of the name of this ritual, is commonly understood as making or installing various geometric paper figures and banners that represent or contain the contents of the scriptures. By making *seolwi*, scriptures are materialized and their power is made visible and physically available. Though the scriptures themselves in book form are rarely visible in the ritual place, the sacred status and power of scriptures that suppress the evil spirits are made clearly visible by their materialized contents and the embodiment of their main characters.

Furthermore, in *seolwi-seolgyeong* we can see how various rituals privilege and distinguish scriptures from other things.[2] First, scriptures themselves as well as their words are distinguished from other texts when lay participants as well as shamans agree that scriptures are the words of divine beings. As a result, the performative activity of reciting the scriptures is equated with proclaiming divine words. Ritualized scriptures distinguish themselves as sacred and as able to exercise the power of "realities thought to transcend the powers of human actors" (Bell 1992, 74). The recitation is a ritualized act that is differentiated as important, powerful, and sacred (Bell 1992, 90). The success of *seolwi-seolgyeong* relies heavily on vari-

---

1. This work was supported by the Seoul National University Research Grant in 2018.
2. The term "ritualization" is usually used to describe certain social actions that distinguish and privilege themselves in comparison to other actions (Bell 1992, 74, 88-93). According to Catherine Bell, "ritualization is a matter of various culturally specific strategies for setting some activities off from others, for creating and privileging a qualitative distinction between 'sacred' and 'profane,' and for ascribing such distinctions to realities thought to transcend the powers of human actors" (Bell 1992, 74). Ritualized acts are differentiated as more important or powerful and often have a dominant status (Bell 1992, 90). Though scriptures themselves are not actions or activities, they are objects in ritual activities and sometimes their presence makes ritual activities effective. Therefore, as Watts persuasively showed (Watts 2006 [2008]; Watts 2017, 257–260, 266), it can be said that scriptures are ritualized.

ous recitation techniques which are necessary in order to defeat evil spirits and heal patients efficiently. This ritualization is more effective when the recitation is performed more skillfully. Finally, the contents of scriptures are ritualized when shamans materialize them into paper figures on the basis of their interpretation of the cosmology and theology in scriptures. This material ritualization makes the contents seem so sacred that they are able to subdue evil spirits and resolve human problems.

Scriptures used in *seolwi-seolgyeong* rituals

Though there are different interpretations of the name of this ritual according to local shamans, the first half of the name, *seolwi*, usually designates figures and banners that are used in shamanistic rituals in the Chungcheong area or the activity of making and installing these figures and banners, while the second half, *seolgyeong*, is understood as reciting scriptures (Gu 2009, 21). Paper figures reflect the core contents of scriptures and are believed to help defeat evil spirits. Paper banners, on which are written the names of gods appearing in scriptures and sometimes words, phrases, or passages from scriptures, carry out the same function. The second part of the title, "*seolgyeong*," signifies the recitation of scriptures that is performed

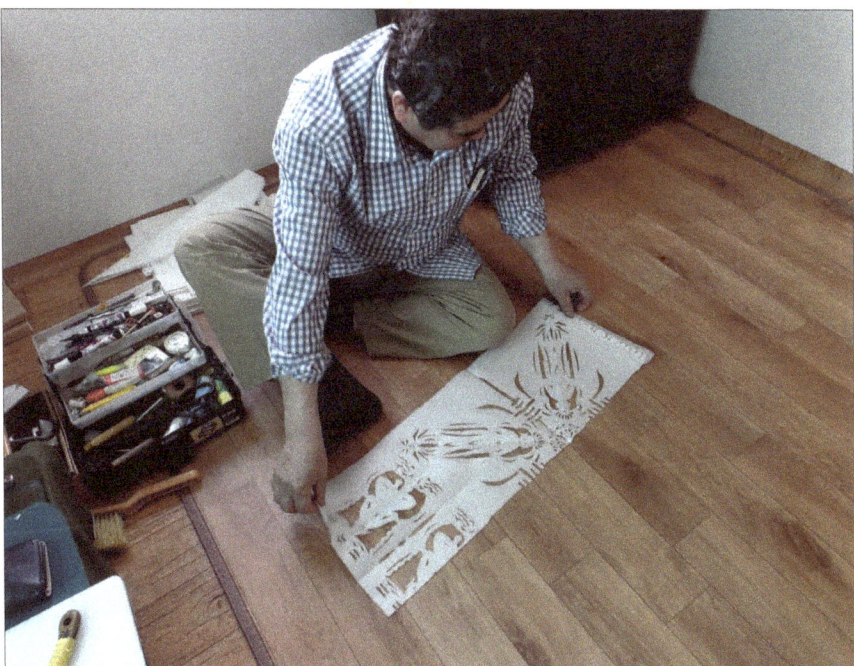

Figure 2.1 *Seolwi*, making or installing paper figures and banners. Photo: author.

for the purpose of solving human problems with the aid of the gods (Lim 2011, 12–13; Jang 2013, 342). Shamans and participants in the Chungcheong area often refer to the *seolwi-seolgyeong* as an *anjeungut*, the "sitting rite." But strictly speaking, *anjeungut* is a more comprehensive term than *seolwi-seolgyeong* because sometimes it designates simpler rituals in which shamans are seated and recite scriptures without making and installing paper figures or banners. A *gut* is a general term for a Korean traditional shamanistic ritual of propitiating the gods, performed by shamans for the benefit of individuals, families, and village communities. The name *anjeungut* underscores the fact that the "sitting" (*anjeun*) dimension of this particular *gut* is what sets it apart from other *gut*s (Lim 2011, 14).

In *anjeungut*s, shamans generally do not read from texts, but rather recite from memory. By the early twentieth century, the job of reciting scriptures to repel evil spirits was often taken on by blind persons, who naturally could not read books in the literal sense (Gu 2009, 36–37; Yi 1989, 264–265). However, shamans and participants also use the term *dokgyeong*, literally meaning "reading scriptures," to signify the main activities in the ritual. This term emphasizes the literal, textual, bookish dimension of scripture, because the activity of reading requires a book in its physical form. "*Dokgyeong*" can refer to the actual recitation activity within the *gut* but can also simply refer to the whole *anjeungut* (Gu 2009, 178), demonstrating that the recitation of scripture is the basic component of the ritual.

Some scholars think that performers of *anjeungut* should not be included in the category of shamans because they are not possessed by gods during the ritual, unlike shamans in many other areas in Korea.[3] However, the view that *anjeungut* should be regarded as a shamanistic ritual is more prevalent. Western and Japanese scholars who visited Korea in the late nineteenth century or early twentieth century considered *anjeungut* a kind of shamanistic ritual. More contemporary scholars also include *gyeonggaek*s among shamans who stand between gods and human beings, who try to alleviate human suffering with the help of the gods, and who carry the gods' messages to human beings (Kim, Park, and An 2012, 15; Lim 2011, 52; Park 2014, 604). Most of all, *gyeonggaek*s themselves think that they are *musogin*s, Korean shamans. They are active members of the Korean federation of shamans. *Gyeonggaek*s of Chungcheong Provinces whose main ritual job is the seated recitation of scriptures have played the same role

---

3. Though I am aware that "shaman" is highly controversial because of the variety of people this term encompasses, I decided to use it to translate *musogin* or *mudang* in Korean. In most Korean-English dictionaries, the first word suggested for their translation is "shaman."

Figure 2.2 A *gyeonggaek* reciting scriptures while remaining seated in a local festival. Photo: author.

as shamans in other areas, that is, as a mediator between the divine realm and the human realm. They play the role of a healer who treats human suffering or a diviner who tells clients' fortune with the aid of the gods or sometimes on the basis of sacred knowledge that is unknown to lay participants (Kim, Park, and An 2012, 29–30). It is true that they are not possessed by gods or spirits during the ritual, but they invite gods to the ritual place and consult them in order to be given divine messages. On the other hand, *gyeonggaek*s were sometimes more respected than other shamans because they were literate and performed rituals while sitting demurely, in contrast to the "primitive" gesticulations associated with most *gut*s. While conservative Confucian scholars of the late Joseon period (seventeenth to nineteenth centuries) abhorred and prohibited *gut*s performed by the shamans possessed by spirits who often danced and hopped during the ritual, they did not ban *anjeungut*s where scriptures are read by persons seated decently (Kim, Park, and An 2012, 16).

*Anjeungut*s can be divided into two types, according to their purposes. The first type, called *antaekgut*, is conducted to invoke the blessings of the guardian gods who govern the different aspects of the home, such as the building, the plot, the main bedroom, the living room, and the kitchen, asking for the peace and stability of the household. Though these favorable gods are offered a simple meal during this ritual, the whole procedure is mainly carried out verbally. For instance, the purification ritual that is performed at the beginning of the *antaekgut* is comprised of recited scriptures, mostly the *Bujeonggyeong* ("Scripture for Impurity") that is recited to remove the impurity of the ritual place, and the *Bosingyeong* ("Scripture of Self-protection") which proclaims that the shaman reciting the scripture is a descendent of the heavenly gods and thus possesses divine mysterious power (An 2009, 106-108; 148-150).[4] The core part of *antaekgut*, calling the gods and communicating with each god, also consists of reciting relevant scriptures.

The second type of *anjeungut* is conducted for the purpose of warding off misfortunes or calamities. *Byeonggut*, "the ritual for sick persons," is the most commonly performed of this second type of *anjeungut* rituals. While the first type of *anjeungut* can be carried out without paper banners and figures, they are usually required for the second type. The main part of the *byeongguts* is, again, the recitation of scriptures, but in these rites the *gyeonggaeks* also perform dramatic actions. *Gyeonggaeks* recite scriptures to invoke the power of Cheonjon, the highest god of Heaven, to summon warrior gods who help subdue the evil spirits to the ritual place, and to repel the evil spirits that cause illness and other misfortunes (Kim, Park, and An 2012, 35–41). It is the power of scriptures that subdues the evil spirits called *dongto* and *sagwi*, expels them from the home, and cures sick persons. Sometimes scriptures are recited in *byeongguts* for the purpose of appeasing dead ancestors' deep-rooted rancor and sending them peacefully to the otherworld. *Byeongguts* are usually conducted for three, five, or seven days depending on the severity of the conditions. The god Seongju, who governs the house building, decides the necessary period of time by means of an oracle. It is said that in particularly severe circumstances, the ritual could take up to one hundred days. Before a *byeonggut* is conducted, an *antaekgut* is performed to purify the house and invite the household gods. During the *byeonggut*, the recitations are punctuated by intermittent dramatic performances, such as dispatching ancestors to the otherworld after quelling their grudges, beckoning the warrior gods to descend from the heavens, and subduing evil spirits by trapping them in a bottle and physically removing them from the house.

---

4. Shamans and the house owners are also required to bathe themselves in preparation for the ritual but their bathing is not a part of *antaekgut*. While *antaekgut* usually begins in the evening and ends at dawn, bathing, along with cleaning the house, is done in the morning on the day the ritual is performed. Purifications conducted as a part of *antaekgut* consists just of reciting scriptures (Kim, Park, and An 2012, 79).

The scripture that shamans recite most often for repelling evil spirits is *Okchugyeong*, originally a Daoist scripture. The second most important scripture for the same purpose is *Cheonjipalyanggyeong*, originally an apocryphal Buddhist scripture. But there are much shorter texts in the form of incantations or prayers which are recited in each sequence of *seolwi-seolgyeong*. The last text recited in the ritual is *Toesingyeong*, a brief scripture for sending back the gods away from the ritual place. The contents of many texts used in *seolwi-seolgyeong* threaten evil spirits. Though some are crude incantations, most of them are scriptures that have their own logic derived from other religious traditions, such as the Confucian theory of five elements or Buddhist cosmology (Kim, Park, and An 2012, 46–47). The contents of threats against evil spirits that are contained in scriptures are "not simple intimidation but are explained by cause-and-effect relationships and secure their legitimacy firmly by citing from Confucian, Buddhist, and Daoist thought" (An 2010a, 146). By reciting these scriptures, shamans therefore invoke deities not only traditional to Korean shamanism, but also those who originated in Daoism and Buddhism, and they subdue evil spirits by their power (Lim 2011, 17).

However, obvious threats do not appear at all in the two most important scriptures for removing evil spirits and misfortunes, *Okchugyeong* and *Cheonjipalyangsinjugyeong*. These two scriptures are mainly composed of teachings given to human beings by transcendental beings, Cheongjon and the Buddha. Originally, the revealer and the speaker of *Okchugyeong*, the Gucheon-eungwon-noeseong-bohwa-cheonjon, "the heavenly god of universal transformation of the sound of the thunder of responding origin in the nine heavens," was one of the three major deities of the Shenxiao Daoist tradition in China. He represents life and the esoteric practice of the thunder, and shows the explicit influence of Buddhism (*vajra*) (Schipper and Verellen 2004, 1082–1083). Shamans pray to this heavenly god for resolving troubles in human lives. He is believed to save human beings by revealing his true way. This Daoist scripture is thought to have been adopted by Korean shamans because of its postscript, which states: "if you recite this scripture, you can annihilate all evil spirits and overcome all kinds of illness" (An 2009, 97).[5] This is the most powerful scripture that

---

5. *Okchugyeong* or *Okchubogyeong* (*Yushubaojing* 玉樞寶經 in Chinese) is the most important scripture in Korean shamanism. It consists of 6 divine incantations (or prayers), 9 chapters on heaven, 11 chapters on earth, 15 chapters on humans, and 15 talismans (Gu 2009, 253). It was originally a scripture of the early Shenxiao (神霄) tradition, one of the Chinese Daoist schools in Southern Song period (1127–1279). This book is regarded as a work of the early thirteenth century but the earliest extant version has a colophon dated 1333. Since *Okchugyeong* is mentioned in *Suhoji*, a very popular Chinese novel written in the fourteenth century, this scripture seems to have circulated

can "melt down" evil spirits (or their bones) by being recited (Gu 2009, 44). In *anjeunguts*, shamans repeatedly recite parts of *Okchugyeong* that they think are appropriate for their clients' situation. *Cheonjipalyangsinjugyeong* begins with the words "thus I have heard," just as in other Buddhist sutras, and it takes the form of the Buddha's teaching, but reflects a Daoist understanding of the cosmos and human beings. There are no direct threats against evil spirits in these two scriptures. They are about understanding the world and the ideal lives of human beings, as explained by Cheonjon and the Buddha (An 2010b, 16, 21).

It is fairly understandable that people think evil spirits can be subdued by the recitation of the scriptures in which divine beings rebuke and threaten them. Scriptures can be "the most important symbol of power" through which gods talk and act (Wimbush 2012, 163). As shown above, however, a scripture can subdue evil spirits even if it does not speak against evil spirits directly, because of the divine authority and power that is present in it. Scriptures can "convey mysterious power that has its origin in another realm—from God—and that can be employed to influence others" (Wimbush 2012, 177). This is the power of the sacred scripture. Reciters and hearers, as well as readers, think that "scriptures are relevant, cryptic, and perfect because they think scriptures come from God [gods]" (Watts 2017, 256 citing Kugel 1997, 14–23). In the ritual space of *seolwi-seolgyeong*, hearers of recited scriptures, as well as the reciters themselves, believe that the scriptures come from the gods. Because participants think scriptures come from gods, they assume that scriptures not only contain divine messages but also divine power. Though human hearers may not understand the meaning of a scripture being recited, its power can be utilized as long as people believe it to be of divine origin. Thanks to the ritualization of this belief through recitation and materialization, scriptures are recognized as

---

in China in this period at the latest (An 2009, 92). This book is included in the Fourth Daozang (Daoist Canon) which was collected mainly in 1444 during the Ming dynasty. Its original full name, *Jiutianyingyuanleishengpuhuatianzunyushubaojing* is translated into English as "Precious Book of the Jade Pivot, Spoken by the Heavenly Worthy (God) of Universal Transformation of the Sound of the Thunder of Responding Origin in the Nine Heavens." Concerning the Shenxiao tradition and this scripture, see Schipper and Verellen 2004, 1081–1095.

Okchugyeong seems to have come into Korea in the fourteenth century at the latest, since *Gyeonggukdaejeon*, the royal law book of the Joseon dynasty (1392–1910) that was compiled during the mid-fifteenth century, attests that this scripture was recited by Daoist priests. Though in the early Joseon period, Daoist rituals were performed by Daoists who held government office, Daoism was considered heretical by Confucian scholars and Daoist offices were closed from the sixteenth century on. This Daoist scripture was accepted by Korean shamans, however, and became the most important shamanistic scripture. See An 2009, 96–98; Gu 2009, 96; Jang 2013, 354–356.

sacred beings. Shamans who have special knowledge of scriptures exert divine authority and the power of scriptures by reciting them.

In *seolwi-seolgyeong*, we find the belief expressed that scriptures recited by shamans can mobilize the gods appearing in the scriptures, subdue evil spirits, and solve human problems. The power of scriptures enables shamans to threaten and defeat evil spirits, rather than merely propitiate them. It is certain that reciting, or literally "reading," scriptures is at the center of this ritual. However, *seolwi-seolgyeong* has also devised other means of maximizing the power of scriptures through the visualization and materialization of scriptures.

Maximizing sacred status and power of scripture by recitation and materialization

Many Korean Buddhists have claimed the power of scriptures by reciting and copying them (see Yoo 2010 [2012][6]). However, it is rare among Korean religious traditions for scriptures to be recited, written, and materialized within the space of a single ritual. Because *seolwi-seolgyeong* involves reciting, writing, and materializing scriptures, it can be said that *seolwi-seolgyeong* is a comprehensive example of the performance of scriptures. Though nowadays there are fewer and fewer shamans who are well acquainted with the contents of the scriptures, traditionally it was necessary for shamans in the Chungcheong Provinces to be versed in the contents in order to be qualified to perform *seolwi-seolgyeong*.[7] Even if the

---

6. References to *Postscripts* are dated as follows: cover date [publication date].
7. It is necessary to master shamanistic scriptures in order to become a *gyeonggaek*. Applicants master scriptures by learning from established *gyeonggaek*s both orally and in writing. In the past, when blind persons often played the role of *gyeonggaek*s, they had to learn everything orally but nowadays there are few blind persons who take the job. Applicants listen and learn by heart what their teachers recite, then they write it in notebooks and memorize it (Park 2010, 68). Some applicants receive the manuscripts that their teachers wrote and recopy them in order to memorize them (An 2010a, 150). Those who have little acquaintance with classical Chinese cannot learn scriptures written in classical Chinese characters with Korean endings, but can only listen to what is recited and write its phonetic pronunciation in Korean (Oh 1997, 98). Recently two noticeable changes among *gyeonggaek*s and the scriptures they are using have been observed. First, the number of experts in shamanistic scriptures is decreasing drastically. A survey conducted in 1976 showed that there were two thousand and fourteen *gyeonggaek*s practicing in North Chungcheong Province, while the number of other types of shamans in that area was only sixteen (Seo 1991). But nowadays this proportion has reversed in Chungcheong Provinces, perhaps because the shamans who perform *gut*s more dynamically are more popular. Second, the proportion of the shamans who do not understand the contents of scriptures in classical Chinese rises year by year. This change is predictable, as the study of Chinese characters has declined drastically since the modernization of Korea beginning in the late nineteenth century.

performers and the audience in the ritual arena may not understand the recitation, the evil spirits do, and they are influenced by it. *Gyeonggaek*s should also be skilled in the recitation techniques thatare required for inviting gods and subduing evil spirits efficiently in various situations. In addition, they should be expert in making paper banners and figures, that is, in materializing scriptures. In *seolwi-seolgyeong*, scriptures are materialized in order to threaten, trap, and expel evil spirits by making and displaying the banners on which are written the names of the gods in the scriptures or in important scriptural passages and figures that reflect the contents of scriptures.

Shamans and the laity in the Chungcheong region say that the most important skill in the performance of *anjeungut*s is recitation technique, the second is playing the drum and gong, and the third is knowledge of the texts. The recitation techniques are considered most important in the first place because they have a decisive effect on the outcome of the ritual. In *seolwi-seolgyeong*, various reciting techniques and methods should be utilized according to the purpose of the ritual and the condition of the patient. The recitation techniques making use of rhythm, tone, pitch, tempo, and dynamics are all crucial for pleasing gods and threatening evil spirits. *Gyeonggaek*s are aware that the better their recitation techniques, the more efficacious the ritual (Han 2017). For instance, in the invocation of the warrior gods and the subduing of the evil spirits, reciters must use urgent and commanding tones with a quick tempo and beat the drums and gongs intensely in order to achieve the goal. They cannot successfully placate the deep-rooted rancor of the ancestors unless they recite the relevant scripture in an appropriately plaintive voice.

Recitation techniques are also counted as most important among the three skills of *gyeonggaek*s because the divine beings are believed to come to the ritual place and work there only through skillful recitations. Many religious traditions in which scriptures are recited tend "to use tone and rhythm to project the voice and make the reading more memorable" (Watts 2017, 259). But tone and rhythm are important here not only for hearing and memorizing scriptures but also for fulfilling the purpose of the ritual and for having the divine be involved in the ritual. In *seolwi-seolgyeong*, these techniques are necessary in order for the gods to become the

---

As these shamans recite scriptures in classical Chinese without knowing their meaning just like uttering incantations, more changes in the text of scriptures come about (An 2010b, 9). Though it is true that changes and the creation of new scriptures have always taken place because the efficacy of the ritual recitation is regarded more highly than its accuracy, those who know only the phonetic values of the text venture to change scriptures more quickly on the basis of their own suppositions about the contents of scriptures (Gu 2009, 137).

subjects and agents of the ritual. As Kimberley Patton properly points out, we often forget that the divine is not just the object but "the subject and agent of the religious action" (Patton 2009, 15). The gods who listen to the skillful recitation are persuaded to come to the ritual place and do their work as the main characters of the ritual; they give orders to *gyeonggaek*s, overpower the evil spirits, heal patients, and give notice if the ritual was successful or not. The recitation, the activity of performing scriptures, is distinguished as more important and powerful than other ritual acts when people equate it with proclaiming the divine words. But this ritualization of the recitation must be completed and consolidated by proper techniques. Without them, the divine words are not efficacious and the sacred power of scriptures is not revealed.

Some scholars do not agree with the view that recitation techniques are the most important among the three skills. They argue that the importance of recitation techniques is overemphasized due to the fact that lay participants do not understand what is recited (An 2010a, 150; Kim, Park, and An 2012, 48–49; Oh 1997, 100–101). These scholars emphasize the contents of scriptures rather than the technique for reciting them, asserting that knowledge of the texts should be counted as the most important skill. It is understandable that the host, the owner of the house where the ritual is performed, and other participants who have not had professional training cannot understand recited scriptures, which are mainly composed of Classical Chinese words with Korean endings. It is true that some *gyeonggaek*s are proud of their specialized knowledge of the texts and their ability to choose and recite specific texts depending on the situation. However, it should be noted that shamans' competence with scriptures matters mainly because it is an efficient tool for inviting the gods and defeating evil spirits, not because the knowledge itself has more value than recitation techniques. Gods and evil spirits are thought to understand the meaning of what is recited and respond to it. The contents of scriptures are privileged, not because they are learned and studied by human beings but because they are efficacious in expelling evil spirits and healing patients.

The conduct of *seolwi-seolgyeong* employs not only the sound of reciting scriptures but also the visualization and materialization of scriptures to call the gods and subdue evil spirits. Traditionally, *gyeonggaek*s are trained to be skillful in making *seolwi*s, paper banners and figures in *changhoji*, traditional Korean paper made from mulberry bark (Oh 1997, 113). They write on it the names of gods or phrases from scriptures and they cut into it images of gods or symbolic traps reflecting the contents of scriptures. These banners and figures therefore show the words of the gods and their majestic world to evil spirits. A *byeonggut*, which is the most common ritual among the second type of *anjeungut*s and is performed to heal sick persons, begins by writing the names of gods or words of scriptures and making paper figures. Scriptures are materialized through these banners and figures, which are important material ingredients in a successful performance of *seolwi-seolgyeong*.

Many *gyeonggaek*s say that they make paper figures on the basis of their understanding of the contents of *Okchugyeong* (Lim 2009, 83, 90–91). In this sense, the process of creating them can be said to be interpreting the scripture.[8] When they make these figures, they embody and visualize the divine wisdom and the cosmology shown in scriptures, especially that of *Okchugyeong*, as they understand it (Lim 2009, 93). *Gyeonggaek*s represent their interpretation of scriptures as paper figures. In other words, the semantic dimension of scriptures is ritualized iconically in the creation of *seolwi*s.

Paper banners, on which the names of gods and important passages from *Okchugyeong* or other scriptures are written, extend the recitation visually (Lim 2009, 95). Paper figures, which are materialized scriptures, have the power of trapping evil spirits in them as well as scaring them away (Park 2010, 74). They enable the power of scriptures to be exerted in full measure. Lim explains how recited scriptures, written scriptures, and materialized scriptures work together, in the following way:

> In hearing the scripture for expelling evil, the evil spirit begins to be frightened. And its fear doubles when it sees the banners of the words from scriptures, which are installed in the hall in which the ritual is conducted. Eventually, it is trapped in the *jinbeop* [battle array] of the paper figures. Now it can be put in a bottle by the *beopsa* [*gyeonggaek*].[9] The voice of the *beopsa* reciting scriptures makes a sound effect that threatens the evil spirit and the *seolwi* produces a visual one. The patient and his or her family who watch the ritual become convinced that the evil spirit will soon be controlled. Basically, therefore, the *seolwi* that is installed in the ritual place works together with the content of scriptures that is recited by the *beopsa*.
> (Lim 2011, 22)

---

8. Though these *gyeonggaek*s argue that their paper figures come from the scripture, it should be noted that most paper figures of the Chungcheong region are not much different from those of other areas in Korea where shamans do not claim scriptures as the basis of paper figures. It is possible that *gyeonggaek*s, at least sometimes, ascribe meanings extracted from the scripture to the preexisting paper figures rather than create the figures on the basis of the scripture.

9. "*Beopsa*" originally means a Buddhist monk who is an expert and teacher of dharma. But the meaning of this term has been extended to designate a male shaman, or more specifically in Chungcheong Provinces a *gyeonggaek*. It is thought that Korean shamanism accepted this term to show more respect for shamans by equating them with respectable Buddhist monks (Oh 2016).

Figure 2.3 *Seolwis* reflecting the contents of scriptures. Photos: author.

Evil spirits understand what is recited, written, or materialized and are overwhelmed by its power. They are frightened and subdued when they hear the recitation of scriptures and see words from scriptures and materialized forms of scriptures.

To utilize the power of scriptures to the utmost, shamans should recite scriptures by using various techniques, write the names of gods that appear in scriptures or important passages from scriptures on paper banners, and materialize scriptures by making figures that reflect their contents.

Conclusion

In the *seolwi-seolgyeong* ritual, scriptures are considered so powerful that they can take over the other dynamics of shamanistic rituals, such as possession or dance. In this ritual, scriptures are performed mainly by recitation. But the recitation is supplemented with other ways of performing scriptures, namely writing and materializing them in paper, to maximize their power. When scriptures are written and materialized to be used as the shaman's tool, as well as recited in the ritual, their contents are realized and simultaneously their sacred status is established. Recitation of scriptures is the nucleus of *seolwi-seolgyeong*. Properly performed recitations are believed to invite the gods to the ritual place and enable them to work there, as well as to subdue evil spirits. During most of the ritual, shamans are seated and recite scriptures to pray for peace in the household and expel evil spirits from it. Though lay participants do not understand the meaning of recited scriptures, it is still regarded as important because gods and evil spirits understand it. There are scriptures whose contents are related to threatening or defeating evil spirits. But the most powerful scriptures that can even melt down the bones of evil spirits are those that focus on the teachings of the heavenly god and the Buddha concerning the cosmos and the human beings. For *seolwi-seolgyeong* to be most efficacious, recitation of scriptures should be supported by materializing and visualizing scriptures. Evil spirits become frightened and weakened when they see and read paper banners on which the names of gods appearing in scriptures and passages from them are written. The paper figures that visualize gods scare evil spirits and those that reflect the cosmology and theology of scriptures can hedge them in and trap them.

In this ritual process, scriptures are privileged and distinguished as sacred beings in several ways. First, scriptures are distinguished as sacred beings when shamans and other participants in *seolwi-seolgyeong* agree that the words in them are no less than the words of divine beings. Scriptures ritualized as such can exert transcendental power. Second, the ritual activity of performing scriptures, the recitation, is believed to be the proclamation of the divine words. This ritualization should be completed and consolidated by proper techniques, without which the divine words cannot be efficacious. Third, the contents of scriptures are also ritualized when the teachings of the divine beings in the scriptures are considered so sacred that the contents can defeat evil spirits and heal the patients and when shamans materialize them as paper figures on the basis of their interpretation of the cosmology and theology in scriptures.

References

An, Sanggyeong. 2009. *Anjeungut Mugyeong*. Seoul: Minsokwon.

———. 2010a. "Chungcheong-do Anjeungut Jikyeo-on Gono Gyeonggaeng-ui Hanseureon Chugwon." *Minjok* 21(5): 146–151.

———. 2010b. "Gyeryongsan Samsindanggut Mugyeong-ui Gujo-wa Uimi." *Urimalgeul: The Korean Language and Literature* 50: 129–159.

Bell, Catherine. 1992. *Ritual Theory, Ritual Practice*. Oxford: Oxford University Press.

Gu, Junghoe. 2001. *Gyeryongsan Gutdang Yeongu*. Seoul: Gukhakjaryowon.

———. 2009. *Gyeongchaek Munhwa-wa Yeoksa*. Seoul: Minsokwon.

Han, Jeongdeok. 2017. "Seolwi-seolgyeong-gwa Gyeongjeon." Interview with Yohan Yoo conducted on May 18.

Jang, Inseong. 2013. "Chungcheong Jiyeok-ui Anjeungut-gwa Jeong-ilgyo." *The Journal of Humanities Studies* 93: 341–360.

Kim, Yeongjin, Hyejeong Park and Sanggyeong An. 2012. *Chungcheong-do Anjeungut*. Cheongju: Chungcheongbuk-do Munhwa Yusan Yeon-guhoe.

Kugel, James L. 1997. *The Bibel As It Was*. Cambridge, MA: Belknap.

Lim, Seungbeom. 2009. "Chungcheonggut-ui Seolgyeong Yeon-gu." *Korean Shamanism* 18: 83–107.

———. 2011. *Taean Seolwi-seolgyeong*. Seoul: Minsokwon.

———. 1997. "Buyeo Jiyeok-ui Anjeungut." *The Journal of Korean Historical-folklife* 6: 91–121.

Oh, Munseon. 2016. "Beopsa." In *Han-guk Minsok Daebaekgwa Sajeon (Encyclopedia of Korean Folk Culture)*. http://folkency.nfm.go.kr/kr/topic/%EB%B2%95%EC%82%AC/2168

Park, Hyejeong. 2014. *Yangban Go-eul Yangban Gut: Chungnam-ui Anjeungut Eumak*. Seoul: Minsokwon.

Park, Jong-ik. 2010. "Daejeon Anjeungut Munyeo Songseonja-ui Gyebo-wa Seolgyeong." *The Journal of Humanities Studies* 79: 63–88.

Patton, C. Kimberley. 2009. *Religion of the Gods: Ritual, Paradox, and Reflexivity*. Oxford: Oxford University Press. https://doi.org/10.1163/156852712x630842

Peters, F. E. 2007. *The Voice, the Word, the Books: The Sacred Scriptures of the Jews, Christians, and Muslims*. Princeton, NJ: Princeton University Press. https://doi.org/10.1515/9780691190471

Schipper, Kristofer and Franciscus Verellen, eds. 2004. *Taoist Canon* Vol 2. Chicago, IL: University of Chicago Press. https://doi.org/10.1017/s0021911807001465

Seo, Daeseok. 1991. "Dokgyeongsinang." In *Han-guk Minjok Munhwa Daebaekgwa (Encyclopedia of Korean Culture)*, Volume 7, edited by Han-guk Jeongsin Munhwa Yeonguwon, 42–44. http://encykorea.aks.ac.kr/Contents/Index?contents_id=E0015943

Watts, James W. 2006 [2008]. "The Three Dimensions of Scriptures." *Postscripts* 2(2–3): 135-159.

———. 2017. *Understanding the Pentateuch as a Scripture*. Oxford: Wiley-Blackwell.

Wimbush, Vincent L. 2012. *White Men's Magic: Scripturalization as Slavery*. New York: Oxford University Press.

Yi, Neunghwa. 1989 [1959]. *Joseon Dogyosa*. Seoul: Boseongmunhwasa.

Yoo, Yohan. 2010 [2012]. "Possession and Repetition: Ways in which Korean Lay Buddhists Appropriate Scriptures." *Postscripts* 6(1–3): 243–259.

— 3 —

Embodying the Qur'an

KATHARINA WILKENS

An aesthetics of religion approach to texts

There has been a rise in recent research on material and bodily aspects of practices surrounding the Qur'an. These include recitation, calligraphy and illumination, but also the rules surrounding the handling of the physical book (the *muṣḥaf*) as well as production and use of amulets and Qur'anic medicine.[1] Aesthetics of religion is a fairly young field of research that is interested in precisely such sensual, embodied and material aspects of religious thought and practice. Religious traditions have developed an impressive variety of theories on sensual perception, the materiality of the world and the functioning of the human body.

We learn and know about the world not just through intellectual learning, but—quite obviously—also through sensual perception, the imitation of peers and elders and simply by doing things. Philosopher Alexander Baumgarten (in conversation with Schelling and Kant) argued that intellectual knowledge is always complemented by aesthetic (sensual) knowledge and thus merits philosophical inquiry in its own right (Cancik and Mohr 1988; Gross 2011). Aesthetics of religion is indebted to this approach in its quest to describe and analyze sensual bodies of knowledge in the history of religions. As the history of philosophy, of the humanities and of science is intimately tied up with the history of religion in Europe (and of Christianity in particular), a self-reflective view of our discipline's genealogy must by necessity be part of the endeavor (Promey 2014).

---

1. For some recent studies see Kermani (2014), Perho (2006), Suit (2010 [2012]), Wilkens (2012 [2017]).

Katharina Wilkens is a Research Associate and Lecturer in the Study of Religion at Ludwig Maximilians University, Munich, Germany

Western academic research is bound up in its own epistemological history of materiality, embodiment and sensual perception. The Cartesian divide between body and mind, the intellectual emphasis on disembodied reason, semantic knowledge and anti-ritualism has led to a focus on texts and on theologies as thought systems. Ritual studies and performance studies were among the first research fields that questioned the dominant paradigm of philology in the study of religions. Aesthetics of religion takes up the "material turn" and adds a specific focus: Sensual or bodily ways of knowing. My focus in this paper lies on ways of knowing encoded in sacred texts. Thus, the questions arising here are: How can we conceive of texts in a way that includes aesthetic aspects of knowledge? What academic ideologies exist around this subject, and what different types of intellectual and aesthetic knowledge can be found among religious practitioners (including diverse schools of theology)?

Rudolf Ware speaks of an "epistemic chasm" (Ware 2014, 68; see also Gril 2006) dividing Western and traditional Islamic ideologies of what the text of the Qur'an is all about. Contrasting Western colonial ideologies of language and those of the local Indonesian population, Webb Keane (2003) has differentiated between different semiotic ideologies. Annette Hornbacher (2016) further differentiates between local Balinese, Hindu, and colonial scriptural paradigms while simultaneously deconstructing oppositional approaches to literacy by anthropology and philology. While the former paradigms involve layers of meaning and efficacy embedded in the graphic signs, sounds and written texts, the latter distinction refers to differences attributed to ritual and semantic meaning within Western academic tradition. She concludes that studying traditional Balinese scripture is a methodological challenge forcing scholars to refine their analytic approach to different types of scripturality. Intertwining religious and intellectual history more closely, Robert Yelle (2013) traces the ideological shift in semiotics and literacy that occurred with the rise of modernity. He documents shifting linguistic practices in the fields of religion and law that showcase the process of Western secularization. For example, repetitive oral formulas considered as binding juridical pronouncements were discredited as magic, which was premised on older Christian supercessionist theology that denounced Jewish religion. With a view to educational paradigms in Islamic countries, Robert Launay (2016b) aptly distinguishes between writing boards and blackboards. While the former are used in some more traditional Qur'an schools and are representative of a corporeal episteme governing their approach to the Qur'an, the latter stand for a semantic episteme favored in Western-style colonial schools. Jonas Svensson (2014), who has researched the handling of *muṣḥaf* in Kenyan schools, has put forward a theory which distinguishes between two approaches to the sacred text of the Qur'an. He distinguishes between two cognitive systems: a theory of mind with a view to the deity speaking through the Qur'an, and a system of contagion responsible for the material sanctions implemented to protect the *muṣḥaf*. He argues that the contradictions between the two approaches "become understandable if viewed from the perspective of distinct mental systems operating in different situations and on the basis of different cues, and of one system overriding the other in particular circumstances" (Svensson 2014). I have argued that we can differentiate between various literacy ideologies, especially with regard to texts considered to be sacred. The literacy ideology most common in academic environments, but also in reformed Christianity or in current movements of reformist Islam, can be characterized as semantic-purist, while more Catholic Christian or traditional (Prophetic) Islamic approaches to sacred images and texts can be characterized as somatic-iconic (Wilkens 2012 [2017][2]).

The double perspective of reconstructing religious aesthetics and deconstructing the Western aesthetic paradigm has been fruitfully applied to sonic theology in Hinduism (Wilke and Moebus 2011). The example I want to present here is equally intriguing. Well established Islamic teachings as well as locally accepted practices surrounding the nature and the usage of the Qur'an demonstrate an aesthetic ideology about the text that is far removed from intellectual reason alone.

The "walking Qur'an": Embodying the Qur'an through memorization

There is a widely-known Islamic saying that Aisha, the wife of the Prophet, characterized Mohammed as a "walking Qur'an."[3] Because Mohammed was the medium of revelation and thus knew the Qur'an by heart, his whole being, body and mind, are thought to reflect the teachings of the sacred text. This saying is generally used to denote Mohammad as an exemplary character and a model of a pious Muslim in general, but also specifically in the context of Qur'an memorization and schooling (for example, Balouch 2013).

The image of a "walking Qur'an" is most consistently applied, however, to the educational principle of Qur'anic schools, or *madrasas*. Qur'anic schools are a central feature of Islamic education, especially for younger children.[4] The ostensive purpose of the schools is to teach children the

---

2. References to *Postscripts* are dated as follows: cover date [publication date].
3. This narration is based on several *hadīth*, of which the most commonly cited is found in the Sunan of Ibn Majah, chapter 15. http://ahadith.co.uk/ibnmajah.php
4. For an overview of *madrasa* education in general see Hefner and Zaman 2007; for the situation in Africa see Launay 2016a. The classic study on the "art of memorization" and madrasa education in pre-colonial Morocco is Eickelman 1978.

Qur'an by memorizing its text. The English phrase "learning by heart" comes closest to the idea of a walking Qur'an: memorization is a process of incorporating the sacred words in a quite literal sense. The entire body is involved in the learning process and as a result the person who learns the Qur'an is thought to be sanctified in body and soul. Building a "good character" and memorization are always co-equal aims of Qur'anic education (Launay and Ware 2016, 258).

The transmission of a textual corpus (such as the Qur'an, but also other texts of theology or law) through memorization usually entails a very close master-disciple relationship. The text embodied by the teacher is passed on physically to the body of the disciple through the sounding of the words. Authority is derived from a lineage of teachers in addition to the mastery of the text. Accordingly, the "chain of transmission" (*silsila*) is the foundation of the theological validity of any Prophetic saying or interpretation of the Qur'an. Launay and Ware (2016, 260) argue that "religious authority is entirely personalized, indeed personified. It is not possible to distinguish clearly between the content of knowledge and the person who possesses it." Normally, children will only learn the most commonly used *sūrah*s from the Qur'an and then quit the school after a few years. Some people, though, commit the entire body of the text to memory. These people are honored by being given the title of *ḥāfiẓ*. They carry special blessings that can be passed on to their listeners and disciples.

But while the human body is heavily involved in the learning process, the body of the holy book, the *muṣḥaf*, is also accorded special respect. The children are habituated to the physical handling of the holy book. The actual book is treated quite differently from all other religious or secular books. This includes the bound book, all kinds of notebooks or scraps of paper used during classes or, in other countries, the wooden boards on which the text is written during school. Over the centuries, elaborate theological debates have theorized the ritual handling of the book and many debates over practical problems have been conducted. The *muṣḥaf* must be kept ritually pure. It must not be dirtied by being placed on the ground or by being taken to the bathroom. People who touch the *muṣḥaf* must be ritually pure themselves. A *muṣḥaf* may not be destroyed other than by fire. These and some further rules are taught and learned in Qur'anic schools.

The text of the Qur'an is (almost) never read out in a speaking voice, but is chanted. Children learn a simplified version, but those who continue on to higher education will learn professional chanting. As William Graham (1987, 113 *et passim*) has pointed out, chanting and listening are sensual, even visceral experiences often moving people to tears.[5] It is this chanting

---

5. The study by Navid Kermani (2014) on the aural, oral and sonic aspects of Qur'anic

that is considered to be the essence of the beauty of the Qur'an as the word of God (Kermani 2014). Listening to the chanting is an emotional and bodily experience (Scheer 2012). Listening to the sonic quality of the text is an attitude of attention that one learns in mosques and also in the Qur'anic schools. Thus, the memorization of words is not just an intellectual exercise, but a synesthetic experience of seeing the words written down, of touching and handling the material on which the words are written, and of hearing them being recited while rocking rhythmically to their cadence.

Children in Qur'anic school learn the holy text in its original ancient Arabic language, the only version of the Qur'an used liturgically throughout history and in all countries. This means that the text that is actually memorized is not understood by the children, nor even by speakers of modern Arabic. But since most parts of the Qur'anic text are written in a poetic style with rhythm and occasional rhymes and since the text is chanted, these poetic features function as vital mnemonic devices enabling children to learn the sound of the text rather than its meaning.

It should be noted, however, that the meaning of the text is always discussed alongside its memorization. But understanding the meaning is not actually the explicit aim of Qur'anic education, it is rather a side product arising as a matter of course, just like literacy in the Arabic script. Besides the Qur'anic text, a number of set prayers and other liturgical elements are taught and practiced in schools, as well as the central narratives from the Qur'an and Islamic history, the meaning of the Islamic feast days, the rules of Ramadan, and the main features of the pilgrimage to Mecca (for a Swedish curriculum, see Berglund 2010). But this formal knowledge of Islamic history and ritual practice is considered to be secondary to the memorization of the text. In the hierarchy of Islamic academic disciplines, textual interpretation with the help of rational arguments follows after memorization, pronunciation and grammar. A semantic-hermeneutic approach to texts is thus always part of academic thinking, but it is premised on first having memorized the text in order to secure its sacred quality.

The didactic emphasis on memorization in Qur'anic schools was always heavily criticized by Western educators because it reverses the Western, or rather semantic, emphasis on rational argument and on studies independent of a specific teacher. In particular, the repetitiveness of memorization and the recitation of unintelligible texts was regarded as "parrot talk" (Loimeier 2009, 244–245). This derisive attitude against "vain repetition" is

recitation of the Qur'an is considered to be one of the founding works in the field of aesthetics of religion. The central argument of the sonic and somatic-sensual quality of the spoken Qur'an alongside its semantic content was previously discussed at length by William Graham (1987).

characteristic of the modernization and secularization process as a whole, first in seventeenth century Europe and later in the European colonies, including India and Africa (Yelle 2013). It remains a central characteristic of the semantic-purist approach to literacy that dominates academic discourse, especially in the fields of philology and hermeneutics. Recent studies in Islamic education, however, have argued that rather than dumbing down the pupils, the practice of memorization inculcates a synesthetic experience of the text which is then employed in theological, political and cultural debates. Theoretical emphasis is laid on the concept of embodiment. Authors such as Boyle (2006) and Sabki and Hardaker (2014) align modern theories of embodiment in pedagogy and cultural phenomenology with theological arguments of incorporating sacred words through memorization – such as al-Ghazali's theory of learning linking the physical heart with the metaphysical heart, a connection of subtle, spiritual quality.[6]

Embodying the Qur'an as medicine

Another practice involving material aspects of the holy text was described as abhorrent superstition by a number of Western travelers and Orientalists in the early twentieth century: Drinking the Qur'an as medicine.[7] There is a widespread understanding among Islamic scholars that the Qur'an itself has healing powers. The Word of God is thought to have an immediate and physical effect on human beings and the material environment—which is why memorization is conceptualized in such a physical way as described above. This physical effect can also be utilized to heal diseases. An oft-quoted hadith from the Sahih of al-Bukhari states that "there is no disease that Allah has created, except that He also has created its remedy."[8] The Qur'an itself states, "And We sent down in the Quran such things that have healing and mercy for the believers" (an-Najm 17:82). In the well-established and very popular tradition of Prophetic medicine, the Qur'an has established itself as a physical remedy for the treatment of afflictions of body, mind and soul. The most common application involves reading the verses and breathing these verses onto the body. This is most commonly

---

6. It should be noted that memorizing the Qur'an is no longer regarded as the only educational principle recommended for children. In the Arab countries that have adapted French schools, modern reformed madrasas (Arabic schools) combine elements of the French curriculum with some elements of specifically Islamic education such as memorization. For quite diverse examples, see Launay 2016a for an overview of the situation in various African countries or Berglund 2010 for curriculum developments in Islamic schools in Sweden.

7. For a more detailed overview of drinking the Qur'an, see Wilkens (2012 [2017]).

8. Sahih of al-Bukhari, Book 76 "On Medicine," opening hadith. https://sunnah.com/bukhari/76

referred to as *ruqya*. There are long lists of verses considered to be effective for specific ailments.

The verses can also be read over water after which the water is drunk. The Qur'anic words can be given material form by writing them down and then fumigating the paper and ink. Or the verses can be written down with saffron and rosewater ink onto a plate, then rinsed off with water that is drunk as medicine. One or the other of these remedies is known and practiced throughout the Islamic world while being adopted to local tastes, hygienic expectations and availability of materials.

In most South Asian cultures, for example, an Islamic specialist writes specific verses onto a white porcelain plate with ink made from saffron and rosewater. The ink is then washed off the plate with some more water; the mixture is collected, bottled and given to the patient to drink, usually over a period of a week or two. In India, fumigation is more popular, but I also know of examples of fumigation in Sudan. In Turkey and many Arab countries, Qur'anic verses are spoken over water which is then drunk. In East Africa, two types of remedies exist. On Zanzibar, people prefer writing on plates though the red color of the ink is achieved by adding food dye to the water rather than expensive saffron. In most mainland areas of East Africa, people more often write some verses onto plain paper, immerse that paper into a glass of water and then drink that. Both methods are attested in medieval handbooks of Prophetic medicine.[9] In West Africa, wooden boards are still used in the children's Qur'anic schools. The school teacher is often the same person who is consulted in cases of affliction, so the board is used just as in school: the verses are written onto the board with black ink made from ashes, then washed off, collected, bottled and given to the patient to drink over a period of a week or so.

It must be noted that Islamic scholars do not agree whether this type of medicine is allowed or not. Many classify it under "forbidden magic" and prohibit its use. This fight over textual and material authority in Islamic tradition has been waged since the very beginning and continues to influence modern-day practice. But neither side has ever won conclusively. Quite often, the practice is forbidden publicly, but engaged in privately. Because the treatment of family illness often falls under the purview of women, there is also an element of gender division in the demand for Qur'anic medicine. The sociological differences between the clientele and critics thus complements the distinction between semantic-purist and somatic-iconic literacy ideologies. Both can exist in different milieus of the same culture or even within the same families.

---

9. Such as in the handbook on prophetic medicine *Ṭibb al-Nabbi* by al-Suyūṭī (1445–1505), translated in Elgood 1962,155f.

Hanna Nieber summarized the beliefs in Zanzibar about the medical efficacy of drinking the Qur'an in the following way: "For Talib Ali [an Islamic healer], the heart's belief and trust are constitutive for the unfolding and efficacy of the embodied Qur'an to work against affliction. When seen in this light, drinking *kombe* [Qur'anic verses immersed in water] could be understood as a practice that presupposes and requires a body with a heart in which belief/trust in the Qur'an's efficacy are situated – a heart that understands" (Nieber 2017, 12). Thus the basis for a literacy ideology of the somatic-iconic type is a heart, or body, that understands the words of the Qur'an in a sensuous way rather than in an intellectual way. Healing efficacy and such an understanding of an embodied text go hand in hand.

Conclusion

I have presented two aspects for understanding the Qur'an within the framework of a somatic-iconic literacy ideology, the somatic and personalized aspects of Qur'anic education and the materiality of Qur'anic medicine. In Islamic theology, the Qur'an is thought to have two forms, the text in its divine form, co-eternal with Allah as his word, and the material manifestation of the text as book made of paper and binding called the *muṣḥaf*.[10] The former manifests itself most readily in the form of recitation, in its sonic quality – the word "Qur'an" literally means to "recite". Qur'anic readings are a constant acoustic backdrop in many Islamic cities through radio broadcasts or cassettes turned up in public busses or via the loudspeakers of the mosques. Just as the sonic quality of the words is conceptualized as having such material effects as to merit the effort of memorizing them in the *madrasas*, the same material quality is guarded in the form of the book.

The rules of the *muṣḥaf* generally apply only to a complete Arabic-only Qur'ans. But to a lesser degree, this kind of ritual sanctification is also accorded to all materials on which Qur'anic verses are written, including translations, notebooks in schools and other scrap material. Circling back to Qur'anic education, the *muṣḥaf* concept has consequences for the materials used during schooling. The verses the children write down and read are usually discarded after some time. Most teachers and students find pragmatic ways of dealing with such day-to-day materials (for a Kenyan example, see Svensson 2006). In West Africa and Sudan, the children wash off their writing boards, catch the washing water in bowls and then drink the concoction in order to reinforce the memorization of the lesson of the day. In this case, the multiple consequences of a somatic-iconic approach to the holy text become immediately clear: drinking the ink saves the verses

---

10. For an excellent summary of the concept of *muṣḥaf*, see Suit 2010 [2012]. For an historic overview of the development of the concept, see Zadeh 2009.

from touching the ground in accordance with the rules of ritual purity pertaining to the *muṣḥaf*. Drinking the ink also reinforces the somatic aspect of memorization as an incorporation of the sacred words into the character of a person. And finally, the somatization of the text is put to work as a medicine for heart, body and soul. For Rudolph Ware (2014), washing the writing board is the primary example of a textual episteme completely at variance with both Western academic and Salafi reformist ideologies which reduce the text to an intellectual exercise alone. The aesthetic way of knowing a text, this somatic-iconic literacy ideology, needs further explorations to theorize more fully the multiple layers of efficacy and meaning a sacred text can have.

References

Balouch, Asif. 2013. "How To Be A Walking Quran." On *Islamic Learning Materials*, directed by Muttaqi Ismail. 27 October. http://islamiclearningmaterials.com/walking-quran/

Berglund, Jenny. 2010. *Teaching Islam. Islamic Religious Education in Sweden*. Münster: Waxmann.

Boyle, Helen N. 2006. "Memorization and Learning in Islamic Schools." *Comparative Education Review* 50(3): 478–495. https://doi.org/10.2307/4091412

Cancik, Hubert and Mohr, Hubert. 1988. "Religionsästhetik." In *Handbuch der religionswissenschaftlichen Grundbegriffe*, edited by Hubert Cancik, Burkhard Gladigow and Matthias Laubscher, 121–156. Stuttgart: Kohlhammer. https://doi.org/10.1017/s0395264900059370

Eickelman, Dale F. 1978. "The Art of Memory: Islamic Education and its Social Reproduction." *Comparative Studies in Society and History* 20: 485–516. https://doi.org/10.1017/s0010417500012536

Graham, William A. 1987. *Beyond the Written Word. Oral Aspects of Scripture in the History of Religion*. Cambridge: Cambridge University Press.

Gril, Denis. 2006. "Le corps du Prophète." *Revue des mondes musulmans et de la Méditerranée* [online] 113–114. http://remmm.revues.org/2966

Gross, Steffen W. 2011. *Cognitio sensitiva. Ein Versuch über die Ästhetik als Lehre von der Erkenntnis des Menschen*. Würzburg: Königshausen & Neumann.

Hardaker, Glenn and Sabki, Aishah Ahmad. 2014. "Islamic Pedagogy and Embodiment. An Anthropological Study of a British Madrasah." *International Journal of Qualitative Studies in Education* 28(8): 873–886. https://doi.org/10.1080/09518398.2014.917738

Hefner, Robert W. and Zaman, Muhammad Qasim, ed. 2007. *Schooling Islam. The Culture and Politics of Modern Muslim Education*, Princeton, NJ: Princeton University Press. https://doi.org/10.7146/tifo.v3i1.24561

Hornbacher, Annette. 2016. "Introduction. Balinese Practices of Script and Western Paradigms of Texts. An Anthropological Approach to a Philological Topic." In *The Materiality and Efficacy of Balinese Letters*, edited by Richard Fox and Annette Hornbacher, 1–22. Leiden: Brill. https://doi.org/10.1163/9789004326828_002

Keane, Webb. 2003. "Semiotics and the social analysis of material things." *Language & Communication* 23(3–4): 409–425. https://doi.org/10.1016/s0271-5309(03)00010-7

Kermani, Navid. 2014 [1999]. *God is Beautiful: The Aesthetic Experience of the* Quran. Translated by Tony Crawford. Cambridge: Polity.

Launay, Robert, ed. 2016a. *Islamic Education in Africa. Writing Boards and Blackboards.* Bloomington and Indianapolis: Indiana University Press. https://doi.org/10.1111/amet.12535

Launay, Robert. 2016b. "Introduction: Writing Boards and Blackboards." In *Islamic Education in Africa. Writing Boards and Blackboards*, edited by Robert Launay, 1–26. Bloomington: Indiana University Press. https://doi.org/10.2307/j.ctt1zxz0gv.4

Launay, Robert and Ware III., Rudolph T. 2016. "How (Not) to Read the Qur'an? Logics of Islamic Education in Senegal and Côte d'Ivoire." In *Islamic Education in Africa. Writing Boards and Blackboards*, edited by Robert Launay, 255–267. Bloomington and Indianapolis: Indiana University Press. https://doi.org/10.2307/j.ctt1zxz0gv.16

Nieber, Hanna. 2017. "'They all just want to get healthy!' Drinking the Qur'an between forming religious and medical subjectivities in Zanzibar." *Journal of Material Culture* 22(4): 453–475. https://doi.org/10.1177/1359183517729427

Perho, Irmeli. 2006. "Medicine and the Qur'an." In *Encyclopaedia of the* Qur'an, volume 3, edited by Jane Dammen McAuliffe, 349–367. Leiden: Brill.

Promey, Sally M. 2014. "Introduction." In *Sensational Religion. Sensory Cultures in Material Practice*, edited by Sally M. Promey, 1–21. New Haven, CT: Yale University Press. https://doi.org/10.1017/s0009640715000402

Scheer, Monique. 2012. "Are Emotions a Kind of Practice (And Is That What Makes Them Have a History)? A Bourdieuian Approach to Understanding Emotion." *History and Theory* 51(2): 193–220. https://doi.org/10.1111/j.1468-2303.2012.00621.x

Suit, Natalia K. 2010 [2012]. "Muṣḥaf and the Material Boundaries of the Qur'an." *Postscripts* 6(1–3): 143–163.

Svensson, Jonas. 2006. "Have you all got your copy of the Qur'an? Rationalisation, Ritual and the Role of God's Word in a Kenyan Islamic Educational Setting." *Tidsskrift for Islamforskning* 1: 1–27. http://lnu.diva-portal.org/smash/get/diva2:272961/FULLTEXT02.pdf

———. 2014. *The Double Scripture: Explaining Diversity and Conflict in Muslim Perceptions and Practices in Relation to the* Qur'an (conference abstract). http://lnu.diva-portal.org/smash/record.jsf?pid=diva2%3A734090&dswid=1056

Ware III, Rudolph T. 2014. *The Walking Qur'an. Islamic Education, Embodied Knowledge, and History in West Africa.* Chapel Hill: The University of North Carolina Press. https://doi.org/10.5149/northcarolina/9781469614311.001.0001

Wilke, Annette and Moebus, Oliver. 2011. *Sound and Communication. An Aesthetic Cultural History of Sanskrit Hinduism.* Berlin: De Gruyter. https://doi.org/10.5149/northcarolina/9781469614311.001.0001

Wilkens, Katharina. 2012 [2017]. "Infusions and Fumigations: Literacy Ideology and Therapeutic Aspects of the Qur'an." *Postscripts* 8(1–2): 115–136.

Yelle, Robert. 2013. *The Language of Disenchantment: Protestant Literalism and Colonial Discourse in British India.* Oxford: Oxford University Press. https://doi.org/10.1093/acprof:oso/9780199924998.003.0006

Zadeh, Travis. 2009. "Touching and Ingesting: Early Debates over the Material Qur'an." *Journal of the American Oriental Society* 129(3): 443–466.

— 4 —

Scriptures, Materiality, and the Digital Turn: The Iconicity of Sacred Texts in a Liminal Age

Bradford A. Anderson

Introduction: The digital turn

When asked several years ago about his thoughts on eBooks and Amazon Kindle, author Ray Bradbury responded:

> Those aren't books. You can't hold a computer in your hand like you can a book. A computer does not smell. There are two perfumes to a book. If a book is new, it smells great. If a book is old, it smells even better. It smells like ancient Egypt. A book has got to smell. You have to hold it in your hands and pray to it. You put it in your pocket and you walk with it. And it stays with you forever. But the computer doesn't do that for you (Weller 2010).

Many people, I suspect, sympathize with Bradbury. At one level, physical books seem irreplaceable—the dogeared pages, the coffee stains, the attendant aromas. However, at another level, books appear to be very much replaceable. While recent signs have suggested that the sale of e-books has slowed somewhat (Flood 2016; Cain 2017), we nevertheless live in an age when digital texts not only exist, but are becoming more commonplace. Mobile readers such as the Amazon Kindle along with tablets, apps, and other digital devices have shifted how both producers and consumers think about books, texts, and reading (Ingram 2015). Whatever the actual numbers, it is clear that how people think about and use written texts is changing (McGann 2014).

Similar questions arise in relation to sacred texts where, for many people, the stakes are higher. Critical analysis of the use of scriptures in digital culture has to this point largely focused on digital scholarship (see for example: Parker 2003; Clivaz, Dilley, and Hamidović 2016), though recent

---

Bradford A. Anderson is Head of the School of Theology, Philosophy, and Music of Dublin City University in Dublin, Ireland, and the Editor of *Postscripts: The Journal of Sacred Texts, Cultural Histories, and Contemporary Contexts*

years have witnessed a growing interest in the digital use of these texts outside of academia (Hutchings 2015; 2017; Richardson and Pardun 2015). This essay contributes to this conversation by exploring two related questions. First, how might we begin thinking about the use of scriptures in digital culture, particularly in light of the iconic function of sacred texts? And second, how might the material dimensions of sacred texts contribute to this analysis, specifically in relation to the texts of Judaism, Christianity, and Islam?

The iconic function of scriptures

While analysis of sacred texts is a practice with ancient roots, scholarship on these writings has focused primarily on their content rather than phenomenological issues such as the functional use of such texts. However, a growing number of scholars have, in recent decades, begun reflecting on the diverse uses of scriptures (Graham 1987; Cantwell Smith 1993; Malley 2004; Parmenter 2006 [2008][1]; Bielo 2009). Among these is James Watts, who has proffered a helpful three-dimensional model for understanding the functional dimensions of scriptures, where the ritualized use of scriptures can be classified heuristically in terms of a semantic dimension, a performative dimension, and an iconic dimension. Drawing on Smith (1987) and Bell (1992), among others, Watts notes, "the otherwise trivial practices involved in reading a book are, in the case of scriptures, given sustained attention. [...] The *more* a book or text is ritualized in *all three* dimensions [...] the more likely it is to be regarded as a scripture. Thus the functional identification of scriptures depends not on a difference in kind from other books and writings, but on the *degree* to which a particular book or writing is ritualized as text *and* as performance *and* as icon" (Watts 2006 [2008], 146).

The semantic dimension has to do with the content and meaning of what is written, and engagement with the written word. This "includes all aspects of interpretation and commentary as well as appeals to the text's contents in preaching and other forms of persuasive rhetoric" (Watts 2006 [2008], 141). Meanwhile, the performative dimension of scriptures, Watts suggests, is the performance of what is written, be it the performance of the words or the contents of scriptures. This can take the form of ritualized public readings, recitation of texts, musical performance or singing of scriptures, dramatic presentation, and artistic illustration (Watts 2006 [2008], 141–142).

Beyond the semantic and performative levels, Watts notes that scriptures function as icons. These texts are iconic in that they point to something beyond themselves. As such, their physical forms are treated

---

1. References to *Postscripts* are dated as follows: cover date [publication date].

differently from other books. "They are often displayed prominently on podiums or tables, hung on walls, or else hidden within special cases that call attention to them" (Watts 2006 [2008], 142). Further, we also see such texts "manipulated in political ceremonies—displayed or touched as part of oath ceremonies and waved in political rallies and protests" (Watts 2006 [2008], 142). As a result, scriptures often come to be identified with the tradition as a whole, and so also with the legitimization of particular traditions. The issues of scriptural iconicity and legitimacy lead to another issue, which is the potential desecration of scriptures. Watts notes that "the iconic dimension of scriptures [...] can be manipulated by anyone who gains access to a copy of the book. [...] Ease of access also means that the iconic dimension is most easily attacked by deliberately mishandling the scripture. Such ritual abuse is called 'desecration'" (Watts 2009, §1). Such use "also explains the explosive social power of desecrating scriptures. Insofar as the scripture has become identified with the religion to the point that the tradition's legitimacy is conveyed by [...] the material book, its ritual abuse can feel like an attempt to delegitimize the whole religious tradition" (Watts 2009, §1).

The rise of digital media has undoubtedly altered the textual landscape and the way in which people interact with sacred texts. What happens, though, when we think about these technological changes in light of these theoretical reflections on the diverse use of scriptures, particularly the iconic function of such texts? How has the digital turn impacted this aspect of scriptural use?

The iconic dimension

Digital usage

As access to digital texts has increased, there are now numerous examples of engagement with the semantic domain of scriptures in the digital world: from apps that contain the sacred texts, to digital study materials, to the use of digital tools in preaching and instruction. But what about the iconic dimension? As outlined above, the iconic dimension focuses on how scriptures point to something beyond themselves, are treated with special reverence, and often come to symbolically represent the larger traditions of which they are a part. Examples of digital use that reflect the iconicity of scriptures are more difficult to find than semantic counterparts, though a few instances might be noted.

To begin, there have been several instances over the past few years where officials have been sworn in on an iPad containing a sacred text. New Jersey firefighters were sworn in on an iPad in 2013 (Drinkwater 2013), a New York county executive was sworn in using a digital version of the Bible in 2014 (Rodriguez 2014), and a United States ambassador to Switzerland and Liechtenstein likewise took her oath on an e-reader (Levenson 2014). All of these cases garnered national and international headlines.

There have also been some interesting discussions regarding the proper disposal of digital texts. In many traditions, including Judaism, the scriptures or parts thereof that contain the divine name, should be treated with reverence, and this includes their proper disposal. The question arises: how do you properly dispose of a digital sacred text? You can find many fascinating online discussion forums on these issues, often between religious leaders and members of the community. One particular forum had a very interesting discussion of what to do with an email that contains scriptures including the name of God. A rabbi notes, "This issue was discussed in the 1950s regarding audio cassettes. Rabbi Moshe Feinstein ruled that he saw no reason to forbid erasing a tape with Torah content, but still advised 'perhaps not to erase since it appears like erasing G-d's name.' He—and others—therefore advised that it would be ideal to do the erasing in an indirect manner, such as asking a child to do it" (Posner 2015).[2] The implication here is that an email is similar to an audio cassette, in that it is not a permanent form of the text. Thus, an email containing scripture can be deleted—but better to have someone else delete it for you, just in case.

A further example of the iconicity of digital sacred texts involves questions of purity. In Islam, one has to be purified (*Taharah*) before picking up and reading the Qur'an. But what about the Qur'an as an app on your phone? Much depends on whether or not the text can be considered a *Mushaf* (a codex officially recognized as the Qur'an) in this form, and there is some disagreement on the issue (ibn Adam 2010). One fatwa reads as follows: "These mobile phones in which Qur'aan is put in written or recorded form do not come under the same ruling as the Mus-haf, so it is permissible to touch them without having purified oneself and it is permissible to take them into the washroom with one, because writing Qur'aan on the mobile phone is not like writing it in a Mus-haf. It takes the form of waves that appear and disappear, and its letters are not fixed, and the mobile phone may contain Qur'aan and other things" (al-Munajjid 2007; *cf.* 'Abdullaah 2018; Suit 2015).

There is, then, some evidence for the ritualization of the iconic dimension of scriptures in digital form: Swearing of oaths on digital texts, the proper disposal of electronic sacred texts, and questions of purity in relation to these formats are just a few examples.

---

2. For more about ritual disposal of sacred texts, see the essays in Myrvold 2010.

Continued physical usage

While the developments noted above are both interesting and noteworthy, it is also worth highlighting a series of events from recent years that point to the continued importance of physical, material scriptures as iconic artefacts in the contemporary world. I offer here a few scenes and snapshots drawn from the headlines that demonstrate just how prevalent and diverse such usage of material Scriptures continues to be. I have divided these into examples of oath swearing, desecration, talismans, and social engagement and protest.

1. For his second inauguration, Barack Obama used three Bibles while taking his oath of office as President of the United States: a Bible from the Robinson family (his wife's family), Abraham Lincoln's Bible, and Martin Luther King Jr.'s travelling Bible (Levy 2013). These choices received a good deal of attention and critique, including a robust response from Cornel West, who criticized Obama for appropriating King (Savali 2013). In January 2017, meanwhile, Donald Trump used two Bibles while taking his oath of office: His own personal Bible, and Abraham Lincoln's Bible, the latter a choice which some found surprising given Trump's noted disdain for Obama (McCann 2017).

2. London's mayor, Sadiq Khan, took office as the city's first Muslim mayor in May 2016. At the time of his inauguration, an anecdote from Khan' previous 2009 appointment to the Privy Council was making the rounds. At that time, he was to be sworn in before the Queen at Buckingham Palace. He chose to be sworn in on a Qur'an, but had to bring his own text for the ceremony as there was none available at the Palace. When officials tried to return the Qur'an to Khan he responded, "No, can I leave it here for the next person" (The Economist 2016).

3. In 2016, Irish solicitors were told to always carry with them both Bibles and Qur'ans in case they have to administer an oath for a sworn affidavit, as instructed by the High Court. This was front page news in Ireland at the time, and received a good deal of attention in various quarters of the media as a signal of the growing presence of Islam in Ireland (O'Regan 2016).

We also see various examples of desecration that draw attention to the materiality of sacred texts.

1. In 2010–2011, Terry Jones, the pastor of a small church from Florida, threatened to burn a Qur'an on the tenth anniversary of 9/11 in protest of what he decried as the text's violent tenden-

cies. There was much publicity, and even President Obama weighed in, citing the possibly destructive implications of such an event for international relations. Finally, Jones relented, and did not go through with the burning. On March 20, 2011, however, Jones and his family did burn the Qur'an after holding a court trial in their own church and finding the Qur'an guilty of encouraging violence. Jones' actions did lead to violence, as twelve people ended up dying when people took to the streets in Afghanistan to protest this desecration (Najafizada and Nordland 2011).

2. In February 2012, several days of protests led to the deaths of thirty Afghans and four American soldiers after it became known that American soldiers had burned Qur'ans at the Bagram Air Base (Rubin and Bowley 2012).

3. Bishop Eddie Long, the pastor of New Birth Baptist Church in DeKalb County, Georgia, was wrapped in an actual Torah scroll by the charismatic messianic rabbi Ralph Messer, who claimed the ritual was an ancient one symbolizing enthronement and new birth. This event led to both publicity and controversy: the story was highlighted by CNN, and after renunciation from a number of sectors, Bishop Long issued an apology to the Jewish community for showing disrespect to their sacred text (Oster 2012).

4. In March of 2016, footage surfaced of what appeared to be ISIS destroying Christian bibles and books in a bonfire in Mosul. This was seen by many as deliberate desecration of Christian texts and part of a larger pattern of hostile persecution of Christians in the region.

Meanwhile, stories continue to appear in the news regarding scriptures and their talismanic properties.

1. In 2016, a story made headlines in the United States when a man was pulled from his burning car following an accident—along with an unscathed Bible (Hanks 2016). Here we see the ancient trope of Scriptures functioning as a talisman, protecting people and bringing good luck because of their association with the divine (Parmenter 2012 [2017]). There have been no such stories, to my knowledge, about iPads with Bible apps installed.

2. Local and national news outlets also reported on the following scene: "When a tornado battered southern Mississippi in January 2017, it yanked trees out of the ground and tore through buildings at William Carey University. When staffers combed the cam-

pus, sifting through the damage, they said they happened upon a stunning scene: An open Bible on the pulpit of the campus church, undisturbed by the surrounding debris" (Holcombe 2017). Again, no mention was made of digital texts surviving the storm.

Finally, the presence of physical sacred texts in social engagement and protest is also noticeable.

1. After the US retailer Target announced a new policy regarding use of bathrooms, including allowing those who are transgender to choose which restroom to use, Target faced considerable backlash to this decision. One prominent example appeared on YouTube, as a mother paraded through a Target store, her kids in tow, warning shoppers of the new policy. During the entire video, the woman holds high above her a Bible. As Brent Plate (2016) notes,

   there's really nothing 'biblical' in her soliloquy [...] She doesn't quote scripture, nor does she really even claim anything particularly 'Christian' [...] What she does do is firmly hold high a bible. [...] It stands as a visible beacon that guides them [...] But the bible is never mentioned, never quoted from, never used for anything other than a visual display of some, unknown, power.

2. In March 2017, police arrested a thirty-five-year-old man, suspected of throwing rocks and a Bible at a Colorado mosque. Surveillance video captured a person overturning benches, breaking windows, and hurling objects—including a Bible—into the prayer area of the Islamic Center of Fort Collins, police said (Le Miere 2017).

Oath swearing, desecration, scriptures as talismans, social engagement and protest: In each case, we find a focus on the material and physical dimensions of these scriptures and the iconic role that they continue to play in the world today. Thus, in spite of the rapid increase in and accessibility of digital scriptures, it is important to note that ritualizing the iconic dimension of scriptures has seen less drastic change as physical forms continue to play a significant role. We should keep in mind that scriptures function in different ways, and the impact of the digital turn on these diverse uses is far from uniform.

Reflecting on a changing landscape

How might we begin to account for this scenario? Here it is worth reflecting on the work of Jonathan Westin (2012). Westin, who works in the field of critical heritage studies and conservation, has developed what he calls the vocabulary of limitations as a way to reflect on the translation of books to digital formats. Westin's work draws on Bruno Latour's notion of objects as actants, as well as Latour's focus on the importance of times of transition and innovation. Before looking at Westin's analysis, it is worth describing the work that Latour and others have done on objects and questions of agency.

One aspect of Latour's work is the recognition that networks and social formations include more than human subjects; these networks also include non-human objects, and they too play a part in networks (1993; 1994; 2007). As Latour notes, "*any thing* that does modify a state of affairs by making a difference is [...] an actant. [...] Does it make a difference in the course of some other agent's action or not?" (2007, 71). This is not to assign agency (as normally understood) to objects, but rather to recognize that such objects do matter in the networks which we form and the way in which we live our lives. This, Latour clarifies,

> does not mean that these participants 'determine' the action, that baskets 'cause' the fetching of provisions or that hammers 'impose' the hitting of the nail. [...] Rather, it means that there might exist many metaphysical shades between full causality and sheer inexistence. In addition to 'determining' and serving as a 'backdrop for human action,' things might authorize, allow, afford, encourage, permit, suggest, influence, block, render possible, forbid, and so on. (2007, 71–72)

Elsewhere Latour (1993) refers to these as *quasi-objects*—not subjects in the traditional sense, but not to be relegated to the background as "mere" objects as so often is the case.[3]

Second, a key theme in the work of Latour and others is that objects become particularly visible as actants during times of change and innovation (Latour 2007, 79–80). Objects that normally work in the background become noticeable, and their place in social formation becomes more conspicuous, when there is a change in context or when modes or formats are altered. The implications for reflections on scriptures in a liminal age are readily apparent: in the shift from print culture to digital media, we begin to notice the object itself and the role it plays in networks and social formations.

With these issues in mind, we return to the suggestions made by Westin, who draws on the work of Latour to reflect on the translation of books to digital formats. To begin with, Westin draws our attention to the fact that all formats embody cultural values:

> As the concept of digital books [...] has become ubiquitous, questions arise regarding how those cultural values which are negotiated around a physicality translate to a digital sphere. [...] Few would argue that nothing has been lost in translation when a phenomenon is moved from an analogue to a digital format. Expressed through digital means, the content is detached

---

3. Others who have reflected on the biography and agency of objects include Preda (1999); Hoskins (2006); Bennett (2010); and Connolly (2011).

from the 'culture' to which it was bound by the context of its traditional physicality [...] something that demanded certain networks in operation with established ties with society. (2012, 130)

Indeed, Westin points that such cultural values associated with material artefacts is the product of networks and stakeholders. Such networks

> champion the positive connotations and authenticity of their format, rather than the content itself, by invoking cultural values in a context tied to time and space. This ensures the longevity of the format and consequentially their investment in it, while the content is deemed lessened in other contexts. As a consequence, the cultural values of a format stand in proportion to the cultural values put into that format by the stakeholder. (2012, 135)

Second, Westin suggests that we pay attention to the limitations of a format, and the way these limitations shape the cultural use of and values associated with these objects. Such limitations become significant in light of translation, in part because translation to a new format often takes place *precisely because* of what is seen as a limitation. For example, a primary reason that bibles are translated into digital formats is to make the text more accessible, not limited by the cumbersome physical object. Similar issues were at work historically in other shifts, such as the move from scroll to codex. However, the formats that impose "limitations" also embody sociocultural values, so the new format must eventually negotiate these aspects of the object: "When the limits of a format's ability to communicate a content is reached, and there is a detour to another format, these cultural values enter the negotiation as actants, to be enrolled or ignored" (Westin 2012, 135). Thus, Westin notes,

> in the negotiation process,, a new format can either follow the absolute limitations of the new format or partially emulate the limitations of the previous format. [...] While content can be moved from one format to another, the 'culture' present in the combination of format and content must be translated and in that act branches are created that take the content in new directions. (2012, 137–138)

Consequently, according to Westin, the process of translating to a digital format is a negotiation that includes engaging with cultural values of physical forms, values (and limitations) which may or may not be inherent in new textual formats.

The implications of Westin's research are suggestive for reflecting on the translation of sacred texts to digital contexts. The examples that I highlighted above indicate that while attempts are being made to negotiate the cultural values represented by the iconic dimensions of material scriptures —swearing oaths on iPads, for example—many of these values retain attention to the physicality of printed scriptures, and translating these cultural values, these limitations, will continue to be a challenging and complex endeavour. The fact that these are sacred texts, with a special place in their respective traditions, makes the issue that much more complex and, for scholars of religion, that much more interesting.[4]

Conclusions

How is the digital turn affecting the use of sacred texts? This is an important question, and one we need to keep in mind as Judaism, Christianity, and Islam, amongst other traditions, embrace in diverse ways the emerging digital landscape. I conclude with three points.

First, while the scholarly classes, not to mention the religious traditions themselves, have long privileged the content of these collections, we need to continue to think critically about how and why scriptures are actually used: They are read, studied, performed, sung, painted, revered, processed, marched, waved, displayed, and desecrated. These uses are a reminder that scriptures are employed in a multiplicity of ways, and such uses go well beyond a simple focus on the semantic content of these texts.

Second, when this complex usage of sacred texts is borne in mind, our attention is also drawn to the object, the physical form in which the text is embodied, whether scroll, codex, digital format, or countless other forms. This focus on issues of materiality highlights the role these objects play as actants, which might, as Connolly notes, "encourage us to rethink the dicey problematic of agency, to convert a dichotomous view that bestows agency upon humans only [...] into a more *distributive* image of agency" (Connolly 2011, 21, italics in original). Such an approach raises suggestive possibilities for the study of scriptures, including new perspectives from which to reflect on the social lives of these books as "sacred beings."[5]

Finally, approaching questions of digital culture from the vantage point of the diverse uses of scriptures is informative: While we are witnessing a rapid change in how scriptures are used in the semantic dimension in the emerging age of digital texts, we also see, if we pay close attention, that physical scriptures continue to play important roles, particularly in the iconic dimension. Westin's work is suggestive for reflecting on why this might be the case: The act of translation to digital formats involves engaging with the limitations of material scriptures, while also pointing out how these same material features carry socio-cultural values. As we are witnessing, translating these socio-cultural dimensions to a new format is not a simple, straightforward

---

4. For another perspective on such transitions which focuses on ritual dimensions of sacred texts in particular, see Watts 2010.
5. For some related reflections on sacred texts and actants, see Suit 2015.

task. Can a digital scripture be desecrated? Can it function as a talisman, or be used as an icon in a protest? These are questions we need to keep in view as we continue to analyze the role of scriptures in this liminal age.

References

ʿAbdullaah, Abu. 2018. "Reading the Qurʾan from a Mobile Phone." *Fatwa Online*. 3 January. http://www.fatwa-online.com/reading-the-quraan-from-a-mobile-phone/

Al-Munajjid, Muhammand Saalih. 2007. "Is Purity Essential for Reading Qurʾaan from One's Mobile Phone?" *Islam Question and Answer*. https://islamqa.info/en/106961

Bell, Catherine. 1992. *Ritual Theory and Ritual Practice*. Oxford: Oxford University Press.

Bennett, Jane. 2010. *Vibrant Matter: A Political Ecology of Things*. Durham, NC: Duke University Press.

Bielo, James S. 2009. *Words Upon the Word: An Ethnography of Evangelical Group Bible Study*. Qualitative Studies in Religion. New York: New York University Press. https://doi.org/10.1177/00084298100390040603

Cain, Sian. 2017. "Ebook Sales Continue to Fall as Younger Generations Drive Appetite for Print." *The Guardian*. 14 March. https://www.theguardian.com/books/2017/mar/14/ebook-sales-continue-to-fall-nielsen-survey-uk-book-sales

Clivaz, Claire, Paul Dilley and David Hamidović, eds. 2016. *Ancient Worlds in Digital Culture*. Digital Biblical Studies 1. Leiden: Brill. https://doi.org/10.21071/mijtk.v0i3.10782

Connolly, William E. 2011. *A World of Becoming*. Durham, NC: Duke University Press.

Drinkwater, Doug. 2013. "New Jersey Firefighters Sworn Into Office With iPad." *Mashable*. 11 February. https://mashable.com/2013/02/11/new-jersey-firefighters-ipad/#mTNZPQIbsPq1

The Economist. 2016. "Donald Trump's Nightmare." Bagehot. 14 May. https://www.economist.com/news/britain/21698682-sadiq-khans-win-london-was-victory-enlightened-grown-up-indifference-donald

Flood, Alison. 2016. "Ebook Sales Falling for the First Time, Finds New Report." *The Guardian*. 3 February. https://www.theguardian.com/books/2016/feb/03/ebook-sales-falling-for-the-first-time-finds-new-report

Graham, William A. 1987. *Beyond the Written Word: Oral Aspects of Scripture in the History of Religion*. Cambridge: Cambridge University Press.

Hanks, Henry. 2016. "Bible, Driver Survive After Car Bursts Into Flames." CNN. 22 February. http://edition.cnn.com/2016/02/22/us/car-in-flames-bible/index.html

Hillerbrand, Hans J. 2006. "On Book Burnings and Book Burners: Reflections on the Power (and Powerlessness) of Ideas." *Journal of the American Academy of Religion* 74: 593–614. https://doi.org/10.1093/jaarel/lfj117

Holcombe, Madeline. 2017. "Amid the Tornado Wreckage in Mississippi, a Bible is Left Untouched." *CNN*. 25 January. https://edition.cnn.com/2017/01/25/us/bible-survives-tornado-trnd/index.html

Hoskins, Janet. 2006. "Agency, Biography, and Objects." In *Handbook of Material Culture*, edited by Christopher Tilley, Webb Keane, Susanne Kuchler, Micheal Rowlands, and Patricia Spyder, 74–84. London: Sage. https://doi.org/10.1080/08949460701424395

Hutchings, Tim. 2015. "E-Reading and the Christian Bible." *Studies in Religion/Sciences Religieuses* 44: 423–440. https://doi.org/10.1177/0008429815610607

———. 2017. "Design and the Digital Bible: Persuasive Technology and Religious Reading." *Journal of Contemporary Religion* 32: 205–219. https://doi.org/10.1080/13537903.2017.1298903

Ibn Adam, Muhammad. 2010. "Qur'an Application on an iPhone: Can I Touch My iPhone Without Ablution?" *Seekers Hub*. 28 July. http://seekershub.org/ans-blog/2010/07/28/quran-application-on-an-iphone-can-i-touch-my-iphone-without-ablution/

Ingram, Matthew. 2015. "No, Ebook Sales Are Not Falling, Despite What Publishers Say." *Fortune*. 24 September. http://fortune.com/2015/09/24/ebook-sales/

Latour, Bruno. 1993. *We Have Never Been Modern*. Translated by Catherine Porter. Cambridge, MA: Harvard University Press.

———. 1994. "On Technical Mediation." *Common Knowledge* 3(2): 29–64.

———. 2007. *Reassembling the Social: An Introduction to Actor-Network-Theory*. Oxford: Oxford University Press.

Le Miere, Jason. 2017. "Colorado Mosque Attack: Bible and Rocks Used to Smash Prayer-Room Windows." *Newsweek*. 27 March. http://www.newsweek.com/mosque-attack-bible-colorado-muslim-prayer-574767

Levenson, Eric. 2014. "New U.S. Ambassador Swore Her Oath on an E-Reader." *The Atlantic*. 2 June. https://www.theatlantic.com/national/archive/2014/06/us-ambassador-swears-oath-of-office-on-e-reader/371974/

Levy, Gabrielle. 2013. "Obama's Inauguration: Everything You Wanted to Know About the 57th Inauguration and the 56 Before It." *United Press International*. 21 January. http://www.upi.com/blog/2013/01/21/Obamas-inauguration-Everything-you-wanted-to-know-about-the-57th-inauguration-and-the-56-before-it/8011358757175/

Malley, Brian. 2004. *How the Bible Works: An Anthropological Study of Evangelical Biblicism*. Walnut Creek, CA: AltaMira. https://doi.org/10.1080/10508610701572887

McCann, Erin. 2017. "The Two Bibles Donald Trump Used at the Inauguration." *The New York Times*. 18 January. https://www.nytimes.com/2017/01/18/us/politics/lincoln-bible-trump-oath.html

McGann, Jerome. 2014. *A New Republic of Letters: Memory and Scholarship in the Age of Digital Reproduction*. Cambridge, MA: Harvard University Press.

Najafizada, Enayat, and Rod Nordland. 2011. "Afghans Avenge Florida Koran Burning, Killing 12." *The New York Times.* 1 April. http://archive.nytimes.com/www.nytimes.com/2011/04/02/world/asia/02afghanistan.html

O'Regan, Mark. 2016. "Solicitors Told to Carry Bible and Koran." *Irish Independent.* 24 April. https://www.independent.ie/irish-news/courts/solicitors-told-to-carry-bible-and-koran-34654171.html

Oster, Marcy. 2012. "Bishop Eddie Long Apologizes for Torah Scroll Ceremony." *Jewish Telegraphic Agency.* 6 February. https://www.jta.org/2012/02/06/news-opinion/united-states/bishop-eddie-long-apologizes-for-torah-scroll-ceremony

Parker, David. 2003. "Through a Screen Darkly: Digital Texts and the New Testament." *Journal for the Study of the New Testament* 25: 395–411. https://doi.org/10.1177/0142064x0302500401

Parmenter, Dorina Miller. 2006 [2008]. "The Iconic Book: The Image of the Bible in Early Christian Rituals." *Postscripts* 2 (2–3): 160–189. https://doi.org/10.1558/post.v2i2.160

———. 2012 [2017]. "How the Bible Feels: The Christian Bible as Effective and Affective Object." *Postscripts* 8(1–2): 27–38. https://doi.org/10.1558/post.32589

Plate, S. Brent Rodriguez. 2016. "Waving Bibles, Protesting Bathrooms." *Iconic Books Blog.* 15 May. http://iconicbooks.blogspot.ie/2016/05/waving-bibles-protesting-bathrooms.html

Posner, Menachem. 2015. "Proper Disposal of Holy Objects." *Chabad.* 30 July. https://www.chabad.org/library/article_cdo/aid/475304/jewish/Proper-Disposal-of-Holy-Objects.htm

Preda, Alex. 1999. "The Turn to Things: Arguments for a Sociological Theory of Things." *The Sociological Quarterly* 40: 347–366. https://doi.org/10.1111/j.1533-8525.1999.tb00552.x

Rodriguez, Salvador. 2014. "Elected Official Takes Oath of Office on an iPad." *Los Angeles Times.* 3 January. http://www.latimes.com/business/technology/la-fi-tn-politician-sworn-in-ipad-bible-20140103-story.html

Rubin, Alissa J., and Graham Bowley. 2012. "Koran Burning in Afghanistan Prompts 3 Parallel Inquiries." *The New York Times.* 29 February. https://www.nytimes.com/2012/03/01/world/asia/koran-burning-in-afghanistan-prompts-3-parallel-inquiries.html

Savali, Kirsten West. 2013. "Cornel West: President Obama Doesn't Deserve To Be Sworn In With MLK's Bible." *News One.* 20 January. https://newsone.com/2153928/cornel-west-obama-mlk/

Smith, Jonathan Z. 1987. *To Take Place: Toward Theory in Ritual.* Chicago: University of Chicago Press. https://doi.org/10.1017/s0360966900040421

Smith, Wilfred Cantwell. 1993. *What Is Scripture? A Comparative Approach.* London: SCM.

Suit, Natalia. 2015. "Enacting 'Electronic Qurʾans': Tradition Without a Precedent." *Material Religions*. 18 November. http://materialreligions.blogspot.ie/2015/11/enacting-electronic-qurans-tradition.html

Watts, James W. 2006 [2008]. "The Three Dimensions of Scriptures." *Postscripts* 2(2–3): 135–159.

———. 2009. "Desecrating Scriptures." *A Case Study for the Luce Project in Media, Religion, and International Relations*. http://surface.syr.edu/rel/3/

———. 2010. "Disposing of Non-Disposable Texts." In *The Death of Sacred Texts: Ritual Disposal and Renovation of Texts in the World Religions*, edited by Kristina Myrvold, 147–159. Farnham: Ashgate. https://doi.org/10.4324/9781315615318

Weller, Sam. 2010. "Ray Bradbury: The Art of Fiction. Interviewed by Sam Weller." *The Paris Review* 192 (Spring). https://www.theparisreview.org/interviews/6012/ray-bradbury-the-art-of-fiction-no-203-ray-bradbury

Westin, Jonathan. 2012. "Loss of Culture: New Media Forms and the Translation from Analogue to Digital Books." *Convergence: The International Journal of Research into New Media Technologies* 19(2): 129–140. https://doi.org/10.1177/1354856512452398

— 5 —

Being the Bible: Sacred Bodies and Iconic Books in Bring Your Bible to School Day

DORINA MILLER PARMENTER

In 2014, the American Christian evangelical ministry Focus on the Family organized the first Bring Your Bible to School Day in response to a few instances where public school teachers in the United States prohibited students from reading their Bibles during free time (Daly 2014a; Strauss 2014). The planning and recruitment for the ritual, now every first Thursday in October, provides students and parents with information about personal religious freedoms in public schools. It encourages kids to "let your light shine" against the "cultural censorship" of Christianity (Daly 2015) by carrying their Bibles to school, placing them on their desks for others to see, and discussing their faith with their peers (Focus on the Family 2019). Participation in Bring Your Bible to School Day has been bolstered with social media videos from celebrities like Sadie Robertson (of *Duck Dynasty* fame, in 2018) and Kentucky Governor Matt Bevin (in 2017 and 2018), and online photos and videos of Bible-carrying kids themselves (identified by #BringYourBible). This annual, nation-wide event has grown from 8,000 students in the first year to over 650,000 in 2018 (Daly 2015, 2018b).

This article addresses the actions and rhetoric of Bring Your Bible to School Day in relation to theoretical frameworks related to iconic books and bodies, both human and divine. More specifically, the act of carrying a Bible to school as an organized ritual practice, often accompanied by an online testimonial and/or portrait to commemorate the event, will be examined through conservative Protestants' attitudes toward the material world and the lenses of icons, iconicity, and indexes.

Dorina Miller Parmenter is Professor of Religious Studies at Spalding University in Louisville, Kentucky, and a co-founder and Vice-President of the Society for Comparative Research on Iconic and Performative Texts (SCRIPT)

Bibles, icons, and sacred beings

In previous studies, I have drawn upon examples from Ancient Near Eastern, early Christian, and Byzantine texts, rituals, and images to demonstrate how the Christian Bible functions as an icon of Christ (Parmenter 2006 [2008];[1] 2009). Here the term *icon* is specific to how the concept functions in Eastern Orthodox Christianity as an image that resembles and represents a heavenly figure, made visible through a material medium, which then functions as an intermediary between humans' earthly embodiment and divine power[2] (Onasch and Schnieper 1995, 17–19; Stuart 1975). Significant to how icons operate as mediators of the divine are the myths that demonstrate the connection between the prototypes of the icons and their referents, and the rituals that activate the icon, or call upon the living presence of the figure represented (Belting 1994, xii, 4; Marty 1982, 13–14, 16). While not a representational portrait, the Christian Bible functions as an icon in the same way as a portrait icon because it follows the Ancient Near Eastern mythologies of books that reside in heaven but are given to humans to reveal the will of the god or gods (Parmenter 2009). This connection is explicit in Christian depictions of Jesus Christ as both the divine Word "made flesh" to live among humans (John 1:14) and the heavenly Book of Life (Rev 13:8; see Parmenter 2006 [2008]; 2009). The Christian Bible (or metonymically, a book of the Gospels) also functions as an icon in ritual practice when the book is used to connect to the presence and/or power of Christ, as seen in both public and private rituals that began in the early Christian period and continue today.[3] Thus the Bible is an icon because it represents the divine original (the heavenly Word of God), both through its mythological origins and through specific ritual practices. As a material manifestation of the sacred, the holy book is treated as the body of Christ, a connection made in several early medieval images where a jeweled Gospel-book is iconographically substituted for the image of Christ's

---

1. References to *Postscripts* are dated as follows: cover date [publication date].
2. Essential to the connection between material uses of the Bible and icons are the cases made by Byzantine iconodules in the eighth and ninth centuries, such as John of Damascus (675–749) and Nicephorus (d. 828), who argued that the same image was revealed through portraits of Christ and the text of the Gospels and therefore both should be legitimate aids for worship. This view was affirmed at the Second Council of Nicaea in 787 (see Parmenter 2006 [2008], 173).
3. For example, Gospel books were enthroned in early Christian churches, councils, and Justinian courtrooms in order to bring Christ into the proceedings and thereby legitimate the activities and the outcomes (Humfress 2007, 148–151; Mathews 1971, 141–150; Walter 1970, 114, 147; see Parmenter 2006 [2008], 165–170). The most obvious private rituals with Gospel books that began in the early Christian period and continue today relate to divination, protection, and healing (Parmenter 2006 [2008], 177–184; 2012, 28–32).

human body (Brown 2010 [2012], 59; Parmenter 2006 [2008], 170–172), but also evident in how Bibles or Gospels have been clothed (Ganz 2019), liturgically processed (Lowden 2007, 28), displayed (Walter 1970), and disposed (Parmenter 2010).

Examining Bibles as icons, treated as the body of Christ, is a helpful interpretive framework for explaining some particular ways that Christians interact with their Bibles as powerful and effective material objects rather than solely as texts to be read. In more recent studies I have applied ideas of how Bibles function as icons in early Christianity to (somewhat heterodox) Protestant biblical practices such as Bible burials, where the book is interred as a sacred being (Parmenter 2010) and Bibles carried as protective and apotropaic objects (Parmenter 2012 [2017]). In relation to the present study of Bring Your Bible to School Day, one can see hints of the Bible as a vehicle for divine presence in some of the informal language surrounding the event. Following evangelical rhetoric that the Supreme Court "kicked God out of the schools" in rulings against teacher-led Bible reading and prayer in the 1960s, leading to "almost every social ill, from schoolhouse shootings to drug addiction" (Haynes 2012), a news article from the Christian Broadcasting Network that was picked up by many Christian websites opened with the line: "Students from across the US are bringing God back in schools for Bring Your Bible to School Day" (Jones 2018). In an Instagram video, Bring Your Bible to School Day honorary chair Sadie Robertson said that "if you have this book [the Bible] in your hands, you have no reason to be afraid, [...] we can be as confident as ever" (legitsadierob 2018). These examples show the popular rhetoric of Bible use that grants the book agency as a sacred being who is present or absent in the physical book itself. However, the documents published by Focus on the Family do not use this rhetoric of biblical agency and emphasize that it is the students' activity in their exercise of free speech—to be empowered as "modern-day Esthers and Daniels to be courageous in standing up for their faith" (Focus on the Family 2019)—that brings "God into the tough situations" (legitsadierob 2018). Ever-mindful of turning material objects into idols, careful evangelical rhetoric does not see divine activity within material objects of paper and ink (Malley 2004, 70; Parmenter 2010); instead, "the word of God is living and active" (Daly 2014b, quoting Heb 4:12) and related but not limited to the Bible (Malley 2004, 2009). Therefore, due to the Protestant disdain of a sacramental view of the divine working in the material world, looking at Bibles as icons (that is, as material vehicles for divine presence) provides only a limited analysis of Bring Your Bible to School Day and requires additional nuance.

Bibles, icons, and the attempted dematerialization of Protestantism

Just as Protestants attempt to dematerialize Christianity, the term *icon* has undergone a similar abstraction, so that in common use today an icon is an image, object, or person that is widely recognized by name and visual appearance, represents a movement or particular aspect of culture, and is worthy of admiration or veneration.[4] Bibles are ubiquitously icons in this way, and especially function as icons of bibliocentric Protestantism. This section addresses the iconoclasm of the Reformation period to help explain the shift from a sacramental view of how God operates in the material world to conservative Protestants' prophetic assertion of the Word of God as unmediated and immediately available through the Bible. This illuminates a shift in how the Bible functions as an icon in many Protestant contexts and how the Bible relates to sacred beings and bodies in Bring Your Bible to School Day.

Sixteenth-century reformers of the Christian Church complained that the Medieval Latin Bible was used in the liturgy as an object of power rather than a text to be read and understood by the people (Wilson 2008, 79–82). Thus when writing and preaching about scripture, reformers like Martin Luther insisted that the importance of the Bible lay in the message it contained about the *Logos,* the divine spoken word and God's communication to humans incarnate in Jesus Christ, and not as a canon of texts authorized by humans and housed in an elaborate liturgical codex. For Luther, the Bible was "the Holy Spirit's own special book, writ and word" (Graham 1987, 152), a complex interplay between writing and reading, speaking and hearing. Luther insisted that the Word is primarily spoken and only derivatively written. The writing of the gospel itself, resulting in the New Testament and the Christian Bible, is a sign of sin or lack in Luther's narration of apostolic events.

> [B]efore [the apostles] wrote they preached to the people with their physical voice and converted them. And this was their proper apostolic and New Testament work. The fact that it became necessary to write books reveals that great damage and injury had already been done to the Spirit. [...] Instead of godly preachers[,] heretics, false teachers, and all sorts of errorists arose who fed poison to the sheep of Christ. This made it necessary to attempt everything possible so that some sheep might be rescued from the wolves. And then [the apostles] began to write and thus—insofar as this was possible—to lead the sheep of Christ into the Scriptures so that the sheep would be able to feed themselves and preserve themselves against the wolves.
>
> (*WA* 10 in Althaus 1966, 73)

---

4. This definition of *icon* was added to the Oxford English Dictionary online draft editions in 2001. See http://www.dictionary.oed.com.

While the need to commit the gospel to writing arose due to damage in the transmission of the message, according to Luther, the writing itself became a corrective, and the assured, although not ideal, means for keeping the true gospel alive. However, Luther's view of the written Scriptures as a necessary evil—as a failure to maintain the command to spread the message verbally—did not preclude the Word of God as witnessed by the written words living and speaking to individuals. He stated that "[t]he Holy Spirit speaks to those who read the Word of God. In this way speaking and writing become identical, only that the oral Word is more powerful than the written Word" (*LW* 22 in Luther 1960, 473). And not only by writing, but also with the aid of the printing press, Luther could attempt to free many more "sheep" from the "wolves" than he could reach through the pulpit.[5]

Sola scriptura operated at several different levels for Luther. Perhaps foremost, salvation through scripture alone was symbolic of taking authority away from the interpretations and requirements of Catholic clergy. All that one needed to know about God and the world could be found in the message of the Old and New Testaments, not in the added traditions of the Church. Salvation was not dictated by ritual requirements or assent to Church authority, but, as evidenced in scripture, salvation was the working of God's grace through the death and resurrection of Christ. The written Bible was "assurance in tangible form [...] of the stupendous act of God in Christ" (Bainton 1978, 202). While the words of the Bible were not sufficient in themselves for salvation, the message they convey was external evidence for God's relationship with humans, and provide the necessary ground for faith. According to Roland Bainton (1978):

> "The Scriptures assumed for Luther an overwhelming importance, not primarily as a source book for antipapal polemic, but as the one ground of certainty. [...] He was completely lost unless he could find something *without* on which to lay hold. And this he found in the Scriptures." (288, italics added)

Luther's view of the Bible as the witness to the revelation of the Word of God, and not the revelation itself, has remained representative of a *liberal* Protestant attitude toward the Bible (Marty 1972, 120–126) that

---

5. Many historians have attributed Luther's success to his strategic manipulation of the printing press. Just as leaders of the Church were becoming wary of the possible increase in errors of faith due to the many vernacular Bibles in press before 1520, Protestants manipulated the new technology to their advantage. "Protestantism," according to Eisenstein, "was the first movement [...] to use the new presses for overt propaganda and agitation against an established institution. By pamphleteering directed at arousing popular support and aimed at readers who were unversed in Latin, the reformers unwittingly pioneered as revolutionaries and rabble rousers" (Eisenstein 1979, 304).

resists being treated as an icon of Christ. Luther is famously quoted as saying that the Bible is the cradle where Christ is laid (*LW* 35 in Luther 1960, 236; see Bainton 1963, 20), an image that has resonated with liberal preachers throughout the ages who make a distinction between the written book and the living Word (for example, Kaurin 2004). But while credit goes to Martin Luther for elucidating many of the theological assertions of Protestant Christianity, his views on the status and usefulness of images and material objects, including the Bible, were quite moderate compared to the Swiss "Reformed" positions of Ulrich Zwingli and John Calvin, which later carried over into American Puritanism and American Evangelicalism. Whereas Luther found images, objects, and rituals to be generally impotent and neutral (Hardy 1999, 11; Koerner 2004, 28),[6] as he thought would be evident after one's transformation by freely-gained faith and not by forced iconoclasm (*LW* 51 in Luther 1960, 76–77; see Michalski 1993, 1–42), Zwingli and Calvin took the idea of God's freely given grace unperturbed by human works to an aesthetic extreme.

Calvin thought that Christians should disengage from the arts for religious use, for God's accommodation "to human capacities through the Word (and by the Spirit) in preaching and sacraments [...] is so full that any addition or substitution is unnecessary; images can only be a substitute for the Word, and they are no genuine aid to devotion" (Hardy 1999, 12). Because "everything respecting God which is learned from images [is] futile and false" (Calvin 1998, 94; see Michalski 1993, 183), Calvinist churches were stripped of visual elements except for inscriptions from scripture so that the faithful could hear the voice of God (Michalski 1993, 70).[7] Pictorial altarpieces were replaced with written words, and eventually the altar was supplanted by the pulpit, where the Word was proclaimed (see Koerner 2004, 42, 426). Zwingli was even more iconoclastic than Calvin, and advocated an atmosphere of worship directed solely at prayer "in spirit and in truth" (John 4:24), "free of visual arts and music, which were powerless to aid the worshipper and tended always to distract" (Hardy 1999, 13).

This more radical, Reformed approach to *sola scriptura* and Protestant iconoclasm, which attempts to shatter the sacramental theology of the Roman Catholic Church and the perception that God works through objects and bodies that engage in the Church's rituals, also includes a change in

---

6. Luther, like Byzantine iconodules, felt that "the spirit works by fleshly means. To save us, God became a man, and to proclaim that he needs a medium—the Bible, a preacher's voice, the elements of water, bread, and wine" (Koerner 2004, 185).

7. Calvin did not object to the display of religious images in private homes, particularly for the depiction of historical narratives, which "are of some use for instruction or admonition." Pictures "which merely exhibit bodily shapes and figures [...] are only fitted for amusement" and are of little value (Calvin 1998, 100; see Joby 2007, 1–28).

the interpretation of the Eucharist. This has been explored thoroughly by Sergiusz Michalski (1993), who writes that,

> as a rule the opponents of the Real Presence of Christ in the sacrament were supporters of religious aniconism. During the Reformation this pattern was very clear: the views of Luther as a supporter, though moderate, of religious art and of the Real Presence collide here directly with the iconophobia of Karlstadt, Zwingli, and Calvin, all of whom denied (though in different ways) the Real Presence of Christ in the Host. (169)

This "characteristic convergence of iconophobia [that is, iconoclasm] with a symbolic view of the Eucharist" (Michalski 1993, 169) follows the Swiss Reformed view of Calvin and Zwingli, who sharply divided the spirit from the flesh, the internal from the external, the ear from the eye, and the living from the dead (Michalski 1993, 184–187). From the Reformed perspective, the Eucharist is a sign through which humans remember or a symbol that represents Christ's sacrifice and not a vehicle through which salvation is offered (Michalski 1993, 183–184; Stephens 1992, 98–109). In this view, the transcendent God does not accommodate to human capacities through material objects, including the sacraments; instead, God is known through language. It is incidental that immaterial divine language is embodied in the Bible (McGrath 1990, 130), or in the words of Harold Lindsell (1976) in the twentieth century, that the historical revelation "has become inscripturated" (30).

Ironically, in their denial of transubstantiation (of the Eucharist transformed into the literal body and blood of Christ which imparts grace to the recipient) and affirmation of iconoclasm (that the material world can only signify the sacred, not be sacred itself), Calvin and Zwingli generated a *literal* attitude toward the Bible. *Literal* is a highly problematic term in the study of scripture, and rarely refers to textual interpretation that is exclusively straightforward, without metaphor, allegory, or exaggeration. Instead, the appeal to literalism connotes an *a priori* position that the Bible and the texts therein *contain the truth* by following the "normal" ways that language signifies meaning (Malley 2004, 92–103). Martin Marty advocates this choice of the label *literal* for the Reformed position toward the Bible. He makes the distinction between a liberal attitude toward the Bible (represented by Luther) and a literal attitude (represented by Calvin) in this way:

> If for Luther the sequence was: first I have come to faith in Christ and then I find the whole Bible compelling, for Calvin the question was: how can I come to faith in Christ, unless first I have faith in the reliability of the only testimony I have to Him as a figure from the past. Therefore a view of the inspiration of Scripture had to come first. (Marty 1972, 123)

For Calvin, faith "originate[s] in obedience" to Scripture, through which "God, the Maker of the world, is manifested" (1998, 65–66). This view is sustained through the assurance that God dictated orally to the biblical authors what God intended to be written scripture (Calvin 1998, 72). "God took such a strong initiative in this act of revelation that he literally gave men word-for-word accounts and they merely acted as secretaries" (Marty 1972, 124; see Zachman 2006, 2–5). Thus one pays "homage" to "the volume of sacred Scripture" (Calvin 1998, 71) because "the Scriptures are the only records in which God has been pleased to consign his truth to perpetual remembrance." These truths are "are believed to have come from heaven, as directly as if God had been heard giving utterance to them" (Calvin 1998, 68). For Calvin and others tending toward biblical literalism, one gives reverence to the written Word of God as one would to God's presence. In this literal view, according to Marty, the Bible "*is* the Word of God. The Book is not the testimony to a revelation but it is the revelation" (Marty 1972, 124; see Lindsell 1976, 30).

This Protestant *sola scriptura*, which demotes the material world as impotent with regards to salvation yet promotes the Bible as the primary object for Christian belief and practice, has shaped American Protestantism and has been amplified further by it. The American colonies were populated by many Europeans seeking religious freedom with only the Bible as their guidebook. Puritans imagined the New World as their Promised Land, the fulfillment of their new covenant with God to create a Calvinist Christian society comprised of free individuals. Religious revivals of the mid-eighteenth and early-nineteenth centuries affirmed the idea that American society would progress through a non-sectarian, individualistic form of Protestantism that, while diverse, was unified around the Bible.

However, the fundamentalist-modernist controversy of the nineteenth century divided American Christians' views on the Bible and how it would be used to shape society. Liberal forms of Christianity, influenced by biological and geological science and historical biblical criticism, viewed the Bible as a guide in need of human interpretation, and "the materiality of the Bible became recognition of its historicity, which signals both its human crafting and [...] the limits of human understanding" (Engelke 2007, 22) much as it did for Martin Luther. For more conservative Christians like the Fundamentalists of the early twentieth century who reacted strongly against the liberal tendencies of many American Christians, the Bible "became not only a guide but also the destination" (Engelke 2007, 22). In this literal view that echoes Calvin and the Reformed theologians, "[t]he Bible is the unshakable bedrock of faith and something that, as the Word, cannot be separated from God. In the most stringent of these faiths, the materiality of the Bible became [the] presence of the divine—not representation, but presence; not sign, but actuality" (Engelke 2007, 22). Here the Word of God is not Christ, a mediator between humans and God, but in good Protestant fashion there is a perception of *unmediated* access to God's presence through the Bible.

This twentieth-century reiteration of biblical literalism, or perception that the Bible is the site of God's ongoing activity, has been strengthened even further by the perception of a direct threat from biblical liberalism in American Christianity and secularism in American culture, and remains an essential element of twenty-first-century evangelical biblicism. Recent studies in the anthropology of Christianity explain evangelical biblicism as "patterns of beliefs and practices inherited by individuals as part of their membership in evangelical communities" (Malley 2004, 2; see also Bielo 2009a, 2009b). These analyses of evangelical perceptions and uses of the Bible explain that literalism among evangelicals is not a hermeneutical method applied to specific biblical texts, but instead an expectation that "God might speak to the reader through the text. [...] And they expect that God will say things that are important" and relevant to the reader's life, resulting in personal transformation and action in the world (Malley 2004, 105; see also Bielo 2009b, 49–50). This expectation of relevance and "transitivity between the text and beliefs" combines with an interpretive tradition so that much of what is transmitted about "what the Bible says" is not always attributable to specific texts in the Bible, but gains legitimacy by its general association with biblical discourses (Malley 2004, 73; see also Malley 2009). "The Bible" as a material object used in evangelical practice is also non-specific, with an acknowledgement that there are a variety of editions of the book and translations of the texts (Malley 2004, 37–72).

In Protestant evangelical biblicism, the Bible, as a rhetorical invocation and as a material image and object, works as a "cognitive placeholder" to signal shared evangelical ideas, attitudes, and feelings (Malley 2004, 68–69). These socially communicated attributes include how God works in the world through his Word and how Christians should revere and respond to it. In this valuation of the Bible, the book is not an icon of Christ and a mediator of the saving grace of God; instead, it is *iconic* and operates as a different kind of sign: an index.

Iconic books, indexes, and bringing Bibles to schools

For evangelicals who follow biblical literalism in the tradition of Calvin and Zwingli, God's active and on-going presence—the Word of God—is the Bible itself. While God is not perceived to be in the ink, pages, and covers of the book, individuals and social groups who are physically and visually linked to the book are signified as empowered and transformed by the Word and the words. This evangelical biblicism informs interpretations of the iconic and indexical functions of the Bible in the ritual displays of Bring Your Bible to School Day.

The "iconic dimension of scripture" elucidated by James Watts in "The Three Dimensions of Scriptures" (2006 [2008]), is a valuable expansion upon the significance of the visibility, materiality, and ritualization of scriptures that includes the possibility of scripture as an icon that mediates sacred reality but is not limited by that concept. The iconicity of scripture, which includes the ways that the physical forms of scripture are ritually displayed and manipulated, is one of three interrelated dimensions of sacred texts, along with semantic and performative dimensions (Watts 2006 [2008], 143–145). Investigating Christian rituals like Bring Your Bible to School Day through the lens of the iconic dimension of scripture (as well as the other dimensions) is especially important because in Watts' analysis the functions of different scriptural practices relate to social power, and thus are not dependent upon the assent of the participants, who may perceive other purposes or motives for their actions. Watts writes that publicly "[r]itualizing the iconic dimension of scripture serves purposes of *legitimation*" (2006 [2008], 149) for religious traditions, institutions, and the individuals connected with them. Formal liturgical Gospel processions, informal processions of carrying a Bible to church (or school), and portraits of individuals with their Bibles are iconic because the books as physical objects are positioned to be seen by others "to represent visually the legitimate source of the community's practices and beliefs" and to validate the person connected to the legitimizing object (Watts 2006 [2008], 149). "Bringing God back in schools" for Bring Your Bible to School Day through an iconic display of carrying a Bible and placing it on a desk is thus a claim to social power by the community of evangelicals, perceived to be a reclamation of lost Christian values in American schools and society.[8] Tapping into this social power through the shared practice of carrying an iconic Bible, students feel "uplifted and empowered" (Bring Your Bible 2018c) and "can be as confident as ever" (legitsadierob 2018). Indeed, many of the online testimonials about children's experiences displaying their Bibles at school on Bring Your Bible to School Day are not about persuading or converting others to accept a Christian message, but instead emphasize making connections with other Christians and realizing that their Christian community (that is, people who are legitimized by the same icon) is larger than they thought (for examples, see Jones 2018; Daly 2017).

---

8. For an example of this issue in relation to several US states' proposals to teach Bible classes in public schools, see Richards 2019.

In "Scriptures' Indexical Touch," James Watts (2012 [2017]) probes deeper into the iconic dimension of scripture and adds a helpful concept for interpreting the displays of Bring Your Bible to School Day. Following the semiotic theory of C. S. Pierce, Watts explains how a book indexes its owner, much in the same way that a book indexes its author. *Index* here refers to a causal relationship between a sign (in this case, a book) and its referent (the book's possessor), rather than an association based on resemblance, as with icons (Watts 2012 [2017], 174; see also Engelke 2007, 32). So when a Christian Bible is carried and/or displayed as a personal object, the indexical relationship or the causal connection is between the assumed textual contents of the book and the presumed values and beliefs of its possessor. This connection is heightened by the owner's touching of the book, which conveys an intimate personal possession of and by the text in a way that displaying a book on a shelf does not (Watts 2012 [2017], 176).

A significant aspect of Bring Your Bible to School Day is parents sharing on social media pictures of kids holding their Bibles with an accompanying testimonial about their experiences. These photos, the majority of them consisting of kids wearing and carrying their student gear and holding children's Bibles in front of their chests (see #BringYourBible on Facebook, Instagram, and Twitter), along with the in-school Bible displays, demonstrate how the Bibles index the individual users' identities. Common responses to the pictures are that the kids "love Jesus" or "trust Jesus," showing the presumed values or beliefs associated with the person who holds the book. Victoria, posing with a small, pink, patent leather Holy Bible under her chin, says that she brings her Bible to school "To show my friends that God's Word is true [...] I'm proud of who I'm becoming because of what he says I am" (Bring Your Bible 2018b). She echoes a phrase made popular in a Bible ritual conducted by evangelist Joel Osteen and broadcast to millions of people each week (Blunt 2018): "This is my Bible. I am what it says I am" (Osteen 2019).

This collapse between the biblical text and the Christian's identity is supported further by the common tendency for people to relate to books as bodies and bodies as books. Watts (2012 [2017]) writes that "[t]he indexical link between book and person gains force from the fact that books and people share the quality of interiority. Books have contents and people have thoughts" (182). In a promotional video for Bring Your Bible to School Day, "Ethan's Story" features a high school student who overcomes a difficult upbringing and family tragedy by relying on the Bible for courage, strength, and the will to carry on. The line that is most emphasized in "Ethan's Story" relates to his desire to share his faith with others in "the non-Christian environment" at school. He asks: "What if I'm the only

Bible that these people get in their life?" (Bring Your Bible 2018a) which is slightly transformed in the subsequent advertising for the video: "What if I'm the only Bible that these people *see* in their life?" (Daly 2018a, italics added). Thus the subtitle to "Ethan's Story" is "Being the Bible They See" and that tagline is repeated in multiple promotional venues. This emphasis on seeing (both the Bible and Ethan) demonstrates the importance of the materiality of the index (see Engelke 2007, 32-33). Rather than relying on words as signs (as in making a statement, such as "Ethan is encouraged and strengthened by the Bible"), the object as index provides a material connection between the Bible that is carried to school and seen by others, and Ethan's embodied life. The perception of the living word of God as the animating force of the Bible and the Bible-owner's body closes any gap between them (Watts 2012 [2017], 182).

Conclusion

Looking at how the Bible functions as an iconic book reveals different forms of significations related to different kinds of bodies. As an iconic book, the Bible is a recognizable and venerable object that legitimates its user and the community it represents. This is the most straightforward interpretation of the rituals of Bring Your Bible to School Day—to assert social power and legitimacy for Christians and Christian values in public spheres such as schools. But probing deeper, we can see multiple significations at play under the umbrella of the iconic dimension of scripture. When the Bible is an icon, more akin to Orthodox icons, it is perceived to mediate Christ's powerful and salvific presence through the book. The Bible as the embodied presence of the divine reflects a sacramental view of divinity at work within the physical world, and although it does appear from time to time within Protestantism, it plays a lesser role in Bring Your Bible to School Day. Students are seen to "bring God back" into schools by visibly showing Bibles at school, but the Bibles themselves are not given special treatment as sacred objects that bear the divine presence. Instead, the Bibles presented for Bring Your Bible to School Day are treated as personal and personalized books that exert affects and effects on the bodies of their possessors, and are therefore better understood as indexes. An index implies causality between the sign and its signifier, so that the Bible is perceived to create and shape the possessor. Therefore, for Bring Your Bible to School Day, the sacred body is the student who, following conservative Protestantism biblicism, becomes the book that is seen.

References

Althaus, Paul. 1966. *The Theology of Martin Luther*. Translated by Robert C. Schultz. Philadelphia: Fortress.

Bainton, Roland H. 1963. "The Bible in the Reformation." In *The Cambridge History of the Bible,* Volume 3, *The West From the Reformation to the Present Day*, edited by S. L. Greenslade, 1–37. Cambridge: Cambridge University Press. https://doi.org/10.1017/chol9780521042543.002

Bainton, Roland H. 1978. *Here I Stand: A Life of Martin Luther*. Nashville, TN: Abingdon.

Belting, Hans. 1994. *Likeness and Presence: A History of the Image before the Era of Art*. Translated by Edmund Jephcott. Chicago, IL: University of Chicago Press. https://doi.org/10.2307/3170525

Bielo, James S. 2009a. "Introduction: Encountering Biblicism." In *The Social Life of Scriptures: Cross-cultural Perspectives on Biblicism*, edited by James S. Bielo, 1–9. New Brunswick, NJ: Rutgers University Press. https://doi.org/10.1111/j.1548-1352.2012.01253.x

———. 2009b. *Words Upon the Word: An Ethnography of Evangelical Group Bible Study*. New York: New York University Press.

Blunt, Katherine. 2018. "The Preacher's Son: Joel Osteen and the Making of a Megachurch." *Houston Chronicle*. 31 March. https://www.houstonchronicle.com/news/investigations/article/Joel-Osteen-and-the-making-of-Lakewood-Church-12954518.php

Bring Your Bible. 2018a. "Ethan's Story." *YouTube*. 21 June. https://www.youtube.com/watch?v=vnTpiIZjjeA&feature=youtu.be

———. 2018b. "Why does Victoria bring her Bible to school?" *Facebook*. 8 November. https://www.facebook.com/BringYourBible/

———. 2018c. "We love this pic from Meredyth." *Facebook*. 14 November. https://www.facebook.com/BringYourBible/

Brown, Michelle P. 2010 [2012]. "Images to be Read and Words to be Seen: The Iconic Role of the Early Medieval Book." *Postscripts* 6(1–3): 39–66. https://doi.org/10.1558/post.v6i1-3.39

Calvin, John. 1998. *Institutes of the Christian Religion*. Translated by Henry Beveridge. Grand Rapids, MI: Eerdmans.

Daly, Jim. 2014a. "Elementary School Students Now Being Censored and You Can Help." *Daly Focus*. 29 September. https://jimdaly.focusonthefamily.com/elementary-school-students-now-being-censored-and-you-can-help/

———. 2014b. "Encouraging Stories from 'Bring Your Bible to School Day.'" *Daly Focus*. 3 November. https://jimdaly.focusonthefamily.com/encouraging-stories-from-bring-your-bible-to-school-day/

———. 2015. "WATCH: Exclusive Debut of Newsboys Video Kicks Off 'Bring Your Bible to School Day.'" *Daly Focus*. 23 September. https://jimdaly.focusonthefamily.com/watch-exclusive-debut-of-newsboys-video-kicks-off-bring-your-bible-to-school-day/

———. 2017. "Bring Your Bible to School Day 2017 Update: Close to 500K Students Brought Hope to the Nation!" *Daly Focus*. 24 October. https://jimdaly.focusonthefamily.com/bring-bible-school-day-2017-update-students-brought-hope-nation/

Daly, Jim. 2018a. "It's Legal to Bring This to School." *Daly Focus*. 29 August. https://jimdaly.focusonthefamily.com/its-legal-to-bring-this-to-school/

———. 2018b. "650K Students Set an Example for the Nation—One of Hope, not Division." *Daly Focus*. 10 October. https://jimdaly.focusonthefamily.com/650k-students-set-an-example-for-the-nation-one-of-hope-not-division/

Eisenstein, Elizabeth L. 1979. *The Printing Press as an Agent of Change: Communications and Cultural Transformations in Early-Modern Europe*. 2 vols. Cambridge: Cambridge University Press. https://doi.org/10.1017/s0021121400026225

Engelke, Matthew. 2007. *A Problem of Presence: Beyond Scripture in an African Church*. Berkeley: University of California Press. https://doi.org/10.1017/s0395264900022757

Focus on the Family. 2019. *Bring Your Bible*. https://www.bringyourbible.org/

Ganz, David. 2019."Clothing Sacred Scriptures: Materiality and Aesthetics in Medieval Book Religions." In *Clothing Sacred Scriptures: Book Art and Book Religion in Christian, Islamic, and Jewish Cultures*, edited by David Ganz and Barbara Schellewald, 1–46. Berlin: DeGruyter. https://doi.org/10.1515/9783110558609-001

Graham, William A. 1987. *Beyond the Written Word: Oral Aspects of Scripture in the History of Religions*. Cambridge: Cambridge University Press.

Hardy, Daniel W. 1999. "Calvinism and the Visual Arts: A Theological Introduction." In *Seeing Beyond the Word: Visual Arts and the Calvinist Tradition*, edited by Paul Corby Finney, 1–16. Grand Rapids, MI: Eerdmans. https://doi.org/10.1177/004057360205900119

Haynes, Charles C. 2012. "50 Years Later, How School-Prayer Ruling Changed America." *Freedom Forum Institute*. 29 July. https://www.Freedomforuminstitute.Org/2012/07/29/50-Years-Later-How-School-Prayer-Ruling-Changed-America/

Humfress, Caroline. 2007. "Judging By the Book: Christian Codices and Late Antique Legal Culture." In *The Early Christian Book*, edited by William E. Klingshirn and Linda Safran, 141–158. Washington, DC: Catholic University of America Press. https://doi.org/10.2307/j.ctt2853v4.14

Joby, Christopher Richard. 2007. *Calvinism and the Arts: A Re-assessment*. Leuven: Peeters.

Jones, Emily. 2018. "Sadie Robertson: Celebrate Religious Freedom with 'Bring Your Bible to School Day' Thursday." *CBN News*. 3 October. https://www1.cbn.com/cbnnews/us/2018/october/sadie-robertson-celebrate-religious-freedom-with-bring-your-bible-to-school-day-thursday

Kaurin, Gregory S. 2004. "God's Vocal Plan of Salvation." Sermon for Messiah Lutheran Church, Auburn, West Virginia. 23 May.

Koerner, Joseph Leo. 2004. *The Reformation of the Image*. Chicago, IL: University of Chicago Press.
legitsadierob. 2018. "Hey y'all." *Instagram*. 2 October. https://www.instagram.com/p/Bob-rV3gPpq/?utm
Lindsell, Harold. 1976. *The Battle for the Bible*. Grand Rapids, MI: Zondervan.
Lowden, John. 2007. "The Word Made Visible: The Exterior of the Early Christian Book as Visual Argument." In *The Early Christian Book*, edited by William E. Klingshirn and Linda Safran, 13–47. Washington, DC: Catholic University of America Press. https://doi.org/10.2307/j.ctt2853v4.7
Luther, Martin. 1960. *Luther's Works (LW)*. Edited by Jaroslav Pelikan and Helmut T. Lehmann. St. Louis, MO: Concordia.
Malley, Brian. 2004. *How the Bible Works: An Anthropological Study of Evangelical Biblicism*. New York: Altamira.
———. 2009. "Understanding the Bible's Influence." In *The Social Life of Scriptures: Cross-cultural Perspectives on Biblicism*, edited by James S. Bielo, 194-204. New Brunswick, NJ: Rutgers University Press. https://doi.org/10.1111/j.1548-1352.2012.01253.x
Marty, Martin. 1972. *Protestantism: Its Churches and Cultures, Rituals and Doctrine, Yesterday and Today*. New York: Holt, Rinehart and Winston.
———. 1982. "America's Iconic Book." In *Humanizing America's Iconic Book: Society of Biblical Literature Centennial Addresses 1980*, edited by Gene M. Tucker and Douglas A. Knight, 1–23. Chico, CA: Scholars Press.
Mathews, Thomas. 1971. *The Early Churches of Constantinople: Architecture and Liturgy*. University Park: Pennsylvania State University Press. https://doi.org/10.1080/00043249.1973.10793116
McGrath, Alister E. 1990. *A Life of John Calvin: A Study in the Shaping of Western Culture*. Oxford: Basil Blackwell.
Michalski, Sergiusz. 1993. *The Reformation and the Visual Arts: The Protestant Image Question in Western and Eastern Europe*. Abingdon: Routledge. https://doi.org/10.1017/s039526490004316x
Onasch, Konrad and Annemarie Schnieper. 1995. *Icons: The Fascination and the Reality*. Translated by Daniel G. Conklin. New York: Riverside.
Osteen, Joel. 2019. "This is my Bible." https://www.joelosteen.com/downloadables/Pages/Downloads/ThisIsMyBible_JOM.pdf
Parmenter, Dorina Miller. 2006 [2008]. "The Iconic Book: The Image of the Bible in Early Christian Rituals." *Postscripts* 2(2–3): 160–189. https://doi.org/10.1558/post.v2i2.160
———. 2009. "The Bible as Icon: Myths of the Divine Origins of Scripture." In *Jewish and Christian Scripture as Artifact and Canon*, edited by Craig A. Evans and Daniel Zacharias, 298–309. London: T & T Clark.

Parmenter, Dorina Miller. 2010. "A Fitting Ceremony: Christian Concerns for Bible Disposal." In *The Death of Sacred Texts: Ritual Disposal and Renovation of Texts in World Religions*, edited by Kristina Myrvold, 55–70. Farnham: Ashgate. https://doi.org/10.1163/15685152-1018b0006

———. 2012 [2017]. "How the Bible Feels: The Christian Bible as Effective and Affective Object." *Postscripts* 8(1–2): 27–37. https://doi.org/10.1558/post.32589

Richards, Erin. 2019. "Bible classes in public schools? Why Christian lawmakers are pushing a wave of new bills." *USA Today*. 23 January. https://www.usatoday.com/story/news/education/2019/01/23/in-god-we-trust-bible-public-school-christian-lawmakers/2614567002/

Stephens, W. P. 1992. *Zwingli: An Introduction to his Thought.* Oxford: Clarendon.

Strauss, Valerie. 2014. "Did you know it's 'Bring Your Bible to School Day'?" *The Washington Post*. 16 October. https://www.washingtonpost.com/news/answer-sheet/wp/2014/10/16/did-you-know-its-bring-your-bible-to-school-day/?noredirect=on&utm_term=.6c5d646f38b3

Stuart, John. 1975. *Ikons.* London: Faber and Faber.

Walter, Christopher. 1970. *L'Iconographie des conciles dans la tradition byzantine.* Paris: Institut français d'études byzantines.

Watts, James W. 2006 [2008]. "The Three Dimensions of Scriptures." *Postscripts* 2(2–3): 135–159.

———. 2012 [2017]. "Scriptures' Indexical Touch." *Postscripts* 8 (1–2): 173–184.

Wilson, Derek. 2008. *Out of the Storm: The Life and Legacy of Martin Luther.* New York: St. Martin's.

Zachman, Randall C. 2006. "Calvin as Commentator on Genesis." In *Calvin and the Bible*, edited by Donald K. McKim, 1–29. Cambridge: Cambridge University Press. https://doi.org/10.1017/cbo9780511606908.002

— 6 —

Body Building in the Hindu Tantric Tradition: The Advantages and Confusions of Scriptural Entextualization in the Worship of the Goddess Kālī

RACHEL FELL MCDERMOTT

In this short article I want to effect a slight twist to the theme of this volume. I am interested not in books as sacred beings but in beings as sacred books. I look at what happens when an esoteric system that is based on the interpretation of the human being as a living, ritualized embodiment of scripture becomes exotericized through a devotional framework. Specifically, I am interested in the Hindu philosophical and ritual system of Tantra, arguably meant for individualized practice under the guidance of a guru, and the effects of *bhakti*, or devotion, upon its ideas and ritual techniques. What I find in both worldviews, the Tantric and the devotional, is that the human body is deliberately built up, through spiritual practice, as a living reflection of the tradition's scripture or holy texts. However, the understanding of that body changes considerably from the Tantric to the devotional realms. Indeed, one might argue that, from a Tantric perspective, the devotional layer of interpretation causes the sacred body to be lost.

The material for this investigation stands on a thirty-year involvement in the study of the Bengali religious tradition centered on the goddess Kālī—her textual and philosophical history in Sanskrit from about the eighth century, as well as the Bengali poetry tradition focused on her from the eighteenth century to the present (McDermott 2000, 2001a, 2001b, 2011; McDermott and Kripal 2003). In addition, I build upon the very valuable work of British scholar Gavin Flood, who, in his book, *The Tantric Body: The Secret Tradition of Hindu Religion* (2006), offers an interpretation of

Rachel Fell McDermott is Professor and Chair of the Department of Asian and Middle Eastern Cultures at Barnard College in New York, New York

Tantra that fits my Bengali material, and, happily, the theme of this volume. Perhaps most broadly, this chapter aims to contribute something to the ongoing conversation about the transmission of religious traditions—what is foregrounded and what is forgotten—when vehicles of transmission proliferate, jostle for position, or disappear.

In what follows I first make three introductions: To Gavin Flood's theory of entextualization, to the Hindu goddess Kālī, and to the Tantric elements in her medieval Bengali tradition. Then I present the devotional tradition that was layered onto the Tantric goddess and demonstrate the intriguing consequences for the entextualized body.

Entextualization, the Goddess Kālī, and *Kuṇḍalinī yoga*

Tantra is notoriously difficult to define, but for our purposes we can say that Hindu (and Buddhist) Tantra arose in India from at least the seventh century. The Tantras, or texts in which Tantric ideas are contained, offer a perspective on the religious life that (1) values the acquisition of power over the performance of devotional rites, (2) rests on an equation or homologization of the human body as a microcosm with the universe as a macrocosm, (3) transforms the body through a series of ritual actions taught in secret by an authentic guru in a lineage, and (4) often engenders power through the deliberate flaunting of normative conceptions of Vedic purity/impurity rules. In the scholarly world, there have been various studies and expositions of Tantra and of what "true" Tantra consists—some claiming that at base Tantra is a series of power-producing antinomian sexual rites (White 2000; White 2003), and others asserting that Tantra is derived from and mirrors medieval Indian political conflicts (Davidson 2002). Gavin Flood admits the salience of these arguments but offers a third. For him, the "hallmark of Tantric culture" (2006, 4) is the "divinization" of the human body by the inscription or mapping of Tantric scriptures and their ideas onto the body. This is not done literally, by some form of body-marking or -piercing, but by a dedicated cultivation, in ritual and meditation, of the received tradition. In so "entextualizing" the body, encoding the body with the text (2006, 26–27), the body is "moulded" within the constraints of the historical tradition. In fact, for Tāntrikas (Tantric practitioners), such an empowered, transformed human body actually becomes the deity through the process of entextualization, or becomes a place where the deity may reside.

Flood substantiates his argument by detailed descriptions of three medieval Tantric systems, the Vaiṣṇava Pāñcarātras, the Śaiva Siddhāntins, and the non-Siddhāntin Śaiva monists. We will not review these examples, except to draw out some generalizations from them. Common Tantric divinization techniques include reversing the process of creation in the body by dissolving lower elements into higher ones; cleansing the body by "touching" its various parts with purificatory gestures and mantras; inviting the various deities of the scripture into the body, installing them at certain cardinal points and replicating inside the body an external sacred geography, or *maṇḍala*; and transforming one's own subjectivity into the absolute subjectivity of the principle deity, whether (in his cases) Viṣṇu or Śiva. One striking technique, manifest in a variety of sub-forms from the eleventh century, is the raising of divine power from the base of the spine up to the crown of the head. The spine is the site of a sacred journey, and the body is populated by rest-stops, one might say, with resident beings, along the spiritual, spinal path. In this and other examples, one over-encodes the workaday body, with its normative functions and expectations, with a Tantric cosmology reflective of the Tantric revelation.

Scholars argue over how far back Tantra can be traced in India. Certain ideas that become central to the Tantric episteme can be found as far back as the Upanisadic period, perhaps as early as 1200 BCE (Flood 2006, 112, 159; Padoux 2017, 73–74), such as learning how to control the macrocosm by homologizing it with the human microcosm, which can be manipulated, and the potential for power from antinomian actions. Tantra as a ritual and philosophical approach began to color many sectarian traditions in the Indian subcontinent by the seventh century, and in some cases there were Tantric and rival non-Tantric communities devoted to the same deities.[1]

The goddess Kālī was one such deity. We do not know for sure how far back she can be dated—in the sense of when she came to be worshipped as a deity separate from others—but we know that in her earliest manifestations, in the epic period around the turn of our Common Era, she was a powerful, if not fearful and dangerous, demon-slayer. By the sixth century CE she was identified in the "Devī-Māhātmya" ["Glorification of the Goddess"] section of the *Mārkaṇḍeya Purāṇa* as a form of the powerful and beneficent Ambikā (Coburn 1984; Coburn 1991); after this point she is found in Sanskrit literature as a potent goddess of opposites who can offer salvation as well as destruction. By the medieval period she was enveloped into the Tantric world. We find her in ritual manuals devoted to the gaining of power, where she, together with her consort, the unruly but puissant Lord Śiva, is conceived of as residing in the body of the practitioner. Her standard iconography develops also from this period: she is described in *dhyāna*s, or aids to meditation on her form, as emaciated, with a mini-skirt of cut arms

---

1. Apart from the texts cited above by Davidson, Flood, and White, other introductory texts on Tantra include: Brooks 1990, Goudriaan and Gupta 1981, Harper and Brown 2002, Samuel 2008, Padoux 2017, and Slouber 2017.

and a necklace of decapitated heads, a lolling tongue, blood-shot eyes, and a horrible laugh; she is either standing on a corpse in the cremation or battle ground or sitting on one, while engaged in intercourse with it. And yet, say the texts, her smile outshines the moon, and her power, if gained by the adept, can bestow material gain (*bhutki*) or spiritual emancipation (*mukti*).

We have evidence from Tantric texts composed in eastern India from the eleventh century onward, but especially from the fifteenth to sixteenth, that Kālī was integral to Tantric rituals and ideologies (McDermott 2011, 163-164 and notes). Of course, there were many deities—mostly fierce goddess types—important to the Tantras, but Kālī is perhaps the most important. Certainly, looking from hindsight to the eighteenth century in Bengal, when we see forms of worship that are clear antecedents to what we find today, Kālī emerges as one of the two most important goddesses in the region, the other being Ambikā/Durgā, who is almost entirely non-Tantric. There are many elements to this Tantric fascination with Kālī over several centuries, but for the purposes of this short essay I will choose only one—the meditation technique centered on the raising of the serpent power within the body. This serpent is aligned with Kālī, and the technique is known as *kuṇḍalinī yoga*—popularized in the West today in a rather different garb.

There are at least thirteen different systems of Tantric *kuṇḍalinī yoga* developed throughout India since the eleventh century.[2] All of them assume a central channel (called the *suṣumnā*) flanked by two lesser channels (the *īḍā* and *piṅgalā*) that extend from the base of the spine up to the top of the skull. These are just the main channels in a system that contains hundreds of smaller veins or arteries. Along these channels, up the spinal cord, are ranged a number (from seven to ten) of *cakra*s, or centers, each one a lotus populated with associated subsidiary beings, elements, seasons, shapes, letters of the alphabet, colors, and sounds (Figure 1). The aspirant must learn how to awaken the serpent of dormant spiritual energy at the base of the spine, fan or heat her so as to arouse her, and get her to move up the central channel to the roof of the head, where she, as Kālī, the female energy, unites with her consort Śiva. As she rises, the serpent power absorbs the energies of each *cakra*, and stops to sport with the deities resident there. The *cakra* in the heart region (the *anāhata*) is where one places her on a throne and worships her; the *cakra* between the eyebrows (the *ājñā*) is where the three channels come together in a knot (called a *tribeṇi*) where one can bathe the *kuṇḍalinī* in the channels' river-like spir-

---

2. The first reference to the serpent is the *Tantrasadbhāva Tantra* (eighth century); the earliest reference to the *cakra* system is the *Kubjikāmātā Tantra*, of the eleventh century. See Flood 2006, 157-162.

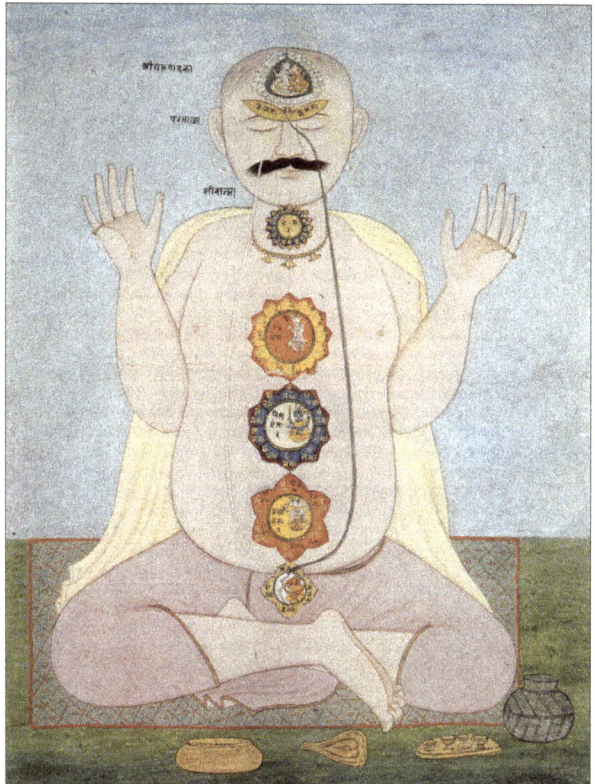

Figure 6.1 Diagram of the *cakra*s in the subtle body. Kangra, Himachal Pradesh, c. 1820. Gouache on paper 12x9 (30x23). From Philip Rawson 1995, ill. 140, p. 169. Reproduced with permission.

itual energies. By the time she reaches the topmost *cakra* (the *sahasrāra*) and unites with Śiva, the experience is non-dual, the aspirant's ego is obliterated, and bliss is said to result.

This is quintessentially Tantric because the entire macrocosm is said to be mapped onto the body, because the pantheon, hierarchically arranged with Kālī at the center, is brought into the body, and because the dual fruits of the experience are what the Tantras promise: material benefit and power, as well as spiritual liberation. The body here is encoded with the visual map of truth, as presented by the Tantric texts and teachings. In this way, one can consider the body as sacred book.

Kuṇḍalinī Yoga in the lives and poetry of eighteenth century Bengali tantric adepts

In the political instability of eighteenth century Bengal, when the Mughal Empire was in decline and local claimants to power were jockeying for posi-

Body Building in the Hindu Tantric Tradition

tion, the powerful goddess Kālī "came out," one might say, from her Tantric realm into a more popular sphere (McDermott 2011, 161–182). Men who called themselves rajas, or kings, but were in reality wealthy landowners responsible for revenue collection, began to project Kālī as a champion of their political aspirations; they built temples to her, sponsored yearly festivals to her, and patronized poets to sing her praise. From about 1750, there arose a group of court litterateurs who expressed in sung poetry their experiences as worshippers of Kālī, sometimes mentioning and celebrating their lives as Tantric practitioners. Of course, just because a poet writes about a certain type of religious activity does not mean that he actually prac-

Figure 6.2 Ramprasad Sen (c. 1718–1775), singing to the goddess Kālī. Popular drawing, Kolkata.

ticed or excelled in it, but in the cases I mention below the poetry so accurately presents Tantric textual imagery, and the hagiographies so clearly narrate the poets' Tantric identities, that I choose to accept the status accorded to them by the tradition.

The genre of Śyāmā Saṅgīt, or songs composed to the black goddess Kālī, began, as I said, in the middle of the eighteenth century with a gifted poet and devotee of the Goddess, Rāmprasād Sen (ca. 1718–1775) (Figure 2). In more than three hundred poems of praise, petition, complaint, self-exhortation, and meditative contemplation, he set the standard for the genre, and his literary followers—over two hundred as of the present—have continued his lead in style and content. Many of these poets have not been Tāntrikas, and have favored a more devotional stance toward the Goddess, but a few have followed Rāmprasād—for instance, in his use of *kuṇḍalinī yoga* imagery—and these we will sample here. It is important to note that the Tantrically-inclined poets also write about love for the Goddess who dwells in their hearts and whom they consider to be their all-compassionate Mother, or Mā.

The first of eight poems I have chosen is "*Kulakuṇḍalinī Brahmamayī*" by Rāmprasād Sen. It represents an early example of the Śyāmā Saṅgīt genre, as the topic is a Tantric meditative system that is just beginning, in the mid-eighteenth century, to emerge into the open through the vernacular.

> Kulakuṇḍalinī, Goddess Full of Brahman, Tārā—
> You are inside me.
> You are inside me, Mā
>   in the *mūlādhāra*, the *sahasrāra*,
>   and the wish-granting *maṇipura*.
> The Ganges flows to the left, the Yamuna to the right:
> in their midst streams the Sarasvati
>   where Śiva and Śakti shine.
> Meditating on You like this
>   a ruby-red snake sleeping
>   coiled around the Lord Self-Born
> a man is blessed.
>
> In each glorious lotus
>   *mūlādhāra*, *svādhiṣṭhāna*, *maṇipura* at the navel,
>   *anāhata*, and *viśuddha*
> You incarnate as letters
>   v to s, b to l, ḍ to ph, k to ṭh,
>   sixteen vowels at the throat,
>   and h and kṣ between the eyebrows.
> My teacher was firm with me;
> he told me to think of You like this in my body.
>
> Brahmā and the four gods, and Ḍākinī and her five *śakti*s
> inhabit the ascending lotuses, supported underneath
> by an elephant, a crocodile, a ram, an antelope, and a second elephant.
> If you hold your breath
>   you can know Her
>   and hear the buzzing hum
> of a drunken bee.
> Earth, water fire, and air dissolve immediately
> when you sound "yaṃ," "raṃ," "laṃ," haṃ," and "hauṃ."
> Then cast me
> a compassionate glance—
>   I keep being reborn!
> Your feet alone drip nectar.
> You are Śakti, cosmic sound,

> and Śiva the dot in "Oṃ"
> > full of nectar like the moon.
> Who can cleave the One Self?
> Ritual worship, controversies over dualism and non-dualism
> these don't bother me,
> for the Great Mistress of Time tramples Time.
> Once sleep is broken
> there is no more sleep, and the soul
> will be turned into Śiva. Could one like this
> > even if reborn
> drown anew in the senses?
> Liberation adores him like a daughter.
>
> Pierce the *ājñā cakra*;
> dispel the devotee's despair.
> Traveling past lotuses
> > four, six, ten, twelve, sixteen, and two
> > to the thousand-petaled flower at the top of the head
> the female swan unites with Her handsome mate
> > in the residence of the Lord.
> Hearing Prasād's words,
> the yogi floats in a sea of bliss.
> > > (McDermott 2001b, 104–105)

Here we get detailed references to the various *cakra*s and what is in them, to the three central channels, called the three rivers, Ganges, Yamuna, and Sarasvati, to the sounds that emanate from the *cakra*s when one is attuned to them, and to the bliss of watching Śiva and Śakti make love in the last *cakra*, in one's own body. At the very end of the poem, the *kuṇḍalinī* and her consort Śiva are likened to graceful swans. In some poems the bliss at the end is such as to make the adept seem spiritually drunk.

Another quite explicitly Tantric poem is "*Badan ḍheke padmanale*" by Mahendranāth Bhaṭṭācārya (1843–1908), who used the pen-name of Premik. Here he presents the material of Rāmprasād's poem more concisely, and in an injunctive voice: you—enter this path to achieve freedom.

> Screening its face among the lotus stalks
> the golden bird
> > contented
> > limbs listless with love
> > > eyes open
> sleeps on the flower with v, ś, ṣ, and s
> emblazoned on its petals.
>
> In a flower bud above

reigns the mantra "raṃ."
Repeat "raṃ! raṃ!"
    and fan the flames red;
surround the swan with heat.
Let no obstacle stand in your way;
get to work—
you are young and fresh.
Break this fake sleep and snap out of your dreams;
then the storms of this world won't concern you.

Oh soul, whip up the wind; let the bird fly
    flower to flower
towards Her mate in the *sahasrāra*.
When that happens the five elements in you
    earth, water, fire, wind, and ether
will dissolve, and you'll be free
    to merge in the Supreme.

                      (McDermott 2001b, 106)

In "*Balo nā ekhan karis ki man?*" a third poem, also by Premik, the poet exhorts his reader or listener to embark upon this path within the body, described as climbing to the top of one's house, where the attic room is strewn with jewels and the moon is full. The Tantric texts state that experiencing the luminous union of *kuṇḍalinī* and Śiva is like being flooded with the light of a full moon in a dark room, or receiving untold riches. But it is a secret path, only for those who have been properly initiated.

Tell me, what are you doing now, Mind,
sitting there with a blind eye?
There's someone in your own house
but you're so oblivious
you've never noticed!
There is a secret path
with a small room at the end –
and what an amazing sight inside:
caskets filled with jewels
that you never even knew about.
There's a lot of coming and going along that path.
Go, upstairs, to the highest room,
and you'll see the moon rising.

Premik says excitedly,
Keep your eyes open;
if you want to be awake in yoga
you must travel this secret way.

                      (McDermott 2001b, 112)

A fourth example of this explicitly Tantric Bengali poetry is again by Rāmprasād Sen. In a poem titled "*Kālī Kālī balo rasanā re*," he makes fun of external pilgrimage, claiming that if one wants to bathe in a holy river, why not do it internally, at the *tribeṇi*, the *cakra* between the eyebrows at the confluence of the three rivers? Tantric meditation trumps all external ritual. The six-wheeled chariot is the body with its six vices, the horse is the mind, and the three reins are the three central channels: the Goddess sits in the body as its passenger.

> Tongue, call out
>   "Kālī! Kālī!"
> Mind, my Śyāmā Mā
> sits in a six-wheeled chariot with three reins
> fastened to the *mūlādhāra*.
> Endowed with five powers, Her charioteer
> drives Her from country to country.
> Her horse
>   charging ahead with the chariot
> can cover ten *krośa*s in a single day
>   though when the chariot breaks down
>   he can't even move his head.
>
> Going on pilgrimage is a false journey, Mind:
> don't be over-eager.
> Bathe at Tribeni; cool yourself
> in your inmost chamber.
>
> When your body's finished, decomposing,
> Prasād will be cast away.
> So, Mind, seize the moment;
> time is running out:
>   call the Two-syllabled One
>   as best you can.
>
> (McDermott 2001b, 94–95)

To return to the theme of this paper, one can say that the Bengali goddess-centered poetry of the late-eighteenth to the mid-nineteenth centuries kept alive, if in the vernacular, and to a larger audience, the entextualization techniques of the Sanskrit, esoteric Tantric tradition. The body is a living territory through which one invites the Goddess to travel, according to a practice passed down from the Tantric scriptures and communicated through the direction of a guru. The body is encoded by the tradition.

Something very interesting happens, however, by the late nineteenth, and especially the twentieth, centuries. Perhaps due to the devotional influence of the very genre that popularized Kālī worship, the poetry itself begins to change, and strange stories are told about the Tantric adepts. New poems added late to the Rāmprasād genre present him decrying Tantric yoga in favor of simple love in the heart. Tales are told about Rāmprasād, Kamalākānta, and other adepts in which they go on pilgrimage to Tribeni (an actual town in Bengal) before realizing their folly and turning back. They are said to be able to make the full moon rise on a dark night, which stupifies their onlookers, and people accuse them of drunkenness. In other words, the esoteric imagery of the internal journey (*tribeṇi* in the *cakra* between the eyebrows, the experience of flooding moonlight when one has reached the highest spiritual state, and the feeling of intoxication) is externalized in such poems and stories. Whether this is a grand attempt at covering up Tantric meanings by effecting a disingenuous ignorance, or a real waning of knowledge and interest in things Tantric (and I assume the latter), the point for us is that the entextualized body changes.

Here are two poems that move us away from the *kuṇḍalinī* system by placing emphasis instead just upon the heart. Both are by modern Bengali poets; the first is "*Māyer nāmer matan dhan ki āche?*" by Kalyāṇkumār Mukhopādhyāy and the second is "*Pūjbo tore aśrunīre*" by Gaṇapati Pāṭhak:

> Is there any treasure like the Mother's name?
> Though She's Consciousness
> though She's Brahman
>   if you call on Her
>   She comes.
>
> Yes, She's in the *mūlādhāra* and *sahasrāra*
> but how many can know Her
> by that route?
> Just fall at Her feet in your heart
>   and find your treasure
>   right close.
>
> You hold no lamp of knowledge in your hand?
> There's no harm in that;
> like a cow missing her calf,
>   Mā runs to find you.
>
> So, Mind, call out "Kālī! Kālī!";
> Meditate on the Mother's form.
> In this way, that cloud-clolored Śyāmā
>   will dance, always
>   dance, in your heart.
>
>   (McDermott 2001b, 98)

> I'll worship You with tears, Mā;
>   why do I need Ganges water?
> With flames from the fire of my sufferings
>   I'll cleanse the altar of my heart.
> Day by day I'll offer You the oblation of my pain
> calling "Mā!"
>   my mantra
> while egotism and envy sizzle in the blaze.
> The five senses and their objects
> the six enemies –
>   I'll even add in my wishes and desires—
> these are the gifts I place at Your feet.
>
> So, Mā, come and stay awhile,
> Wild-Haired One.
>   I reach out to You
> cupped hands brimming full
>   with the flowers of love's devotion.
>   (McDermott 2001b, 102)

It is as if the spiritual physiognomy of the body now is **not** a complex network of channels, lotuses, and regnant deities, with circulating energies, rivers, and serpentine powers, but a much simplified throne in the heart, two eyes that long to see the image of the Mother either outside in a physical image or inside in the heart, and an unruly mind that needs to be cajoled or threatened into giving up its worldly attachments for the love of the Goddess. In some poems, the human chest is said to be an empty cage, into which the Goddess is to be invited—or, in some saucier poems, to be imprisoned. The route from the early Tantric poems to these later poems of devotion is not so difficult to discern: the Tantric body has a heart *cakra*, where the deity is to be installed and loved; this one *cakra*, representing a move away from esoteric to exoteric, from adept practice to temple worship and vernacular poetry, ultimately overrides the others. Indeed, if one searches through the Śyāmā Saṅgīt anthologies that one can buy today, or the new collections of poetry being written in West Bengal and Bangladesh, or the countless recordings of the poetry that one can buy in cd stores or stream on-line, one will find almost no Tantric poems. No one understands them anymore. No one composes new Tantric poetry. No one records them. They turn out to have been a potent vehicle for the slow popularizing of the goddess Kālī in the eighteenth century, but not an enduring legacy. Some poets even glory in their lack of knowledge of Tantra; it becomes a badge of honor "just" to be a devotee. Consider the following poem, "*Mā go āmi Tāntrik nai,*" written by a Muslim devotee of the Goddess, Kāzī Nazrul Islām:

> Oh Mā, I'm no Tantrik;
> > I don't know any *tantra-mantra*.
> My mantra is the practice of meditation;
> > I only chant "Śyāmā Śyāmā."
> I don't go to any cremation or execution grounds,
> I don't put living sacrifice at your feet;
> in order to search for you I don't look, Mā,
> > in the rituals of the new moon or the dread dark night.[3]
>
> Like the cricket at midnight
> > ceaselessly singing a one-tone melody,
> I always repeat your name, Śyāmā.
> > The child easily loves his mother
> > so my spiritual practice is simple;
> > > it will bring me your vision, Mā.
>
> > > > (Islām 2008, 7:223)

In a final poem, Kāzī Nazrul Islām plays with the image of the body, but very differently from the intricately detailed Tantric physiognomy of former poets. Note that in this poem, "*Śyāmā nāmer lāglo āgun āmār dehodhūpkāṭhite*," the full moon symbolism is quite changed: It is not the flooding illumination in the highest *cakra*, but the lovely face of the Goddess, in the heart.

> The fire of Śyāmā's name
> > lights the incense stick of my body.
> As long as I burn, the lovely scent
> > spreads out in all directions.
> My devotion is like incense;
> > ever it rises
> to the temple of Śiva's world, at the touch of the Mother's feet.
> > My inner world becomes pure by that holy, sweet smell.
> Oh, Mā's smiling face floats in my heart like a moon in the blue sky.
> > When will my vices burn to ash
> > > forever?
> > I will take that ash
> > > and draw with it
> > > a dot on Mā's forehead.
>
> > > > (Islām 2008, 7:256–257)

In this devotional turn in the veneration of the Goddess Kālī, one could argue that the body has been newly entextualized, not perhaps with the

---

3. He does not want to seek the Mother in the Amāvasyā night of Kālī Pūjā or in the three three-hour divisions of night, from 7 pm to 4 am, when she is usually worshipped at the Pūjā. In other words, he does not look for auspicious timings.

scriptures of the tradition, but with a new attitude, birthed by a devotional poetry tradition. Here there is no journey to be undertaken but a presence to be adored. As Charles Orzech of the University of Glasgow tells us for Chinese Tantric Buddhism, practices resulting in entextualization actually shape the subjectivity of the participant (Orzech 2017). Indeed, Tāntrikas and *bhakta*s have argued about the way to understand the human being since at least the seventh century: Are we adepts seeking the deity's transformative power, or are we devotee-children, seeking her grace? The significance and crucial differences between these subjectivities, expressed in conceptions of the body, matter in a person's life-trajectory.

Is the emptied map a loss? Concluding reflections

So where does this leave us? With something of an interesting paradox, I think. Most modern-day Kālī-devotees would not dispute that the real scriptures of their tradition are the Tantras. Kālī's ritual worship in temples is done by priests who use ritual manuals culled from Tantric texts. Kālī stands on Tantric ground. Her iconography, no matter how dolled up, derives from the Tantric *dhyāna*s. At her annual festival, which commences ritually at midnight on the dark moon night of the month of Kartik, she is said to arrive with ghosts and ghouls, and to desire blood sacrifice, as mandated by the Tantras. But what I call the "balm of *bhakti*" has indeed changed her, made her more of a domesticated Mother figure, more apt, say her devotees, to love them than to cause them fear. With a move away from esoteric, recondite religious practices towards a more open, public ethos, the bodily divinization that Flood called the hallmark of Tantric practice is no longer aspired to, or at least not by most. It is as if the Goddess's popularization has spread more knowledge about her, but less actual literacy in her tradition. This is true of *kuṇḍalinī yoga* in the West, too: there are countless Kundalini Yoga studios, programs, and retreats on offer in every city, but very few of them require the memorization of and meditative attention to the actual Tantric *cakra* system. One of the reasons Flood wrote his book was to call attention to this disjuncture: real Tantric practice is steeped in specific scriptural traditions and is not something tailored for individual or New Age tastes.

I am reminded here of Jan Assmann's idea of the "stream of tradition," that is, a cultural repository or archive of symbols, ideas, rituals, texts, and traditions that may no longer be of the "everyday" but that transfers across generations and may be usable when appropriate at some future point (Assmann 2006). So the Tantric Kālī may yet rise again.

In conclusion, Tantric entextualization, although very intriguing, is not for the fainthearted or for the person with a wandering memory who desires quick results. This scriptural mapping of body is neither normative nor necessary in the Hindu tradition, nor, I suspect, in any tradition. Sir John Woodroffe, who translated the *Ṣaṭcakranirūpaṇa*, the most well known of the *kuṇḍalinī yoga* texts, stated that "the full discipline is one of difficulty and risk, and can only be pursued under the guidance of a skilled Guru" (Woodroffe 1964, 294). No wonder the *bhakti* tradition has been hailed as the easy way, the wide road, the "simple practice," the invitation to a beloved deity to reside, without complication, in the heart.

References

Assmann, Jan. 2006. *Religion and Cultural Memory: Ten Studies*, translated by Rodney Livingstone. Stanford, CA: Stanford University Press. https://doi.org/10.1177/1750698008097401

Brooks, Douglas Renfrew. 1990. *The Secret of the Three Cities: An Introduction to Hindu Sakta Tantrism*. Chicago, IL: University of Chicago Press. https://doi.org/10.1086/463302

Coburn, Thomas B. 1984. *Devī-Māhātmya: The Crystalization of the Goddess Tradition*. Delhi: Motilal Banarsidass.

———. 1991. *Encountering the Goddess: A Translation of the Devī-Māhātmya and a Study of its Interpretation*. Albany: State University of New York Press. https://doi.org/10.3406/rhr.1993.1438

Davidson, Ronald M. 2002. *Indian Esoteric Buddhism: A Social History of the Tantric Movement*. New York: Columbia University Press. https://doi.org/10.1086/507859

Flood, Gavin. 2006. *The Tantric Body: The Secret Tradition of Hindu Religion*. London: I. B. Taurus.

Goudriaan, Teun and Sanjukta Gupta. 1981. *Hindu Tantric and Śākta Literature*. Wiesbaden: Otto Harrassowitz. https://doi.org/10.1017/s0035869x00159453

Harper, Katherine Anne and Robert L. Brown, eds. 2002. *The Roots of Tantra*. Albany: State University of New York Press.

Islām, Kāzī Nazrul. 2008. *Raṅga Jabā*, collected in *Najrul-Racanābalī*, 12 vols. Dhaka: Bangla Academy.

Padoux, André. 2017. *The Hindu Tantric World: An Overview*. Chicago, IL: University of Chicago Press.

McDermott, Rachel Fell. 2000. "Raising Snakes in Bengal: The Use of Tantric Imagery in Śākta Poetry Contexts." In *Tantra in Practice*, edited by David Gordon White, 167–183. Princeton, NJ: Princeton University Press. https://doi.org/10.1515/9780691190457-015

———. 2001a. *Mother of My Heart, Daughter of My Dreams: Kālī and Umā in the Devotional Poetry of Bengal*. Oxford: Oxford University Press. https://doi.org/10.1086/375102

———. 2001b. *Singing to the Goddess: Poems to Kālī and Umā from Bengal*. Oxford: Oxford University Press.

———. 2011. *Revelry, Rivalry, and Longing for the Goddesses of Bengal: The Fortunes of Hindu Festivals*. New York: Columbia University Press. https://doi.org/10.7312/mcde12918-toc

McDermott, Rachel Fell and Jeffrey J. Kripal, eds. 2003. *Encountering Kālī: In the Margins, at the Center, in the West*. Berkeley: University of California Press. https://doi.org/10.1017/s0041977x04310256

Orzech, Charles. 2017. "Liturgy, Icon, and Text in the Development of Esoteric Buddhism." Talk delivered at the Asian Centre of the University of British Columbia. 9 February.

Rawson, Philip. 1995. *The Art of Tantra*. London: Thames & Hudson.

Samuel, Geoffrey. 2008. *The Origins of Yoga and Tantra: Indic Religions to the Thirteenth Century*. Cambridge: Cambridge University Press. https://doi.org/10.1017/cbo9780511818820

Slouber, Michael. 2017. *Early Tantric Medicine: Snakebite, Mantras, and Healing in the Garuḍa Tantras*. Oxford: Oxford University Press. https://doi.org/10.1163/15734218-12341429

White, David Gordon. 2000. "Introduction." In *Tantric in Practice*, Princeton Readings in Religions, edited by D. G. White, 3–38. Princeton, NJ: Princeton University Press. https://doi.org/10.1515/9780691190457-001

———. 2003. *Kiss of the Yogini: "Tantric Sex" in its South Asian Contexts*. Chicago, IL: University of Chicago Press. https://doi.org/10.7208/chicago/9780226027838.001.0001

Woodroffe, Sir John. 1964. *The Serpent Power, being the Ṣaṭ-cakra-nirūpaṇa and Pādukā-Pañcakā*. Fourteenth edition. Madras: Ganesh.

— 7 —

Saints' Lives as Performance Art

VIRGINIA BURRUS

Jim Watts has argued that we should look beyond the *semantic* dimension of scriptural texts, where scholarly attention has traditionally focused, to consider two other dimensions, namely, the *performative* and the *iconic*. Watts identifies the performative dimension with ritualized practices of reading, reciting, or singing the words of scriptures, as well as dramatizations and visual depictions of their narrative content. He identifies the iconic dimension with the text in its materiality, as an object or thing ritually displayed, manipulated, and/or venerated. For Watts, a text may be considered "scriptural" to the degree that all three dimensions—the semantic, the performative, and the iconic—are in play (Watts 2013).

Here I want to focus on a body of texts that are not usually considered scriptural per se but that partake of certain aspects of the scriptural, namely, Christian Saints' Lives. Watts's model may give us a way to think about this ambiguous status. On the one hand, we can identify semantic, performative, and iconic dimensions in the Lives of Saints, as in scriptural texts; on the other hand, what unifies these three dimensions in the Lives of Saints, it seems to me, is not their textuality per se, as with scriptures, but their performativity. *If scriptures are fundamentally textual* in each of their three dimensions, according to Watts's model, *Saints' Lives are fundamentally performative*, I suggest.

I am obviously using "performative" in a slightly broader sense than Watts,[1] not only to indicate the ways in which written texts can be trans-

---
1. Note that Watts himself has now shifted his labeling of the second dimension from "performative" to "expressive," in order to allow a broader usage for performative; see his essay in this volume.

Virginia Burrus is the Bishop W. Earl Ledden Professor in the Department of Religion at Syracuse University in Syracuse, New York

lated into the media of drama, music, or the visual arts, but also to indicate aspects of both their semantic and their iconic dimensions, as Watts names them. I want to argue first that the literary Lives of Saints are already marked by a distinctive *textual* performativity, and second, that *icons*—here not books, as for Watts, but painted images (*eikones*) and relics—are also distinctly performative qua objects, as expressed above all in an animistic capacity for intimate relationship. In a slight modification of Watts's nomenclature, we might then name the three performative dimensions of Saints' Lives the textual, the visual, and the thingly.[2] Circulating through all of these dispersed media is the presence of the saint's *body*, at once vivid and elusive, unified and plural. For the saint's performance is first and foremost a bodily performance, in all its dimensions.

In order to begin to develop this claim (and I can do no more than begin), I shall juxtapose passages from two late ancient literary Lives of Saints with contemporary performance art. I am wagering that this exercise will help us grasp more fully the highly performative character of the ancient texts, which is present before they are ever read aloud or dramatized or painted. Admittedly, there may seem to be an unbridgeable gap between the immediacy of contemporary performance art and the highly mediated character of the Saint's Life. Yet I would argue that both Saint's Life and performance art sustain a productive tension between the inherent ephemerality of performance and the endurance or persistent iterability of its mediations—in the case of contemporary performance art, the mediations of photography, film, description, or reenactment. Here the medium, with its tensions, meets the message: for both ancient and contemporary performances disturb and challenge the spectator with their insistence on the irreducible corporeality—indeed, the abysmal corruptibility—of human being, while at the same time discovering in those very abject depths a transcendent, enduring strength and beauty, all the more powerful because fragile and flawed. At this point we approach what Tobin Siebers refers to as a "disability aesthetics" that embraces the human as fragmented, broken, or wounded, yet also surprisingly resilient (Siebers 2010). Such an aesthetics arguably begins to shift the terms of what counts as human, what counts as beauty, and what counts as art.

---

2. "Visual" is not entirely satisfactory, as it occludes the multisensory character of this dimension of the performative, but it does have the advantage of uniting both dramatic and visual arts and highlighting the element of spectacle. "Thingly" references a by now extensive theoretical conversation that reaches from Heidegger's 1950 lecture "*Das Ding*" (1971) to Bill Brown's "Thing Theory" (2001) to Jane Bennett's new materialist advocacy of "thing-power"(2010) and Glenn Peers's animist reading of "Byzantine things" (2013).

Having argued for the performativity of Saints' Lives in their textual dimension, I shall consider more briefly the performativity of the visual and thingly dimensions of the lives of saints. Ultimately, we shall see not only how the line blurs between literary Life, on the one hand, and the life of a saint as it emerges across other media, on the other, but also how the three dimensions of the life—the textual, the visual, and the thingly—cross and converge.

Textual performativity

Simeon

Let me begin with two anecdotes from the fifth-century Greek *Life of Simeon the Stylite*, authored by one Antonius.[3] In the first, Simeon (still in his pre-stylite days) steals a rope from the bucket that the monks in his monastery use to draw water and wraps it around his whole body, covering it with a tunic made of animal hair (στιχάριν τρίχινον). He remains bound in the rope for a year or more; as Antonius puts it, "it ate into [κατέφαγεν] his flesh so that the rope was covered by the rotted flesh of the righteous man." Simeon is being devoured by the rope, then (Antonius, *Life of Simeon* 5). An alternative version of this anecdote specifies that Simeon uses a "rope made out of palm-leaves [σχοῖνόν (...) από φοινίκων κατεσκευασμένην]." The language of the text emphasizes the plant-based materiality of this object: Not only is it explicitly said to derive from a palm, but the word used for *rope* itself indicates *rush*, or something woven from rush plants. And there is more: Simeon is said to have "planted [προφύσας] it on his skin," or even more literally, to have *made it grow* upon his skin (Theodoret, *Religious History* 26.5).

The smell of his furrowed flesh is terrible, and worse yet, "his bed was covered with worms," Antonius reports (*Life of Simeon* 5). One of the monks finally goes to the abbot, complaining, "His bed is full of worms, and we simply cannot bear it" (6). Investigating, the abbot confirms that Simeon's bed is indeed "full of worms," and the terrible stench drives him away too. At this point, the abbot chastises the saint roundly, inquiring about the source of his bad smell, accusing him of threatening the discipline of the monastery, and even going so far as to suggest that he is a "phantom" and not "a true man from real parents." Seeking to get to the bottom of the story of Simeon's identity, he orders him stripped (7). This proves easier said than done. Simeon's tunic is completely fused with his putrefied flesh. The monks soak him in water and oil for three days; nonetheless, when they remove the garment, much of Simeon's flesh comes off with

---
3. For both Antonius's and Theodoret's *Lives of Simeon*, I use the editions in Lietzmann 1908; translations follow Doran 1992.

it. What remains of this human is a raw wound in which the rope is still firmly rooted. Moreover, "there was no guessing how many worms were on him" (Maggots or earthworms? we might wonder). Two physicians are summoned and they labor mightily to separate the rope from Simeon; he suffers so much that "at one point they gave him up for dead," and when the rope is finally removed, flesh remains attached to it. Simeon requires fifty days of recuperative care to recover from this virtual flaying. As soon as he is well enough, the abbot orders Simeon to leave the monastery (8).

In less grotesque but perhaps equally unsettling performances, Teresa Murak uses the warmth of her own body to germinate plant seeds. As a student in Warsaw in 1972, she sowed seeds into her clothing, nurturing them until they sprouted leaves on the fabric—a faint echo of Simeon planting rushes in the bloody furrows of his own flesh, covered by a tunic. As Edyta Supińska-Polit notes, "This work anticipated Teresa Murak's nearly thirty-year concern with the phenomenon of life and the process of growth. Seed itself was to become one of her favorite materials" (Supińska-Polit 2002, 317). In a performance in the mid 1970s, Murak lay in a bathtub full of wet seeds for several days, again using the warmth of her body to stimulate germination and thus deliberately weaving her flesh into an unfurling tapestry of cosmic growth. As Peter Herbstreuth describes it, "she allowed the slimy, sprouting seeds to grow on her skin and later arose from the water resembling a hybrid being reminiscent of some of the figures depicted in paintings by the Belgian artist Paul Delvaux: half plant, half woman, her hair and skin barely distinguishable from the plant growth" (Nemitz 2000, 156–157). This performance was subsequently restaged as Seed in Berlin (1989) and New York (1991) (Warr 2000, 131). Murak herself writes, "I lie

Figure 7.1   Teresa Murak. *Seed*. 1976. Photograph courtesy of the artist.

in the bathtub with my soaked, swelling seeds. I am in direct contact with the softened matter whose interior pushes toward the surface. I have realized this work in full knowledge of the power left in the slime by tiny beings as they die [...] a conscious remembrance of former existence as a part of present life. Strength. Energy. Life. WE." (Nemitz 2000, 94)

Like the first, the second anecdote from the *Life of Simeon* involves worms or maggots. When the saint has mounted his final pillar, said to be about sixty feet high, he develops a tumor on his thigh. As a result, Simeon has to stand on one foot for two years. Antonius writes, "Such huge numbers of worms fell from his thigh to the earth that those near him had no other job but to collect them and take them back from where they had fallen, while the saint kept saying, 'Eat from what the Lord has given to you'" (Antonius, *Life of Simeon* 17). Like Christ, he offers his flesh as food, not to other humans but to the lowliest of creatures. Simeon is, rather literally, becoming worm, even as the worms are becoming human—"former existence as a part of present life," as Murak has it. The reader is encouraged to feel not disgust but wonder and to see not monstrosity but beauty in this transformative process: Antonius reports that when a visiting king picks up one of Simeon's maggots, against the saint's initial objections, it is transformed into a pearl (18).

Maggots are also featured in Gina Pane's Death Control (1974), a performance recorded in both photographic and video formats offering close-up shots of live larvae crawling across the artist's face, which remains completely still. Pane recounts, "I was living in posthumous time. Covered with maggots, my flesh detached by maggots: Flesh of my flesh, two fleshes living together, one nourishing itself from the other: process of life in a continuum of time" (Warr 2000, 101). *A reviewer comments that the*

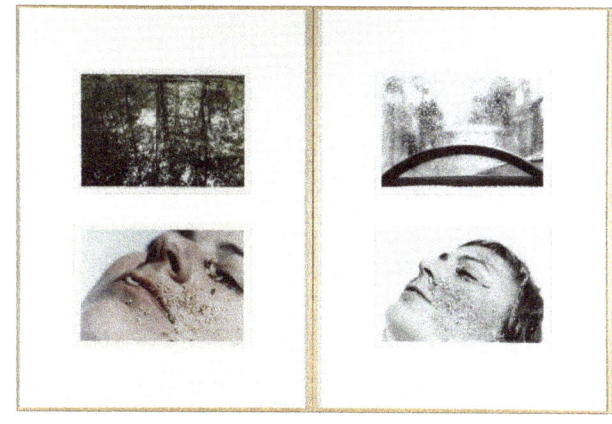

Figure 7.2 Gina Pane. Action posthume de l'action Death Control, 1974. 81 x 80cm. From the collection of Anne Marchand. Photograph courtesy of Frac des Pays de la Loire. Photographer: Cécile Clos / Ville de Nantes, Musée des beaux-arts. © 2018 Artists Rights Society (ARS), New York / ADAGP, Paris.

> videotaped performance is "unbearable" to look at: the maggots "wriggle in her ears and appear to try and get in under her eyelid. The obvious association with death and disease is disturbing—we know flies land on corpses and lay eggs, which develop into maggots, and that they are generally considered vile, disgusting creatures which will eventually burst forth as blowflies" (Black 2002). Like the Life of Simeon, Pane's performance confronts spectators with the unsettling porosity and corruptibility of mortal flesh, evoking a range of possible feelings—horror, disgust, grief, fascination, awe. Death is interwoven with birth—"process of life in a continuum of time." In the photographic version reproduced here, the vividness of color images of verdant trees (seemingly growing downwards, thus into the ground) and rosy (albeit maggot-covered) flesh on the left contrast with the distancing effect of the black-and-white images on the right, harbingers of an impending death.

Syncletica

The second hagiographical text I want to consider is the anonymously authored fifth-century Greek *Life of Syncletica*.[4] Syncletica is a voluble saint, and one of her favorite teaching points is the necessity for cultivating practices of self-humiliation. Significantly, her Life also performs such humiliation, first in the staging of her internal struggles and punishing austerities, then—and most dramatically—in the depiction of an illness that radically transforms her body. Like other female saints, as well as the romantic heroines they resemble, Syncletica is said to have once possessed great beauty: "For she was so exceedingly beautiful physically as to attract to herself from her first youth many suitors," we read. Yet she is unmoved by these attentions; the only bridegroom who interests her is the divine Christ (*Life of Syncletica* 7). After her parents die, she lays aside all "cosmetics" or "adornment" (κόσμησις), going so far as to cut off her tresses (πλόκαμοι)—an act effective on its own terms, we might imagine, but also carrying symbolic freight, as our author emphasizes. "For it was the custom for women to call hair [θρίξ] 'cosmos'" (11). We are thus encouraged to read Syncletica as rejecting not only adornment but order itself (κόσμος). Refusing this conventional canon of beauty, she thereby becomes an "uncosm(et)ic" body—disordered, asymmetrical, disharmonious, disproportionate.

> Hannah Wilke's art likewise displays, and seeks to interrupt and disturb, the female body as the object of a male gaze. Early in her life, her use of her body in her art-making was especially controversial among feminists, some of whom worried that her self-display merely replicated pornographic images. However, Leslie Jones argues to the contrary that "Wilke offered the

---

4. For the *Life of Syncletica*, I have used the edition in Athanasius 1887; translations follow Castelli 1990.

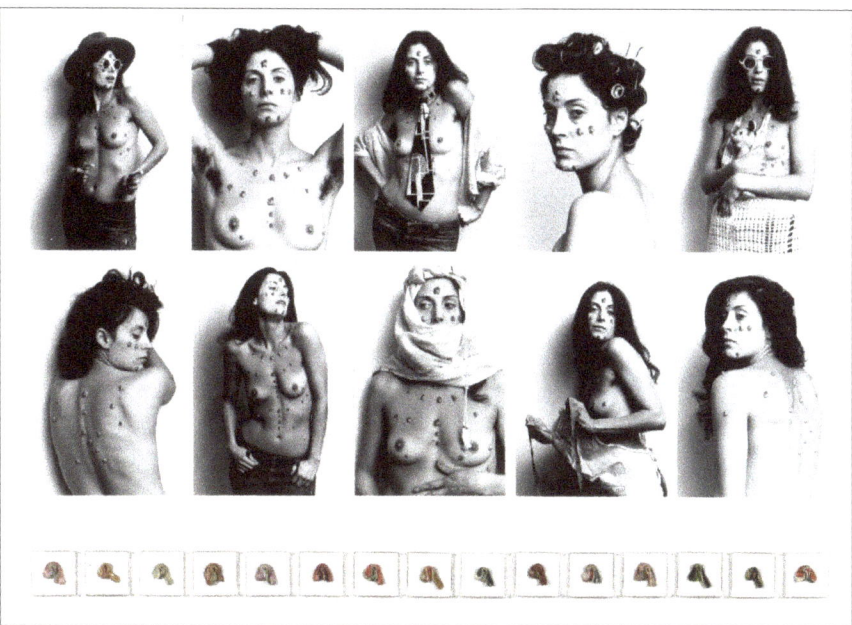

Figure 7.3   Hannah Wilke. S.O.S. - Starification Object Series. 1974–1982. Gelatin silver prints with chewing gum sculptures, 40 x 58 1/2 x 2 1/4" (101.6 x 148.6 x 5.7 cm). Purchase. © Marsie, Emanuelle, Damon and Andrew Scharlatt - Hannah Wilke Collection and Archive, Los Angeles/ VAGA at Artists Rights Society (ARS), NY. Digital Image © The Museum of Modern Art/Licensed by SCALA/ Art Resource, NY.

viewer only blemished or demeaning images of herself," thereby exposing and mocking objectifying representations of women in popular magazines (Wurr 2000, 262). Wilke's performances included covering her naked skin with tiny figures of female genitalia molded from chewed bubble gum—an unsettling act performed live, using gum chewed by the spectators, but also represented photographically as the S.O.S. Starification Object Series.

Syncletica's deconstruction of a "cosmetic body" becomes fully evident in what the author describes as her "final struggle," a protracted illness that ultimately takes her beyond human comfort or cure (*Life of Syncletica* 104–113). Disease first seizes her lungs, advancing gradually; bit by bit, she coughs up her very organs; fevers whittle her body away (105). She is eighty years old when her intestines are consumed with a burning pain that lasts three-and-a-half years (106). Still, she continues to teach her followers (107–109) until her vocal cords are stricken, depriving her of speech (110). Now all that her disciples can do is gaze upon her, and she upon them, but soon Syncletica becomes a sight difficult even to behold. Her teeth and gums are infected with disease, and the corruption moves into her jaw and beyond, causing the bone to fall away; within two months, all that is left of her mouth is a gaping hole surrounded by black putrefaction, and still the corruption spreads. Not only is Syncletica nearly impossible to look at, but she also gives off a "savage" or "inhuman" (ἀπάνθρωπος) stench. Her followers can barely stand to be near her, burning incense when they need to approach her. For three more months she suffers thus, unable either to eat or to sleep yet still strangely strengthened, before she is released from life (111–113).

> *Hannah Wilke's final project, punningly titled* Intra-Venus, *is created in collaboration with her partner Donald Goddard. Not unlike Syncletica's Life, this series of posthumously published photographic and watercolor self-portraits and other related objects displays the body of a middle-aged woman ravaged by cancer and its treatments—hairless, swollen, bruised, bandaged, depleted. Amelia Jones comments: "The beauty here is not that of appearance, but of being—a being that persists, struggles, in the face of death's inexorable and 'untimely' approach" (Jones 2003, 20). That "being" arrives in and as its own appearance, however, an appearance rendered all the more vivid and poignant by the awareness that life's persistence—its transcending beauty—always manifests in the face of impending dissolution. In "Intra-Venus Series Number 4" (July 26, 1992), Wilke's gently tilted head is swathed in a pale blue hospital blanket; her eyes are shut; and the ghost of a*

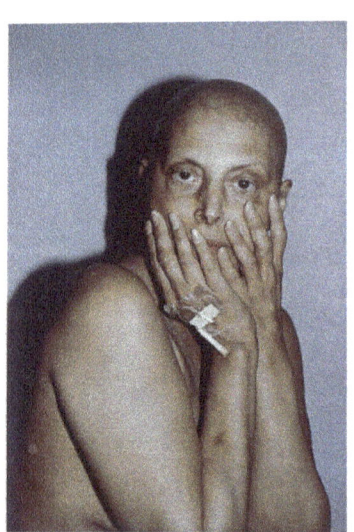 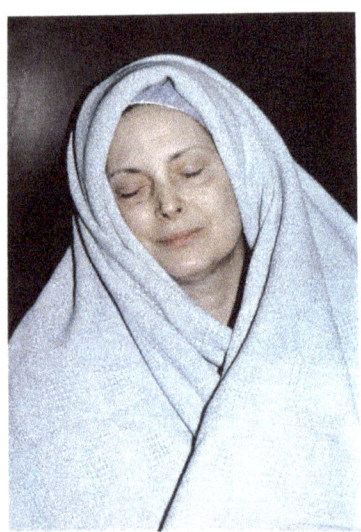

Figure 7.4   Hannah Wilke. "Intra-Venus Series Number 4, July 26 and February 19, 1992–1993." Performalist Self-Portrait with Donald Goddard. Two chromogenic supergloss prints, 71 ½ x 47 ½ inches each. Courtesy of Donald and Hellen Goddard and Ronald Feldman Fine Arts, New York.

smile haunts her closed lips. She "looks like nothing but a Madonna—yet under and around the eyes—an ominous purplish cast points toward trouble," writes Jones. "The smile, on second glance, is tired rather than inspired. The face glows, but perhaps the glow is otherworldly" (Jones 2003, 22). "Otherworldly" is precisely what we would expect from a Madonna. Why, then, the warning "but perhaps" that aligns it with the bruised and the exhausted, making it one more marker of death's proximity? What is the other world that shines through a body that is not long for this world? Is it perhaps "life in process," a fleshly mesh in which our (more or less) discrete bodies are only ever temporarily suspended, from which they arise and to which they return?

Mediated performances

Performance art—and here I include the Life of a Saint—typically values the "live," the immediate, the ephemeral. But at the same time, performance art blurs the distinction between the live and the virtual, the immediate and the mediated, the transient and the persistent. For however much it celebrates its own transience, performance art also wants to leave lasting impressions. Consider the artist self-baptized "Sainte Orlan," whose 1990s project *Reincarnations* involves a series of publicly performed body-altering surgeries—permanent enough, by most standards (Orlan; see also Warr 2000, 185); consider too Ron Athey's blood-letting self-mutilations in "Saint Sebastian," an often-performed segment of a larger work *Martyrs and Saints* (1992) for which Athey's own HIV-positive status is by no means incidental—these also leave lasting marks.[5] Repetition is also courted as a means of temporal extension: in her 2005 *Seven Easy Pieces*, staged at New York's Guggenheim Museum, the famous Marina Abramović reenacts a series of influential performance works from the 1960s and 1970s, thereby exploring "the possibility of redoing and preserving an art form that is, by nature, ephemeral" (Marina Abramović). Photographs and videotapes of performances provide another medium of persistence and preservation, as we have seen. When asked if there is "a strong dividing line" between live and mediated formats in her own work, performance artist Helen Paris replies, "Not really. It comes back to contact and communication. [...] Use whatever lets you tell the story best." She adds, "The relationship between live and mediated formats in performance fascinates me, the visceral and the virtual—the immortality and mortality of both forms" (Hill and Paris 2001, 62).

The immortality *and* mortality of *both* forms. The immediacy and mediated character of *both* as well. Every performance, whether live or mediated, endures beyond its own moment if it has power at all; at the same time, every performance is fundamentally elusive, threatening to slip into

---

5. Athey's work has received extensive treatment in Johnson 2013.

oblivion—we struggle to "capture" it. Finally, every performance is both constrained and enabled by its particular medium, and a living body is a medium too, as saints and other performance artists know well, *precisely because they stretch that body to its limits.*

Visual performativity

I have focused thus far on *textual* performativity, with respect to Saints' Lives. As I have tried to show, by juxtaposing ancient literary works with contemporary performance art, hagiographical texts are inherently performative, not least in their evocative presentations of spectacles of flesh that overload both sense and emotion. Literary Lives of Saints do not so much *represent* as render *present.* Thus, to read such texts aloud on the anniversary of the saint's death is only to reactivate such performativity by bringing it into a different, and perhaps intensifying, audial medium. To dramatize a Saint's Life, even make a film, as Luis Buñuel did in his "Simon del Desierto" (1965), is to reactivate the text in still a different medium, engaging multiple human senses, but perhaps most importantly the visual.

Yet to say that Bunuel's film reactivates the literary Life is perhaps to say both too much and too little. "Simon del Desierto" does indeed implicitly cite, interpret, and contest the textual tradition, but at the same time it also draws on and invokes sacred landscapes long traversed by pilgrims, as well as iconographic traditions, for example. Simeon's Syrian desert merges with the Mexican terrain where Bunuel filmed. The verticality

Figure 7.5 A) The stylite-tower of Umm er-Rassas near Dibhan on the Kings' Road, Jordan. Photo credit: Erich Lessing / Art Resource, NY. B) Luis Bunuel. "Simon del Desierto." 1965. Photo credit: Album: Alamy Stock Photo. C) St. Simeon the Stylite on his column. Mosaic in St Mark's Basilica, Venice, Italy. Photo credit: Werner Forman / Art Resource, NY.

of the classicizing column topped by fenced platform so familiar from Byzantine art is repeated in Bunuel's set. We are reminded again that the performative life of a saint is always dispersed across a diverse, and ever emerging, body of media.

Just so, Byzantine icons themselves need not be thought of as illustrating or dramatizing a text exclusively or even primarily. No text describes the stylite saint as an uncanny hybrid of human and column, flesh and thing, yet that is how the iconographic tradition presents him quite consistently. No text describes a congregation of such hybrid creatures, but a painted icon from the monastery of St. Catherine's is free to imagine just such a meeting, manipulating time and space in its own way, so that holy men rooted in different places and eras may draw close to one another, giving the impression of an endless series, each figure the same and also different. That is to say, the *icon* is performative not because it gives body to a textual narrative but because of its own qualities—the vividness and intensity of the isolated figures set off against the gold background, for example, or the direct address of their frontal posture and gaze, as they crowd in front of the viewer, patient yet persistent.

Thingly performativity

The boundary between what I have called the visual and the thingly quickly blurs, in the lives of saints. The painted panel of six stylite saints from St. Catherine's Monastery does not only offer an arresting visual spectacle of the saints (see Figure 7.6). It also potentially functions as an object of devotion, which is also to say that it invites relation. Glenn Peers argues for a kind of animism, both as a characteristic of the Byzantine view of the world and as a view that we ourselves might do well to adopt. "In Byzantium, divinity infused matter, and when properly activated and perceived, that matter mediated and transformed. [...] The icon is in real relation to the saints, and at certain points of stress, [...] an excess of presence emerges forcefully from the thing" (Peers 2013, 42-43). The icon is in real relation to the saints, and it is also in real relation to the humans who cherish and care for it, gazing, caressing, kissing, transporting, covering, and protecting, while beseeching to be cherished and cared for in turn. The icon does more than represent the six stylite saints; it does even more than render them present. It also exercises a kind of presence and force of its own, in so doing. Active and relational, it is inherently performative.

Most Christians would not have personal access to such a costly thing as the St. Catherine's icon. They might, however, hope to possess a small flask of oil or a pilgrim's token (see Figure 7.7) stamped with an image of the saint. Molded from dirt taken from the saint's shrine, tokens of the Stylite "were not inert pieces of clay but extensions of his own body," as Peers puts it (Peers 2013, 73). Bearing the imprint of their maker's hand on the reverse, such tokens remind us of the intimacy of touch that these objects both offered and invited. "Palm prints on tokens embodied Symeon's own hand and the moment of tactile encounter between saint and pilgrim," as

Figure 7.6 Six Stylite Saints. Icon, date unknown. By permission of Saint Catherine's Monastery, Sinai, Egypt. Photograph courtesy of Michigan-Princeton-Alexandria Expeditions to Mount Sinai.

Figure 7.7 Pilgrim token of Saint Simeon the Younger (front and back), late sixth to early seventh century. Clay, 1-1/4 x 1-1/4 inches (3.2 x 3 cm). Courtesy of The Menil Collection, Houston.

Shannon Steiner argues, with regard to these "touch-loving things" meant to be carried by hand, all the more intimate in their very modesty (Steiner 2013, 109).

Conclusion

To say that saints are performance artists is of course not to say that they are in every sense like contemporary performance artists. The comparison reveals as many differences as similarities. The textual, visual, and thingly dimensions of the saints' performativity have more fully absorbed the "live" performance than is the case for contemporary performance art, which remains more strongly tied to live human bodies, even if not entirely so. Still, we can say of saints, as of their latter-day counterparts, that their bodies, however virtual, however fragmented and dispersed, are their prime performative medium, and that their performances push at boundaries--the boundaries of art, the boundaries of performance, the boundaries of bodies, the boundaries of beauty, the boundaries of humanity itself. Frequently this makes us uncomfortable. *It is supposed to.*

References

Abramović, Marina. 2005. "Marina Abramović: Seven Easy Pieces." http://pastexhibitions.guggenheim.org/abramovic/

Athanasius. 1887. *Opera omnia, tomus quartus*. Patrologia Graeca 28.

Bennett, Jane. 2010. *Vibrant Matter: A Political Ecology of Things*. Durham, NC: Duke University Press. https://doi.org/10.1017/s1537592710003464

Black, Carolyn. 2002. "Gina Pane: Arnolfini, Bristol, 23.02.02 to 13.04.02." *Decode Magazine* (May/June) 11.

Brown, Bill. 2001. "Thing Theory." *Critical Inquiry* 28(1): 1–22.

Castelli, Elizabeth A. 1990. "Life of Syncletica." In *Ascetic Behavior in Greco-Roman Antiquity*, edited by Vincent L. Wimbush, 256–311. Minneapolis, MN: Fortress.

Doran, Robert. 1992. *The Lives of Simeon Stylites*. Kalamazoo, MI: Cistercian Publications.

Heidegger, Martin. 1971 [1950]. "The Thing." In *Poetry, Language, Thought*, translated by Albert Hofstadter, 163–180. New York: Harper & Row. https://doi.org/10.1017/s0012217300036672

Hill, Leslie, and Helen Paris. 2001. *The Guerilla Guide to Performance Art*. London: Continuum.

Johnson, Dominic, ed. 2013. *Pleading in the Blood: The Art and Performances of Ron Athey*. Bristol, UK: Intellect. https://doi.org/10.1017/s0040557415000447

Jones, Amelia. 2003. "Everybody Dies . . . Even the Gorgeous: Resurrecting the Work of Hannah Wilke." *Markszine*. 1–23.

Lietzmann, H. 1908. *Das Leben des heiligen Symeon Stylites*. Texte und Untersuchung zur Geschichte der altchristlichen Literatur 32.4. Leipzig: Hinrichs.
Nemitz, Barbara, ed. 2000. *Trans Plant: Living Vegetation in Contemporary Art*. Berlin: Hatje Cantz Publishers.
Orlan. "Performance." http://www.orlan.eu/works/performance-2/
Peers, Glenn. 2013. "Byzantine Things in the World." In *Byzantine Things in the World*, edited by Glenn Peers, 41–84. New Haven, CT: Yale University Press.
Siebers, Tobin. 2010. *Disability Aesthetics*. Ann Arbor, MI: University of Michigan Press.
Steiner, Shannon. 2013. "Tokens Touched and Touching." In *Byzantine Things in the World*, edited by Glenn Peers, 109–111. New Haven, CT: Yale University Press.
Supińska-Polit, Edyta. 2002. "Seed and Growth: The Art of Teresa Murak." *Analecta Husserliana* 77: 317–326. https://doi.org/10.1007/978-94-010-0538-8_24
Warr, Tracey, ed. 2000. *The Artist's Body*. London: Phaidon.
Watts, James W. 2013. "The Three Dimensions of Scriptures." In *Iconic Books and Texts*, edited by James W. Watts, 8–30. Sheffield: Equinox

— 8 —

Aspiring Narratives of Previous Births in Written and Visual Media from Ancient Gandhāra

JASON NEELIS

Introduction: Buddhist narratives as bodies and sacred beings

Performative and iconic values of Buddhist material and visual texts are significantly enhanced by a "moral economy of merit."[1] In many Buddhist communities, ritualization and "transvaluation" (Appadurai 1986, 23) of relics, texts, images, and other religious commodities with highly charged symbolism factor into the social lives of material objects. According to epigraphical formulae in Gandhāran reliquary inscriptions, the relics of the Buddha's physical body (śarīra) are "pervaded by virtue (śīla), pervaded by concentration (samādhi), understanding (prajñā), liberation, and the seeing and knowledge <*of liberation>" (Baums 2012, 231).[2] Such passages testifying that relics imbued with virtue, concentration and understanding and therefore animated by the "actual living presence of the Buddha" (Schopen 1997, 134) clarify the centrality of Buddhist practices of estab-

1. East Asian Buddhist examples of devotional uses of sutras of miracle tales and hagiographies (Campany 1991), treatment of a miraculous copy of the Larger Perfection of Wisdom Sūtra and benefits of its recitation (Campany 2012, 110–114), writing and venerating the Heart Sūtra to make merit (Kieschnick 2003, 168 ff.), and the "performativity" (Rambelli, 2007, 88–128) of Japanese scripture worship of the Lotus Sūtra and other textual artifacts are abundant. On Buddhist moral economies of merit, see Neelis (2011, 17–19) and Rotman (2009, 6–12).

2. Formulae in the Senavarman Gāndhārī reliquary inscription (Baums and Glass 2019, # 249) are parallel to the Kopśakasa reliquary inscription (CKI # 266): "[These relics are] pervaded by virtue, pervaded by concentration, pervaded by understanding" (Baums 2012, 223), and the inscription of Ariaśrava in year 98 of Azes (?) (CKI # 358): "a relic of that Lord who is pervaded by virtue, pervaded by concentration, pervaded by liberation, pervaded by liberation" (Baums 2012, 227). Fussman (1982, 25) cites a literary parallel in Pāli *Milindapañha* 98: *sīla-samādhi-paññā-vimutti-ñāṇa-dassana-paribhavitaṃ dhāturatanaṃ*.

Jason Neelis is Associate Professor and Chair of the Department of Religion and Culture at Wilfred Laurier University in Waterloo, Ontario, Canada

lishing and enshrining relics in stūpas. The concept of relic extended on a "sliding scale" (Willis 2000, 16) to other material objects the Buddha touched and used (*pāribhogika*) as well as those which commemorated his life and teachings (*uddeśika*).³ Ultimately texts regarded as the Buddha's abstract/concrete "embodiment in Dharma" (*dharmakāya*) were also considered to be "dharma relics" so that "both dharma relics and body relics could be used in similar ways as stand-ins for the Buddha" (Strong 2004, 9) and "the cult of the relics eventually coalesced with the cult of the book" (Harrison 1992, 76). Thus, a wide range of practices emerged for venerating the Buddha's embodied presence in textual relics, with some polemic discourses in Mahāyāna sūtras and associated "para-texts" authorizing scriptural production, establishment and depositions of written texts within a hypothetical "Cult of the Book" (Schopen 2005, 2010).⁴

This article focuses on an early stage when Buddhist texts are first attested in written manuscripts from ancient Gandhāra (ca. first century BCE—third century CE).⁵ During this period, visual and material cultures

---

3. Willis (2000, 13) points out that relics of commemoration were probably accepted as worthy of veneration after the development of the Buddha image in the first century CE, while the two other types of relics (bodily relics and relics of contact) were accepted earlier in the Pāli tradition. Categories of Buddhist relics and practices of relic veneration in literary and archaeological courses are extensively discussed by Skilling 2005, Strong 2004, Trainor 1997, Germano and Trainor 2004, and Stargardt and Willis 2018.

4. Schopen's thesis of a competition between a Mahāyāna "Cult of the Book" and mainstream *stūpa* worship based on textual formulae in the *Vajracchedikā* and other in Mahāyāna sūtras with the phrase "this spot of earth becomes a *caitya* [shrine]" because the "discourse on dharma" (*dharmaparyāya*) effectively sacralises places in different ways than the establishment of non-textual relics in stūpas (1975, 152) has been challenged by Drewes (2007). While Drewes acknowledges that "Mahāyāna sūtras commonly advocate the veneration of written sūtras" (137), he contends that textual formulae ("*caityabhūta* passages") identified by Schopen are not sufficient to support the hypothesis of book shrines, and in any case, "The practice of venerating written texts was thus certainly not peculiar to the Mahāyāna and it seems quite doubtful that it was even original to it" (137). Schopen defends and revises his hypothesis of the "cult of the book" by asserting that the compound *caityabhūta* in these passages "can only mean that the 'spot of earth' is a shrine *tout court*" (2010, 48), while emphasizing that such shrines were likely in private homes and cautioning against generalising the practice too widely across all Mahāyāna traditions. As Hartmann (2009, 101 *ff*.) has observed, the use of Buddhist "Books as Ritual Objects" is certainly not confined to Mahāyāna texts, since "using the manuscript fragment in a context in which a book became a visible representation of the Dharma, the teachings of the Buddha, and even represented the Buddha himself" (2009, 102) is widely attested in the disposition of textual materials with pan-Buddhist formulae. Michael Como usefully discussed how "para-texts" stimulated early Japanese practices of sutra copying and deposition at the "Books as Sacred Beings" conference at Seoul National University (October 13–14, 2017).

5. The author is grateful to Yohan Yoo, organizer of the international conference for Books as Sacred Beings at Seoul National University for an invitation to speak to a

of regionally distinctive Buddhist architecture and art flourished with the patronage of artisanal ateliers responsible for constructing stūpas and monasteries, while scribal workshops produced diverse collections of Gandharan Buddhist literature, which have become available over the last two decades (Salomon 1999; Salomon 2018). After contextualizing the semantic content and performative ritual contexts for viewing early Buddhist manuscripts as "bodies" and "sacred beings," questions related to iconic dimensions of specific genres of rebirth narratives in Gandhāran literary and visual cultures will be addressed. First of all, were these written and visual narratives as preserved in the extent media of birch-bark scrolls and stone sculptures venerated and worshipped as sacred beings embodying the Buddha's presence similar to other types of material and textual relics? If narratives were indeed iconic objects of devotion, in what sense do narratives of the previous and present births of the Buddha and other figures have religious lives? Regardless of whether these questions about Gandhāran narratives can be answered on the basis of the available evidence, thinking about this class of early Buddhist texts and images in these terms helps us to better understand their role in shaping aspirations to Buddhahood by localizing karmic lives and vows in specific regional, ritual and cultural contexts.

Performative and Semantic Dimensions of Gāndhārī Manuscripts as Embodied Sacred Beings

The emerging corpus of Gandhāran Buddhist texts, which includes the oldest extant Buddhist and Indian manuscripts, has greatly enlarged within the last twenty-five years.[6] After Brāhmī and Kharoṣṭhī writing systems emerged in South Asia by the middle of the third century BCE, Buddhists and Jains gradually embraced written media for textual transmission while continuing to orally promulgate their root texts, narratives, and exegetical commentaries. The Kharoṣṭhī script was reserved almost exclusively for writing Gāndhārī, a northwestern Middle Indic vernacular language used in early manuscripts and inscriptions throughout "greater" Gandhāra. Pāli

---

South Korean audience already very familiar with practices of making merit by reading, writing and patronizing the production of Buddhist texts. After this conference, a field trip to Haien-sa organized by James Watts provided inspiration for thinking about texts as embodiments at the center of Buddhist practice. Support for this research was provided by a Collaborative Research Grant from the Robert H.N. Ho Family Foundation for Buddhist Studies.

6. In addition to a brief overview of the major collections (Salomon 2018, 77–79), see more detailed studies from a Stanford conference held in 2009 on Indic Buddhist Manuscripts: The State of the Field (Harrison and Hartmann 2014). An updated Catalog of Gāndhārī Texts and Bibliography of Gāndhārī Studies is available online at https://www.gandhari.org/. An annotated bibliography on Gandhāran Buddhism is available online from *Oxford Bibliographies Online—Buddhism* (Neelis 2013).

literary sources refer to the first written transmission of Buddhist texts in Sri Lanka in the first century BCE, but evidence for initial scribal production of Buddhist manuscripts is from the northwestern borderlands of the Indian subcontinent. Prior to the recent discoveries, only a single incomplete manuscript of a Gāndhārī version of the *Dharmapada* (Brough 1962) found far outside of Gandhāra in Khotan in 1892 hinted at a larger corpus.

The British Library's acquisition of twenty-nine fragmentary birch-bark scrolls in 1995 was the first collection to become available (Salomon 1999), and several texts from this collection have been published as scholarly editions in the Gandhāran Buddhist Texts series.[7] Richard Salomon (1999, 81) compared the deposit of the birch bark scrolls of old and possibly worn-out manuscripts in a clay pot to ritually interment of "dead" documents in a Jewish *genizah*. Although the condition of Gāndhārī manuscripts belonging to other collections varies, he states: "[I]t is clear that the manuscripts were conceived as relics which had to be ritually buried, and it is due to this practice that they have survived to the present" (2014, 2). In "Looking into water pots and over a Buddhist scribe's shoulder—On the deposition and the use of manuscripts in early Buddhism" (2014), Ingo Strauch revisits Salomon's hypothesis of the ritual burial of early Buddhist manuscripts from Gandhāra by focusing on another collection, reportedly from Bajaur in northwestern Pakistan.[8] Since these collections typically lack secure provenance and do not come from helpful contexts of archaeological excavations, Strauch suggests that distinctions should be made between practical reasons for storing birch-bark scrolls in clay pots and other containers to protect the valuable contents, which may have belonged to monastic treasuries, and the deposit of fragmentary texts inscribed with specific verses and protective formulae (which functioned like amulets) in reliquaries and in the hands of Buddhist figures. The fact that birch-bark scrolls belonging to the Senior collection were found in a clay pot with an inscription on the lid clearly indicating establishment in a stūpa in year 12, probably of the Kaniṣka era, which may be calculated as beginning in 127 CE (Salomon 2003, 74–78), is pertinent to the issue of the manuscripts' ritual context. Mark Allon asserts:

> Once the Senior manuscripts were interred in a stūpa, they would have functioned as relics, in this case as Dharma relics ... Like other relics associated with the Buddha and deposited in stūpas, these manuscripts, as

---

7. Rhinoceros Sūtra (Salomon 2000), Anavatapta-gāthā (Salomon 2008), Ekottarikāgama-type sutras (Allon 2001), *Dharmapada* fragments, Previous-birth stories (Pūrvayogas), and Avadānas (Lenz 2003 and 2010) have appeared in the Gandhāran Buddhist Texts series.

8. For overview surveys of the Bajaur collection, see Strauch 2008 and Falk and Strauch 2014.

Dharma relics, would have made present the Buddha, thereby transforming the stūpa which honored them into an object of veneration and the monastic compound associated with the stūpa into a sacred space. (2007, 4)

Although the provenance, disposition, contents, and contexts for discovery of early Buddhist manuscripts in the so-called "Split" collection and over 10,000 Schøyen collection palm-leaf fragments in Kharoṣṭhī, Brāhmī and Bactrian likely to be from caves near Bamiyan in central Afghanistan remain to be clarified,[9] it is hoped that further research and the possibility that future discoveries of manuscripts with known findspots and archaeological contexts will aid in clarifying the ways in which early Buddhist manuscripts functioned as ritual objects.

The semantic contents of textual genres represented in more than 135 Gāndhārī manuscripts exhibit various levels of originality, innovation or fidelity to Indian Buddhist literary parallels in Sanskrit and Pāli (Falk and Strauch 2014, 57). The scope of this article and the preliminary state of research, with several manuscripts yet to be properly conserved and with many texts unidentified and unedited, does not permit a thorough catalog, but the internal semantic content of specific textual examples relates to themes of worship of books as ritual objects. Chapters of the Perfection of Wisdom sūtra in 8000 lines (Sanskrit: *Aṣṭasāhasrikā Prajñāpāramitā*) in the Split collection, a Bajaur collection scroll with descriptions of a Pure Land similar to Abhirati of the Buddha Akṣobhya, and identifications of *Bhadrakalpikā-sūtra* and other Mahāyāna fragments in the Schøyen Gāndhārī collection clearly demonstrate that Mahāyāna texts were circulating in Gandhāra as early as the first three centuries CE (Salomon 2018, 88–90).[10] An intratextual formula in the fifth chapter (*parivarta*) of the Perfection of Wisdom sūtra repeatedly emphasizes that whoever gives this book to others for writing, reciting and teaching gains greater merit than progressing through the four meditations (stages of *dhyāna*), attaining the infinite sublime states (*apramāṇa*) and five special knowledges (*abhijñā*s):

> More than this, Kauśika (i.e. Indra), is the merit that a good man or good woman [would produce] who would write a book of the Perfection of Wisdom and give it to other people. (Salomon 2018, 354–356; Falk and Karashima 2013, 106 *ff*.)

---

9. For brief introductions to the Schøyen collection of Buddhist manuscripts and the Split collection, see Braarvig 2014 (list of titles published in four volumes) and Falk 2011. Matsuda 2014 surveys Japanese collections with manuscript fragments of Gāndhārī texts with other fragments in the Schøyen collection.

10. Allon and Salomon (2010), Strauch (2010), and Falk and Karashima (2012, 2013) discuss recent identifications of Mahāyāna texts in Gāndhārī manuscripts belonging to the Schøyen, Bajaur, and "Split" collections.

A colophon at the end of the fifth chapter reflects the impetus provided by formula in the Perfection of Wisdom for connecting scriptural production with merit making:

> The first volume of the Perfection of Wisdom [property] of Buddhamitra, the monastic companion of Indraśava. And by this root of merit, in honor of all beings, of my mother and father.
> (Salomon 2018, 358; Falk and Karashima 2012, 25)

The oldest attested manuscript fragments of Vinaya monastic codes of any Buddhist ordination lineage have been identified in the Bajaur collection.[11] Two different versions of a part of a Prātimokṣa section on monastic robes are written on the recto and verso by the same scribe, perhaps in something like an exercise of text critical comparison. Since it is not possible to identify an affiliation of either version with a particular ordination lineage, according to Strauch:

> The differences between both versions and their canonical parallels allow us to characterize the Gāndhārī tradition as a witness to a formative state in the textual genesis of the various nikāya versions of the Prātimokṣasūtra which had not yet reached their fully developed and later canonized shape.
> (Falk and Strauch 2014, 59)

This example of versions of a Prātimokṣa rule which was still very much alive in processes of textual interpretation is an apt illustration of Richard Salomon's view of the "tangled" evolutionary bush of early Buddhist literature evidenced in Gāndhārī manuscripts in which "a given Buddhist text, linguistic tradition, or sectarian canon can rarely, if ever, be traced back in a neat line of transmission through other known texts and corpora leading to a single ancestor" (2018, 364).

In addition to Vinaya fragments, versified karmic autobiographies in the "Songs of Lake Anavatapta" (*Anavatapta-gāthā*) (Salomon 2008; 2018, 199–228) and narrative prose texts connected with Śākyamuni's hagiography (Allon 2007, 13–18, 22) circulated widely as individual texts and are embedded in Vinaya collections to authenticate normative monastic rules by providing ideal models for monks and nuns. As Stefan Baums (2015, 49) observes with regard to classifications of Buddhist commentaries, narrative explanations of root texts can develop lives of their own. While literary parallels for the Gāndhārī versions of these narrative texts can be clearly identified, overlaps of these independent texts with other genres of stories linked with Vinaya collections and anthologies of "Karmic Stories" (Salomon 2018, 205) reflect complex intertextual relationships.

---

11. Falk and Strauch (2014, 59–60) and Strauch (2008, 115) address Vinaya fragments in the Bajaur collection.

Paracanonical scholastic texts and commentaries in the British Library collection demonstrate that Gāndhāran authors interacted with root texts by generating their own exegetical techniques of categorical mapping in original compositions without direct literary parallels. According to Collett Cox (2014) and Stefan Baums (2009; 2015, 412), commentarial strategies become increasingly more complex, from glossing of lemmata to formulating sets of doctrinal categories using techniques of numerical categorical reduction. As the Gāndhārī commentaries are "very close to their autographs, and possibly even autographs themselves..." they provide "firsthand unmediated evidence for the state and craft of Buddhist commentary writing in this very early period" (Baums 2015, 412). These very early commentaries "represent the inevitable concomitants of oral methods of teaching and transmission present within the Buddhist tradition from its beginnings" (Cox 2014, 48). In the same sense that Gāndhārī commentaries are witnesses to a transition between oral and written transmission of Buddhist literary genres, they are comparable to secondary texts with summaries of Avadānas and previous-birth stories labeled as Pūrvayogas.

Iconic dimensions of previous-birth narratives

Buddhist scribal storytellers shaped Avadāna and Pūrvayoga narratives to appeal to the cultural milieu of the Northwestern frontier in the first century CE. Two scribes were responsible for writing original summary compositions of 58 Avadānas and Pūrvayogas in the British Library collection of Gāndhārī manuscripts (Lenz 2003, 2010; Salomon 2018, 87–88, 229–263). The performative dimension of oral storytelling underlies the informal abbreviated summaries, which include only skeletal narrative information with formulae typically indicating that the details should be elaborated: "Expansion should be according to the model. It should be told" (Lenz 2003, 89). The large flowing or slanted handwriting of these two writers who scavenged space at the bottom of the recto and on the verso of the birch-bark scrolls is clearly distinguishable from that of scribes who wrote the primary texts. As autograph manuscripts, these stories are "specimens of literature in the making" (Salomon 2018, 234) which belong to an early stage of development when genre distinctions and characteristic structures were still very much in flux. These terse written narratives do not conform to the "standard avadāna package" (Lenz 2010, 6) of Buddhist birth stories in which present lives of characters are explicitly connected with stories of the past and identified with figures from the time of the historical Buddha. While the four narratives explicitly labeled as previous- birth stories (Pūrvayogas) connect past and present lives of figures, Avadānas tend to focus on the present lives, with only a few exceptions of 'karmic tales' with explanations of how current conditions resulted from past actions (Lenz 2010, 7–9). Since Gāndhārī Buddhist manuscripts of the British Library and other collections seem to have been ritually significant with semantic content and performative dimensions reflecting their value as embodied sacred beings, to what extent can these short informal narrative summaries labeled as Avadānas and Pūrvayogas also be considered to have their own religious lives?

In an article on "Narrative as Icon," Robert Brown (1997) provides a framework for answering this question by arguing that Jātakas (birth stories) in Indian and Southeast Asian Buddhist art and architecture serve an iconic function by manifesting the Buddha's presence. In order to develop a holistic view of Gāndhārī Avadānas and Pūrvayogas in the broader context of Gandharan Buddhist material and visual culture, I co-ordinated a collaborative research project with textualists (primarily Timothy Lenz) and historians of Gandharan art (led by David Jongeward).[12] Our collaboration resulted in identifications of over 170 images of at least fifteen Jātaka narratives through a global survey of collections of Gandhāran art, and helps to shed light on both this understudied visual corpus and fragmentary Gāndhārī Avadānas and Pūrvayogas.

However, only the ubiquitous story of the Buddha's previous birth as Prince Sudaṣṇa (Viśvantara in Sanskrit; Vessantara in Pali) is among the Jātakas represented in Gandhāran art and briefly summarized in the series of Pūrvayogas in a British Library Gāndhārī manuscript (Lenz 2003, 23–27; Salomon 2018, 240–245). While this Jātaka has special significance in Pāli literature as Śākyamuni Buddha's penultimate birth before his rebirth as Siddhattha (Siddhārtha) and as the last of 547 Jātakas is the longest (Appleton and Shaw 2015, 2.507–639), it is so generally widespread in Buddhist literature and art that it is not at all surprising to find it in both Gāndhāran art and a Gāndhārī manuscript. We do not have access to Gandhāran ritual re-enactments of the Vessantara/Viśvantara Jātaka in festival processions incorporating visual scrolls and recitation or to living storytelling traditions as case studies demonstrate in contemporary Southeast Asia and the Kathmandu Valley of Nepal (Collins 2016), but Chinese visitors to Gandhāra in the sixth—seventh centuries CE localize this story at Pa-lu-sha (Varṣapura?) in the Peshawar Basin (Beal 1884, xcvii-xcix, 111–113; Chavannes 1903, 413 *ff.*; Foucher 1915, 33–45; Li 1996, 79).

---

12. Buddhist Rebirth Narratives in Literary and Visual Cultures of Ancient Gandhāra received funding from the Robert H.N. Ho Family Foundation for Buddhist Studies through the American Council of Learned Societies from 2015–2017. For brief and provisional survey results, see Neelis 2019.

Gandhāran scribes made these stories their own through "literary domestication" (Lewis 2000, 3-4) of narratives in regional social, political and cultural contexts. Gāndhārī Avadānas and Pūrvayogas with references to regionally distinctive names, titles, ethnonyms, and toponyms belonging to ca. first century CE contexts reflect patterns of cultural and geographical localization. Non-Indic or hybrid Indo-Iranian onomastic elements, exogenous titles, and Northwestern place names tend to be more evident in Avadānas than in Pūrvayogas. Setting Avadānas and Pūrvayogas in their own contemporary milieu was one of the locative strategies adapted by Gandhāran Buddhists to selectively emplace and transpose particular narratives, relics, and divine figures in order to develop a sacred geography outside of Śākyamuni's "Greater Māgadhan" homeland in northern India.[13]

Ex-eventu prophecies of the Dharma's disappearance in Gāndhārī Pūrvayogas and Avadānas serve as interesting examples to illustrate incorporation of local characters. In the fifth story of the Pūrvayoga sequence set in the northwestern metropolis of Taxila, an anonymous character with an Indo-Scythian ethnonym (Gāndhārī Sago corresponds with Saka / Sanskrit: Śaka) engages in discussion with a monk about the decline of the Dharma (Lenz 2003, 182-192; Salomon 2018, 254-255). The Dharma's disappearance is also a theme in the first of two Avadānas featuring a character named Zadamitra, whose name is clearly Iranian rather than Indian (Lenz 2003, 184-186, Appendix 3; Lenz 2010, 82-93; Salomon 1999, 145). In the summary of this story, Zadamitra declares to a monk: "If the true Dharma shall have disappeared, then I will attain solitary enlightenment" (Salomon 2018, 261). As Lenz (2003, 185-186) and Salomon (2018, 254-5) have observed, a different valency is given to these non-Indian characters with foreign names or ethnonyms in Gāndhārī narratives than other Buddhist eschatologies predicting the future decline of Dharma, in which exogenous groups of Scythians, Greeks, Turks, Muslims and other foreigners are lumped together as invading military forces. Zadamitra's aspiration to "attain solitary enlightenment" is followed by the terms "Teacher, Arhat, Mahātmā" which may be understood as an "abridged *praṇidhāna*" (Lenz 2010, 84). An aspirational vow or "solemn resolution" (*praṇidhāna*) to encounter the Buddha and understand the Dharma is also made by a potter after caring for a dying Solitary Buddha (Pratyekabuddha) in the

---

13. In addition to localizing Jātakas, Avadānas and Pūrvayogas of the Bodhisattva's previous births and encounters with previous Buddhas, other narrative strategies for constructing Buddhist sacred places outside of the "greater Māghadhan" homeland of Śākyamuni identified by Shinohara (2003, 90 *ff.*) included conversions of local autochthonous Nāga and Yakṣa deities and enshrining moveable objects used by the Buddha, such as the "contact relic" (*paribhogika dhātu*) of his begging bowl (Shinohara's specific focus).

Pūrvayoga of Ājñāta Kauṇḍinya, one of the foremost disciples of Śākyamuni Buddha, who is the potter's future rebirth (Lenz 2003, 165–177; Lenz 2010, 112-15; Salomon 2018, 246-49). Generally, Pūrvayogas and Avadānas with recognizable figures linked with hagiographies of Śākyamuni Buddha and other prominent disciples or rulers (such as Aśoka) are relatively more likely to be identifiable with other Buddhist literary versions of narratives than the "homegrown" variety of stories localized in Gandhāra, Taxila, and neighboring northwestern regions.

Gandhāran artisans and their patrons also emplaced aspiring visual narratives of Jātakas in the northwestern borderlands. Gandhāran art features hagiographical scenes from Śākyamuni Buddha's lifetime in the iconographic programme of stūpa architecture more prominently than previous-birth narratives, which are typically depicted in small panels in subsidiary positions, such as "stair risers" on the steps leading up the pathway for circumambulation. The major exception is the so-called Dīpaṅkara Jātaka, which dominates the repertoire of identifiable rebirth narratives (provisionally over 130 out of 170 images in our survey) and is among the four or five most widely depicted narratives in Gandhāran art along with the birth, departure, and Mahāparinirvāṇa of Śākyamuni Buddha. In Gandhāran narrative sequences of Śākyamuni's hagiography, the depiction of the encounter between a young Brahmin ascetic and Dīpaṅkara, a previous Buddha, commonly prefaces the events of Śākyamuni's present birth as Siddhārtha. The characteristic features of the visual narrative are the prostration of the young ascetic, who spreads out his matted dreadlocks for the Buddha Dīpaṅkara to walk upon as he is showered with offerings of lotus flowers. In this transformative encounter between the ascetic character named Sumedha (in the Pāli *Nidānakathā*), Sumati (in the Dharmaruci Avadāna of the *Divyāvadāna*) or Megha (in the Dīpaṅkaravastu of the *Mahāvastu*), the previous Buddha Dīpaṅkara gives a prediction (*vyākaraṇa*) that the Bodhisattva will fulfil his aspirational vow (*praṇidhāna*) to attain Buddhahood. Extant Gāndhārī Avadānas and Pūrvayogas in the British Library collection do not include summaries of this aspirational narrative which is so widely depicted in Gandhāran visual culture, but the Buddha Dīpaṅkara's characteristics are listed first in enumerations of fifteen previous Buddhas in a Gāndhārī *Bahubuddhaka Sūtra* birch-bark scroll in the Library of Congress (Salomon 2018, 265-93; Tournier 2017, 129 ff.). Although the relevant encounter is not preserved due to the fragmentary condition of the beginning of the scroll, the genealogy of previous Buddhas and extended macrohistorical lifestory of Śākyamuni essentially begins with Dīpaṅkara. Beginning with Faxian in the early fifth century CE (Deeg 2005, 247–254; Li 2002, 173), Chinese visitors attest that this encounter was localized in ancient Nagarāhāra (around Jalalabad in modern Nangarhar province in northeastern Afghanistan).[14] Emplacement of the Bodhisattva's aspirational vow (*praṇidhāna*) and Dīpaṅkara's prediction (*vyākaraṇa*) of future Buddhahood in the environment of Gandhāra demonstrates that the Bodhisattva path is not restricted to particular chronological or geographical contexts of Śākyamuni's own time and place. This narrative starting point for Śākyamuni's karmic biography with a transformative encounter in one of his previous lifetimes as a Bodhisattva with the lineage of previous Buddhas, effectively telescopes all rebirths of the Bodhisattva and establishes Gandhāra as the place where the extended lifestory begins. Thus, the localization of the encounter with the Buddha Dīpaṅkara and the prominence of the recollection of this narrative event in Gandhāran visual culture strongly support Robert Brown's argument for the iconicity of Jātakas and other rebirth narratives, which are not limited to serving as didactic illustrations.

Can a case also be made for iconic functions of other Gandhāran Jātakas as manifestations of the Buddha's presence in stūpa architecture? Unlike the Dīpaṅkara narrative, these scenes are not integrated into the hagiography of Śākyamuni's present lifetime, but are depicted on panels which were architectural features of staircases leading up to stūpas at sites such as Jamalgarhi, Aziz Dheri, and Chakhil-i Ghoundi in Hadda (Afghanistan). Perhaps as worshippers ascended the staircases, visual narratives facilitated re-enactments of the Buddha's previous births, thus manifesting the Buddha's presence not only in his bodily relics deposited within the inaccessible relic chamber in the stūpa core but also in these more visible forms. In addition to the narratives of Dīpaṅkara's encounter and Sudaṣṇa (Viśvantara/Vessantara), a logic of locality is also apparent in Chinese visitors' accounts of shrines associated with other jātakas depicted in Gandhāran visual culture. The Śyāma and Ekaśṛṅga (or Ṛśyaśṛṅga) jātakas, which both involve sons of ascetics, are examples of previous-birth narratives localized at hilltop shrines on passes between Peshawar Basin and Swat valley, according to Xuanzang's seventh century account (Li 1996, 78–79). Another pair of jātakas which culminate in "gifts of the body" (*dehadāna*) are localized elsewhere in the northwestern borderlands in fifth and sixth century accounts of Faxian and Song Yun: King Śibi's gift of his body in which he cuts a piece of his own flesh to save a pigeon from a hawk is linked to a region near the Swat valley (Deeg 2005, 120–121, 226–228; Li 2002, 169–170), and the Vyāghrī Jātaka, in which a Bodhisattva sacrifices himself to feed a hungry tigress and her cubs, is associated with

---

14. Deeg comments on the localization of the meeting with Dīpaṅkara (§15), with references to further Indian and Chinese textual sources (2005, 247–254).

multiple locations near Taxila and the Swat valley (Deeg 2005, 230–231; Li 2002, 170). When the Korean monk Hyecho visited Gandhara in the eighth century, "Four Great Stūpas" associated with two Jātakas of King Śibi's gifts of his flesh and eyes, the Vyāghrī Jātaka, and Candraprabha's head offering formed part of a network of pilgrimage sites in parallel to the four places of the birth, awakening, first teaching, and parinirvāṇa of Śākyamuni Buddha in the Buddhist heartland of northern India (Deeg 2005, 121–122; Foucher 1915, 25; Lopez 2017, 177–184). While these locations were not the only places where Jātakas were selectively localized, regional linkages aided in consolidating Buddhist pilgrimage networks in Gandhāra, which became a "second holy land" (Foucher 1932, 416 ff. "la seconde terre sainte") where the Buddha's presence was manifest in narratives.

Conclusions

Buddhist storytellers in Gandhāra used stone, birch-bark scrolls, and other physical media to effectively transmit the Dharma. In the qualified sense that Jātaka images may be perceived as relics of commemoration and abbreviated summaries of Avadānas and Pūrvayogas are original secondary compositions with other texts in manuscripts which were treated like Dharma relics, Gandhāran visual and written narratives of previous births embody the Buddha's presence. Scribes and artisans enhanced the significance of selectively appropriated narratives by emplacing them in northwestern regional contexts through processes of literary domestication and localization, which contributed to the consolidation of a network of shrines visited by monastic and lay worshippers, including East Asian visitors. Since Gandhāran rebirth narratives of the present and previous lives of the Buddha(s) and other figures did not only have didactic functions but also had iconic dimensions, can religious lives of these stories be imagined to resemble persons? Certainly the transformation of oral stories in visual and written media gives birth to visible and legible forms. Gāndhārī Avadānas and Pūrvayogas seem to reflect an early phase in the life cycle of rebirth narratives prior to expansion and elaboration in literary anthologies. The visual ties between previous births depicted on staircases of stūpas with the hagiographic cycle of Śākyamuni's present birth preceded by his encounter with the previous Buddha Dīpaṅkara in an earlier birth can be understood as a comprehensive narrative icon of the Buddha's entire lifestory. By retracing and reliving the extended lifestories of the Buddha and other figures whose previous and present narratives have been given shape in written and visual media, those who aspire to supramundane goals are able to follow the maps with paths to Buddhahood taken by Bodhisattvas.

References

Allon, Mark. 2001. *Three Gāndhārī Ekottarikāgama-type sutras: British Library Kharoṣṭhī fragments 12 and 14*. Gandhāran Buddhist Texts 2. Seattle: University of Washington Press. https://doi.org/10.1007/s10783-005-8898-1

Allon, Mark. 2007. "Introduction: The Senior Manuscripts." In Andrew Glass, *Four Gāndhārī Saṃyuktāgama sutras: Senior Kharoṣṭhī fragment 5*: 3–25. Gandhāran Buddhist Texts 4. Seattle: University of Washington Press.

Allon, Mark and Richard Salomon. 2010. "New Evidence for the Mahāyāna in Early Gandhāra." *Eastern Buddhist* 41: 1–22.

Appadurai, Arjun. 1986. "Commodities and Politics of Value." In *The Social Life of Things: Commodities in Cultural Perspective*, edited by Arjun Appadurai, 3–63. Cambridge: Cambridge University Press. https://doi.org/10.1017/s0395264900069420

Appleton, Naomi and Sarah Shaw, trans. 2015. *The Ten Great Birth Stories of the Buddha: The Mahānipāta of the Jātakatthavaṇṇanā*. 2 volumes. Chiang Mai: Silkworm.

Baums, Stefan. 2009. "A Gāndhārī Commentary on Early Buddhist Verses: British Library Kharoṣṭhī fragments 7, 9, 13 and 18." Unpublished PhD thesis, University of Washington.

———. 2012. "Catalog and Revised Texts and Translations of Gandharan Reliquary Inscriptions." In *Gandharan Buddhist Reliquaries*, edited by David Jongeward, Elizabeth Errington, Richard Salomon, and Stefan Baums, 200–251. Seattle: University of Washington Press. https://doi.org/10.1017/s135618631300028x

———. 2015. "Commentary: Overview." In *Brill's Encyclopedia of Buddhism*, Volume 1, edited by Jonathan Silk, 409–418. Leiden: Brill.

Baums, Stefan and Andrew Glass. 2019. Gandhari Language and Literature. Catalog of Kharoṣṭhī Inscriptions [CKI]. https://www.gandhari.org/a_inscriptions.php

Beal, Samuel, trans. 1884. *Si-yu-ki. Buddhist Records of the Western World*. London: Kegan Paul, Trench, Trübner.

Braarvig, Jens. 2014. "The Schøyen Collection." In *From Birch Bark to Digital Data*, edited by Paul Harrison and Jens-Uwe Hartmann, 157–164. Vienna: Österreichische Akademie der Wissenschaften. http://austriaca.at/7581-0inhalt?frames=yes

Brough, John, ed. 1962. *The Gāndhārī Dharmapada*. Oxford: Oxford University Press.

Brown, Robert. 1997. "Narrative as Icon: The Jātaka Stories in Ancient Indian and Southeast Asian Architecture." In *Sacred Biography in the Buddhist Traditions of South and Southeast Asia*, edited by Juliane Schober, 64–109. Honolulu: University of Hawaii Press.

Campany, Robert Ford. 1991. "Notes on the Devotional Uses and Symbolic Functions of *Sūtra* Texts as Depicted in Early Chinese Buddhist Miracle Tales and Hagiographies." *Journal of the International Association of Buddhist Studies* 14(1): 28–72.

Campany, Robert Ford. 2012. *Signs from the Unseen Realm: Buddhist Miracle Tales from Early Medieval China*. Honolulu: University of Hawaii Press. http://austriaca.at/7581-0inhalt?frames=yes

Chavannes, Édouard. 1903. "Voyage de Song Yun dans l'Udyana et le Gandhara (518–522 p.C)." *Bulletin de l'École française d'Extrême-Orient* 3: 379–440. https://doi.org/10.3406/befeo.1903.1235

Collins, Steven, ed. 2016. *Readings of the Vessantara Jataka*. New York: Columbia University Press.

Cox, Collett. 2014. "Gāndhārī Kharoṣṭhī Manuscripts: Exegetical Texts." In *From Birch Bark to Digital Data*, edited by Paul Harrison and Jens-Uwe Hartmann, 35–49. Vienna: Österreichische Akademie der Wissenschaften. http://austriaca.at/7581-0inhalt?frames=yes

Deeg, Max. 2005. *Das Gaoseng-Faxian-Zhuan als religionsgeschichtliche Quelle: der älteste Bericht eines chinesischen buddhistischen Pilgermönchs über seine Reise nach Indien mit Übersetzung des Textes*. Wiesbaden: Harrassowitz.

Drewes, David. 2007. "Revisiting the phrase 'sa pṛthvīpradeśaś caityabhūto bhavet' and the Mahāyāna Cult of the Book." *Indo-Iranian Journal* 50: 101–143. https://doi.org/10.1007/s10783-007-9052-z

Falk, Harry. 2011. "The 'Split' Collection of Kharoṣṭhī Texts." *Sōka daigaku kokusai bukkyōgaku kōtō kenkyūjo nenpō* (Annual Report of the International Research Institute for Advanced Buddhology at Soka University) 14: 13–23. http://iriab.soka.ac.jp/orc/Publications/ARIRIAB/pdf/ARIRIAB-14.pdf

Falk, Harry and Seishi Karashima. 2012. "A First-Century *Prajñāpāramitā* Manuscript from Gandhāra—*parivarta* 1 (Texts from the Split Collection 1)." *Sōka daigaku kokusai bukkyōgaku kōtō kenkyūjo nenpō* (Annual Report of the International Research Institute for Advanced Buddhology at Soka University) 15: 19–61. http://iriab.soka.ac.jp/orc/Publications/ARIRIAB/pdf/ARIRIAB-15.pdf

———. 2013. "A First-Century *Prajñāpāramitā* Manuscript from Gandhāra—*parivarta* 5 (Texts from the Split Collection 2)." *Sōka daigaku kokusai bukkyōgaku kōtō kenkyūjo nenpō* (Annual Report of the International Research Institute for Advanced Buddhology at Soka University) 16: 97–169. http://iriab.soka.ac.jp/orc/Publications/ARIRIAB/pdf/ARIRIAB-16.pdf

Falk, Harry and Ingo Strauch. 2014. "The Bajaur and Split Collections of Kharoṣṭhī Manuscripts within the Context of Buddhist Gāndhārī Literature." In *From Birch Bark to Digital Data*, edited by Paul Harrison and Jens-Uwe Hartmann, 51–78. Vienna: Österreichische Akademie der Wissenschaften. http://austriaca.at/7581-0inhalt?frames=yes

Foucher, Alfred. 1915 [1901]. "Notes sur la géographie ancienne du Gandhâra." *Bulletin de l'École française d'Extrême-Orient* 1: 322–369. https://doi.org/10.3406/befeo.1901.1060

———. 1932. *L'art gréco-bouddhique du Gandhâra; étude sur les origines de l'influence classique dans l'art bouddhique de l'Inde et de l'Extrême-Orient.* Vol. 2. Paris: Imprimerie Nationale. https://doi.org/10.2307/624457

Fussman, Gérard. 1982. "Documents épigraphiques kouchans (III): L'inscription Kharoṣṭhī de Senavarma, roi d'Oḍi: une nouvelle lecture." *Bulletin de l'École française d'Extrême-Orient* 71: 1–46. https://doi.org/10.3406/befeo.1982.1466

Germano, David and Kevin Trainor, eds. 2004. *Embodying the Dharma: Buddhist Relic Veneration in Asia.* Albany: State University of New York Press.

Hargreaves, Harold, trans. 1915. *Notes on the Ancient Geography of Gandhāra: A commentary on a chapter of Hiuan Tsang.* Calcutta: Superintendent of Government Printing, India.

Harrison, Paul. 1992. "Is the *Dharma-kāya* the Real 'Phantom Body' of the Buddha?" *Journal of the International Association of Buddhist Studies* 15(1): 44–92.

Harrison, Paul and Jens-Uwe Hartmann, eds. 2014. *From Birch Bark to Digital Data: Recent Advances in Buddhist Manuscript Research.* Vienna: Österreichische Akademie der Wissenschaften. http://austriaca.at/7581-0inhalt?frames=yes

Hartmann, Jens-Uwe. 2009. "From Words to Books: Indian Buddhist manuscripts in the first millennium CE." In *Buddhist Manuscript Cultures: Knowledge, ritual, and art*, edited by Stephen Berkwitz, Juliane Schober, and Claudia Brown, 95–105. Abingdon: Routledge. https://doi.org/10.1163/001972409x12645171002298

Kieschnick, John. 2003. *Chinese Buddhism and Material Culture.* Princeton: Princeton University Press.

Lenz, Timothy. 2003. *A New Version of the Gāndhārī Dharmapada and a Collection of Previous-birth Stories: British Library Kharoṣṭhī fragments 16 + 25.* Gandhāran Buddhist Texts 3. Seattle: University of Washington Press. https://doi.org/10.2307/4132130

———. 2010. *Gandhāran Avadānas: British Library Kharoṣṭhī fragments 1–3 and 21 and supplementary fragments A-C.* Gandhāran Buddhist Texts 6. Seattle: University of Washington Press. https://doi.org/10.1163/15728536-05800008

Lewis, Todd. 2000. *Popular Buddhist texts from Nepal: Narratives and Rituals of Newar Buddhism.* Albany: State University of New York Press. https://doi.org/10.1016/s0048-721x(03)00037-x

———. 2015. "Avadānas and Jātakas in the Newar Tradition of the Kathmandu Valley: Ritual Performances of Mahāyāna Buddhist Narratives." *Religion Compass* 9/8: 233–253.

Li Rongxi, trans. 1996. *The Great Tang Dynasty Record of the Western Regions*. Berkeley: Numata Center for Buddhist Translation and Research.

———. 2002. "Journey of the Eminent Monk Faxian." In *Lives of Great Monks and Nuns*. Berkeley: Numata Center for Buddhist Translation and Research.

Lopez, Donald S., Carla M. Sinopoli, Chun Wa Chan, Donald S. Lopez Jr., Ha Nul Jun, Keiko Yokota, Kevin Gray Carr, and Rebecca Bloom. 2017. *Hyecho's Journey: The World of Buddhism*. Chicago, IL: University of Chicago Press. https://doi.org/10.1111/rsr.13926

Matsuda, Kazunobu. 2014. "Japanese Collections of Buddhist Manuscript Fragments from the Same Region as the Schøyen Collection." In *From Birch Bark to Digital Data*, edited by Paul Harrison and Jens-Uwe Hartmann, 165–170. Vienna: Österreichische Akademie der Wissenschaften. http://austriaca.at/7581-0inhalt?frames=yes

Neelis, Jason. 2011. *Early Buddhist Transmission and Trade Networks: Mobility and Exchange within and beyond the Northwestern Borderlands of South Asia*. Leiden: Brill. http://www.oapen.org/search?identifier=627414

———. 2013. "Buddhism in Gandhāra." Oxford Bibliographies Online. http://doi.org.10.1093/obo/9780195393521-010

———. 2019. "Making Places for Buddhism in Gandhāra: Stories of Previous Births in Image and Text." In *The Geography of Gandhāran Art*, edited by Wannaporn Rienjang and Peter Stewart, 175–185. Oxford: Archaeopress.

Rambelli, Fabio. 2007. *Buddhist Materiality: A Cultural History of Objects in Japanese Buddhism*. Stanford: Stanford University Press. https://doi.org/10.1086/649531

Rotman, Andy. 2009. *Thus Have I Seen: Visualizing Faith in Early Indian Buddhism*. Oxford: Oxford University Press. https://doi.org/10.3202/caa.reviews.2011.141

Salomon, Richard. 1999. *Ancient Buddhist Scrolls from Gandhāra: The British Library Kharoṣṭhī fragments*. London and Seattle: British Library and University of Washington Press. https://doi.org/10.5860/choice.37-1505

Salomon, Richard. 2000. *A Gāndhārī version of the Rhinoceros Sutra: British Library Kharoṣṭhī fragment 5B*. Gandhāran Buddhist Texts 1. Seattle: University of Washington Press. https://doi.org/10.1007/s10783-005-1693-1

———. 2003. "The Senior Manuscripts: Another Collection of Gandhāran Buddhist Scrolls." *Journal of the American Oriental Society* 123(1): 73–92. https://doi.org/10.2307/3217845

———. 2008. *Two Gāndhārī manuscripts of the Songs of Lake Anavatapta (Anavataptagāthā): British Library Kharoṣṭhī fragment 1 and Senior Scroll 14*. Gandhāran Buddhist Texts 5. Seattle: University of Washington Press. https://doi.org/10.1111/j.1748-0922.2010.01436_3.x

———. 2014. "Gāndhārī Manuscripts in the British Library, Schøyen and Other Collections." In *From Birch Bark to Digital Data*, edited by Paul Harrison and Jens-Uwe Hartmann, 1–17. Vienna: Österreichische Akademie der Wissenschaften. http://austriaca.at/7581-0inhalt?frames=yes

———. 2018. *The Buddhist Literature of Ancient Gandhāra: An Introduction with Selected Translations*. Somerville MA: Wisdom.

Schopen, Gregory. 1975. "The Phrase *sa pṛthvīpradeśaś caityabhūto bhavet* in the *Vajracchedikā*: Notes on the Cult of the Book in Mahāyāna." *Indo-Iranian Journal* 17: 147–181. https://doi.org/10.1163/000000075790079574

———. 1987. "Burial Ad Sanctos and the Physical Presence of the Buddha in Early Indian Buddhism: A Study in the Archaeology of Religions." *Religion* 17: 193–225. https://doi.org/10.1016/0048-721x(87)90116-3

———. 1997. *Bones, Stones, and Buddhist Monks: Collected Papers on the Archaeology, Epigraphy, and texts of Monastic Buddhism in India*. Honolulu: University of Hawai'i Press. https://doi.org/10.1177/000842980203100356

———. 2005. *Figments and Fragments of Mahāyāna Buddhism in India: More collected papers*. Honolulu: University of Hawai'i Press.

———. 2010. "The Book as Sacred Object in Private Homes in Early or Medieval India." In *Medieval and Early Modern Devotional Objects in Global Perspective: Translations of the Sacred*, edited by Elizabeth Robertson and Jennifer Jahner, 37-60. New York: Palgrave Macmillan.

Shinohara, Koichi. 2003. "The Story of the Buddha's Begging Bowl: Imagining Biography and Sacred Places." In *Pilgrims, Patrons, and Place: Localizing Sanctity in Asian Religions*, edited by Phyllis Granoff and Koichi Shinohara, 68–107. Vancouver: University of British Columbia Press. https://doi.org/10.1177/000842980703600237

Skilling, Peter. 2005. "Cutting Across Categories: Relics in Pāli Texts, the *Bhadrakalpika-sūtra*, and the *Saddharmapuṇḍarīka-sūtra*." *Sōka daigaku kokusai bukkyōgaku kōtō kenkyūjo nenpō* (Annual Report of the International Research Institute for Advanced Buddhology at Soka University) 8: 269–332. http://iriab.soka.ac.jp/content/pdf/aririab/Vol.%20VIII%20(2005)%20[rev.4Aug2010].pdf

Stargardt, Janice and Michael Willis, eds. 2018. *Relics and Relic Worship in Early Buddhism: India, Afghanistan, Sri Lanka and Burma*. Research Publication 218. London: British Museum.

Strauch, Ingo. 2008. "The Bajaur Collection of Kharoṣṭhī Manuscripts—a preliminary survey." *Studien zur Indologie und Iranistik* 25: 103–136.

———. 2010. "More Missing Pieces of Early Pure Land Buddhism: New Evidence for Akṣobhya and Abhirati in an Early Mahāyāna Sūtra from Gandhāra." *Eastern Buddhist* 41: 23–66.

———. 2014. "Looking into water pots and over a Buddhist scribe's shoulder—On the deposition and the use of manuscripts in early Buddhism." *Asiatische Studien* 68: 797–830. https://doi.org/10.1515/asia-2014-0063

Strong, John. 2004. *Relics of the Buddha*. Princeton: Princeton University Press.
Tournier, Vincent. 2017. *La formation du Mahāvastu et la mise en place des conceptions relatives à la carrière du bodhisattva*. Paris: École française d'Extrême-Orient. https://doi.org/10.3406/befeo.1997.2475
Trainor, Kevin. 1997. *Relics, Ritual, and Representation in Buddhism: Rematerializing the Sri Lankan Theravāda tradition*. Cambridge: Cambridge University Press. https://doi.org/10.1017/s1356186300016217
Willis, Michael. 2000. *Buddhist Reliquaries from Ancient India*. London: British Museum.

— 9 —

Daoist Writs and Scriptures as Sacred Beings

Jihyun Kim

The Chinese equivalent of "sutra" or "canonical scripture" is *jing* 經, which literally means "vertical thread" in weaving, from which various strata of meaning are derived, such as "the axis of life," "the orthodox way," or "unchanging rule." What are called *jing* are prolific in the Daoist tradition. Since the fifth century CE, when Daoism was recognized as a *jiao* 教 "teaching" of a different system from that of Confucianism and Buddhism, Daoist scriptures have played an important role in enabling Daoism to gain a position on a par with that of the other two teachings. Plenty of evidence shows that the formation and solidification of canonical scriptures facilitated the development of Daoism: the formation of the classification system of the *Daoist Canon* was the core of establishing the Daoist religious tradition (Ōfuchi 1979; Schipper 1985; Kim 2017); many important Daoist rituals were developed in connection with the transmission of scriptures (Kobayashi 2003; Kim 2011); and the recitation of scriptures was placed at the center of Daoist orthodox praxis (Robinet 1993; Kim 2006). However, since Erik Zürcher pointed out that one of the Daoist characteristics that distinguished Daoism from Buddhism is "the idea that texts as such are quintessential things in themselves" (Zürcher 1980, 142), there has rarely been any discussion of this issue. Kamitsuka Yoshiko has tried to explain the logic of the sanctification of Daoist scriptures, mainly by paying attention to the problem of salvation (Kamitsuka 2017). Wang Chengwen has also dealt with this problem, focusing mainly on the Numinous Treasure Scriptures (Wang 2010).

From the perspective of cultural context, Daoist scriptures have a unique aspect closely related to the Chinese writing system. Needless to

Jihyun Kim is Associate Professor in the Department of Religious Studies in the College of Humanities at Seoul National University, Korea

say, Chinese characters are the one and only surviving ancient writing system characterized by pictorial images. In addition, the Daoist concept of scripture is founded on a belief system in which letters and sounds are particular forms of *qi* 氣, the omnipresent "pneuma and energy." Such a way of thinking provides a lead for understanding the Daoist veneration of scriptures.

The aim of this chapter is to explore the characteristics of Daoist canonical scriptures as "sacred beings," mainly through an investigation of the Daoist perspective on scriptures, evidence of scripture-worship, and lastly the relationship between scripture and practice.[1]

The origins of Daoist scriptures and "original writs"

The starting point for discussing Daoist scriptures should be the *Scripture of the Dao and Its Virtue* (*Daode jing* 道德經) and the *Scripture of the Great Peace* (*Taiping jing* 太平經). In brief, the latter reveals that great peace on earth will be brought about through the advent of *dao-qi* 道氣, "the Way and Pneuma," by arguing for the importance of harmony between the Three Powers of the universe, namely, heaven, earth, and humans. The former, the *Daode jing*, has been widely read as a bible for politics as well as self-cultivation since the fourth century BCE. It was transformed into a religious scripture recited by Daoist adepts in the Heavenly Master tradition (*Tianshi dao* 天師道), in which Laozi 老子, "the Old Master," was deified as Taishang Laojun 太上老君, "the Old Lord of Great High" (Seidel 1969a, Kusuyama 1979).

As for Daoist scriptures that developed later, Ge Hong 葛洪 (283–343) writes, "There is nothing more important than the *Writs of the Three Sovereigns* (*Sanhuang wen* 三皇文) and the *Charts of the True Forms of the Five Sacred Peaks* (*Wuyue zhenxing tu* 五嶽真形圖) among the Daoist scriptures" (Ge Hong, 336). As a master of Chinese alchemy, he placed great emphasis on the golden elixir and refined cinnabar (*jinye huandan* 金液還丹, or *jindan* 金丹) as the best way to become a Celestial Transcendent (*tianxian* 天仙). Both scriptures appeared to have talismanic functions to support entering sacred mountains and to protect Daoist adepts from evil spirits, which were inextricably linked with refining the cinnabar (*liandan* 煉丹).

Antiquity is a critical factor for determining the hierarchy of canonical scriptures in Chinese tradition. However, the *Daode jing* and *Taiping jing* were both overlooked in the first *Daoist Canon* (*daozang* 道藏). The Three Caverns (*sandong* 三洞), the classification system of the *Daoist Canon* established by the Daoist master Liu Xiujing 陸修靜 (406–477), included nei-

---

1 This research was supported by the Promising-Pioneering Researcher Program of Seoul National University (2015–2018).

ther of the two oldest Taoist texts. Instead, the core of the Three Caverns was composed of revealed texts from Southern China dating from the late fourth century CE.

The first division of the Three Caverns, titled Cavern of Perfection (*Dongzhen* 洞眞), is the corpus of Highest Clarity (*shangqing* 上清), which appeared through the revelation of Mt. Mao (Maoshan 茅山); the second is Cavern of Mystery (*Dongxuan* 洞玄), which is the corpus of Numinous Treasure (*lingbao* 靈寶), some of which came from Ge Hong's collections, and others from new scriptures that claimed to have been revealed by the Celestial Worthy of Primordial Beginning (Yuanshi Tianzun 元始天尊) and taught by the Transcendent Duke Ge (Ge Xiangong 葛仙公); and the last is Cavern of Divinity (*Dongshen* 洞神), which is the corpus of Three Sovereigns (*sanhuang* 三皇) that elaborates on the *Writs of the Three Sovereigns* and manuals of transmission rituals (Schipper and Verellen 2008, 11–17).

It was only after four more classification categories, known as the Four Supplements (*sifu* 四輔), were added to the Three Caverns that the *Daode jing* and *Taiping jing* were included in the *Daoist Canon*. Indeed, the principle that the antiquity of a text gives it a higher rank was applied in the Daoist classification system. However, antiquity was not historical, but mythical and theological. The newly revealed scriptures occupied the highest ranks because of theological interpretations that they were revealed by more profound and primordial beings than Laozi.

Each of the three divisions of the *Daoist Canon* is subdivided into twelve parts. Because of this three-twelve classification system, the scriptures of the Three Caverns were often called the "Venerable Scriptures of Thirty-Six Divisions" (*sanshiliu bu zunjing* 三十六部尊經). Here, I wish to focus on the twelve-part classification system, because the classification itself is important for the notion of Daoist scripture.

Although the Daoist twelve subdivisions were obviously influenced by those of the Buddhist Canon, Liu Xiujing originally designed them anew in order to classify the corpus of Numinous Treasure (*lingbao jing*). Through modifications by Song Wenming 宋文明 around the sixth century, the twelve divisions have been applied to all divisions and established as subcategories of the *Daoist Canon*. They are *benwen* 本文, Divine Talismans (*shenfu* 神符), Jade Instructions (*yujue* 玉訣), Numinous Charts (*lingtu* 靈圖), Genealogies (*pulu* 譜錄), Precepts (*jielü* 誡律), Liturgical Protocols (*weiyi* 威儀), Methods and Formulas (*fangfa* 方法), Techniques (*zhongshu* 衆術), Hagiographies (*zhuanji* 傳記), Hymns (*zansong* 讚誦), and Petitions and Announcements (*biaozou* 表奏).

According to the main features of the Chinese classification system, in which the most important and oldest text is placed at the start, the first division "*benwen*" designates the most important texts in the Daoist Canon. What, then, does *benwen* mean? It is often rendered as "Basic Text" (Boltz in Pregadio 2008, 1257). However, as has been pointed out by Wang (2010), the Daoist doctrinal explanation gives a different answer.[2]

> '*Benwen*' is [a scripture written in] the script of the Three Primordials (*sanyuan* 三元) and Eight Assemblies (*bahui* 八會). It is like a sutra (*zhangxing* 長行, prose passages) or gatha (*guqi* 孤起, exegetical verse parts) [of the *Buddhist Canon*]. The Lady of Purple Tenuity (*Ziwei furen* 紫微夫人) said that texts written in the script of the Three Primordials and Eight Assemblies are only possessed by the Highest Perfected in the Grand Pole [of the Daoist Heaven]. '*Ben*' is the beginning (*shi* 始), the root (*gen* 根). It is the beginning of canonical teachings and the root of the script. At the same time, it is the origin of attaining the cosmic pattern and the root of myriad beings. '*Wen*' is division (*fen* 分), pattern and principle (*li* 理). [Because of it,] it is possible to differentiate the two aspects (of Yin and Yang) so as to discern the true reality of beings; it is possible to organize myriad things so as to make clear the explanations of the ultimate pattern and principle. Thus, it is called "pattern," just like trees have distinctive patterns. (DZ1032, *YJQQ* 6: 20a–20b, "Twelve Divisions")

> 言本文者，即三元八會之書．長行．［元］〈孤〉起之說，其例是也．紫微夫人云，三元八會之書，太極高眞所有．本者，始也，根也．是經教之始，文字之根；又爲得理之元，萬法之本．文者，分也，理也．既能分辨二儀，又能分別法相；既能理於萬事，又能表詮至理．如木有文，亦名爲理也．

According to this explanation, *benwen* does not mean "contents" or "basic text," but mainly designates a particular type of script. These scripts or writs are considered to be the beginning of writing and the cosmic principle at the same time. The explanation ascribed to the Lady of Purple Tenuity even placed it in the Daoist celestial realm, and this passage is always quoted to explain the origins of Daoist canonical scriptures. It was a part of the fourth century revelations of Mt. Mao, appearing in *Declarations of the Perfected* (DZ1016, *Zhengao* 眞誥).

> Now let me explain the origins of writing. At the beginning of creating writs, **it was when the five colors started to sprout, and writing patterns were demarcated**. [At that time] human relationships were put forth, and the divisions of Yin and Yang were differentiated. Then the scripts of the Three Primordials and Eight Assemblies, flying in the Heavens of all directions, came into being. Again, the patterns of the Eight Dragons and Cloud Seal script with Bright Rays appeared. Later, when it became

---

2 Because my interpretation of the original text is slightly different from Wang's, I have given my own translation here.

the time of the two Sovereigns (*Fuxi* and *Shennong*), they developed the script of Eight Assemblies into the patterns of Dragon and Phoenix and bent and abridged the Cloud Seal script to turn it into the flowing type of Brahmi script. **[Ever since] the two ways [of Heaven and Earth] were divided, they dismantled the true scripts and transformed them into easy forms, and combined parts of the roots and branches to make sixty-four types of scripts**. Finally, they distributed them in the ten directions above and below the Thirty-Six Heavens. [Each domain has] its own writing system and different usage. Even though the pronunciation rules are the same, their forms and appearances became very different. To make a comparison, **the script of Eight Assemblies is the ultimate true form of script, the ancestor of writing patterns; the Cloud Seal script with Bright Rays was established from the root, and it is the beginning of every type of script. Now, the scripts of the Three Primordials and Eight Assemblies are used by Pure Transcendents and High-ranked Perfected in the Grand Pole of the Highest Sovereign. The pattern of the Cloud Seal script with Bright Rays is what we can see now in the characters of divine talismans.** (DZ1016, 1: 8a–9a)

今請陳爲書之本始也．造文之旣肇矣，乃是五色初萌，文章畫定之時，秀人民之交，別陰陽之分．則有三元八會群方飛天之書，又有八龍雲篆明光之章也．其後逮二皇之世，演八會之文，爲龍鳳之章，拘省雲篆之迹，以爲順形梵書．分破二道，壞眞從易，配別本支，乃爲六十四種之書也．遂播之于三十六天十方上下也．各各取其篇類，異而用之．音典雖均，蔚跡隔異矣．校而論之，八會之書，是書之至眞，建文章之祖也．雲篆明光，是其根宗所起，有書而始也．今三元八會之書，皇上太極高眞清仙之所用也．雲篆明光之章，今所見神靈符書之字，是也．

This is the oldest Daoist origin myth of the Chinese script and writing system. It was transcribed by Yang Xi 楊羲 (330–386?) in 365 (DZ1016, 1: 7b). The Three Primordials and Eight Assemblies are regarded as the beginning of scripts. According to the above explanation, they appeared after the cosmos emerged and before Yin-Yang and the Five Phases (*wuxing* 五行) took concrete forms. Interestingly, it is said that the Brahmi script (actually used from the third century BCE to the fifth century CE) was created at the time of legendary kings of ancient China, Fuxi 伏犧 and Shennong 神農; all sixty-four Indian scripts were made by dismantling and recombining the true script of Daoist scripture. All other Chinese scripts are said to have appeared after Heaven and Earth came into existence. It is noteworthy that Daoist scripts are claimed to exist prior to Heaven and Earth. Here we can also see the notion that the writing style of Daoist talismans imitated that of the celestial world.

However, there is no tangible explanation of these scripts in the above passage. Concrete descriptions of them are found in a later Daoist text, one of the Numinous Treasure scriptures, the *Scripture of Esoteric Sounds of Various Heavens of the Cavern of Mystery* (*Dongxuan zhutian neiyin jing* 洞玄諸天內音經) (DZ97, 3: 2a), which gives an explanation of the "Numinous Script of Eight Assemblies" (*lingshu bahui* 靈書八會).

> Suddenly, the celestial script came into being, and its characters were about 3 meters in size. It emerged spontaneously in the midst of five-colored lights up above in the mysterious sky. Its patterns and colors are bright and brilliant; its eight angles shine down rays of light; its dense radiance dazzles one's eyes, so that one cannot look at it. (DZ1138, *WSBY* 24: 3b)

忽有天書，字方一丈，自然而見，空玄之上，五色光中．文彩煥爛，八角垂芒，精光亂眼，不可得看．

Here, Eight Assemblies is described as a "celestial script" (*tianshu* 天書) that appeared by means of a spontaneous concentration of celestial light, which implies *qi* or cosmic pneuma. The above passage is a prototypical explanation of the characteristics of Numinous Treasure scriptures (Wang 2010, Kamitsuka 2017), excerpted even in an official history (*Book of Sui* 35, 1092).

It developed and became established as Daoist doctrine, as we can see in a conversation between the Tang-dynasty Daoist master Pan Shizheng 潘師正 (586–684) and the emperor Gaozong 高宗. Master Pan said:

> I investigated how Daoist scriptures and revelations originated from the Three Primordials. From this origin, phenomenal beings came down and formed the Five Virtues, then Three plus Five, and formed the Eight Assemblies. The script of Eight Assemblies was composed of subtle pneuma, eight sides of which shine down rays of light, and congealed in the form of the Cloud Seal script in the void. The Great Perfected pressed down his writing brush and the Jade Concubine attended the seat; they wrote the letters with yellowish gold, made tablets with white jade, concealed [those scriptures] up in various heavens, and stored them in the mystic tower of seven treasures. [If] there is Dao [in the world, the scriptures] manifest themselves; [if there is] no Dao, they hide themselves. They are spontaneously created celestial scripts and are not related to the earthly script created by Cang Jie. (DZ1128, 1: 4a)

尋道家經誥，起自三元．從本降迹，成於五德，以三就五，乃成八會．其八會之字，妙氣所成，八角垂芒，凝空雲篆．太眞按筆，玉妃拂筵，黃金爲書，白玉爲簡，秘於諸天之上，藏於七寶玄臺．有道卽現，無道卽隱．蓋是自然天書，非關蒼頡所作．

Master Pan defined Eight Assemblies as being composed of Primordial Qi, a spontaneously created celestial script, which preceded the creation of Heaven and Earth. Later, his explanation became a general explanation for

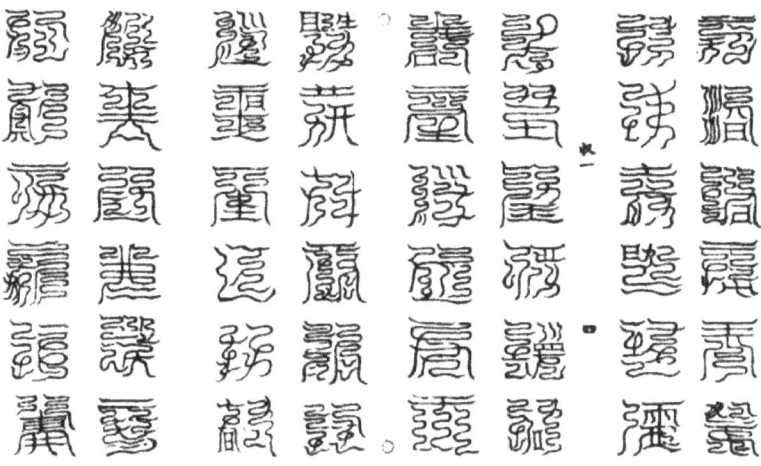

Figure 9.1 Spontaneously Formed Jade Characters (DZ97).

Daoist scriptures (*YJQQ* 3:2b). In Pan's explanation, we can see that interpretations have advanced from those of the Lady of Purple Tenuity. First, Pan adopted the descriptions of Numinous Treasure scriptures in order to understand the Three Primordials and Eight Assemblies. Secondly, he understood Eight Assemblies as the sum of Three and Five.

As a matter of fact, Pan's understanding reflects earlier debates about Daoist writs since the fifth century. Initially, it was Liu Xiujing who interpreted Eight Assemblies as the sum of "Three" Powers (*sancai* 三才) and "Five" Phases (*wuxing* 五行). Song Wenming and later Daoist masters, however, argued against this interpretation. Their debates were summarized in *Great Meanings of the Daoist School* (*Xuanmen dayi* 玄門大義, i.e. *Daomen dalun* 道門大論), and their conclusion is as follows:

> On the basis of these arguments, the Three Primordials are not the Three Powers, and the Five Virtues are not the Five Phases. **Instead, these are the Three Pneumas (*sanqi* 三氣) of the Grandees of the Three Treasures (*sanbao zhangren* 三寶丈人). These Three Pneumas have five virtues for themselves**... Thus, it is clear that the Three Primordials existed when Heaven and Earth had not yet unfolded, before the Three Powers had come into being. **Master Song interpreted the Eight Assemblies as being just [the sum of] the Three Primordials and the Five Virtues:** the Three Primordials are the Primordial of Great Emptiness in Thorough Chaos and the Pneuma of the Highest Jade Sovereign, the Primordial of Great Emptiness in Reddish Chaos and the Pneuma of the Supreme Jade Void, and the Primordial of Mystic Penetration into the Dark Silence and the Pneuma of the Supreme Jade Void. **The Five Virtues are concomitants of the Three Primordials; the assembling of the Three and the Five is [com-

binations of] **Yin, Yang, and Neutral.** There are two types of Yin, Little Yin and Great Yin; two types of Yang, Little Yang and Great Yang. These are combined with Neutral to complete the Five Virtues. (*YJQQ*, 7: 1a–2a)

即此而論，三元應非三才，五德應非五行也．此正應是三寶丈人之三氣，三氣自有五德耳⋯．故知此三元在天地未開，三才未生之前也．宋法師解，八會祇是三氣五德．三元者，一曰，混洞太無元高上玉皇之氣．二曰，赤混太無元無上玉虛之氣．三曰，冥寂玄通元無上玉虛之氣．五德者，即三元所有，三五會即陰陽和．陰有少陰太陰，陽有少陽太陽，就和中之和爲五德也．

The conclusion of the debate is that the Three Primordials and Eight Assemblies are not the Three Powers and Five Phases, for these are later derivations after Heaven and Earth had come into existence. Because they must precede them, it is claimed that the Three Primordials are the *qi* of a trinity of gods (*sanbao jun* 三寶君) who brought forth the Three Cavern scriptures before the emergence of Heaven and Earth. The trinity is composed of Lord of Celestial Treasure (*tianbao jun* 天寶君), Lord of Numinous Treasure (*lingbao jun* 靈寶君), and Lord of Divine Treasure (*shenbao jun* 神寶君). Each deity is again the origin of each of the Three Caverns.

However, the Three Gods are only phenomenal beings, whose substantial being is the Primordial Pneuma (*yuanqi* 元氣) of the cosmos. In other words, they are three differentiations of the One Primordial Pneuma (Mugitani 2005, 135–140). These Three Pneumas formed the script of the Three Primordials, and therefore the script of the Three Primordials is the substance of each of the Three Caverns, located in three Daoist heavens or Three Clarities (*sanqing* 三清).

	Three Primordial Pneumas 三元 (三氣) (Origin/Substance)	Lords of Three Treasures (Phenomenal Beings)	Three Caverns (Scriptures)	Three Clarities (Heavens)
元氣 Primordial Pneuma	Primordial of Great Emptiness in Thorough Chaos Pneuma of the Highest Jade Sovereign	Lord of Heavenly Treasure	Cavern of Perfection	Jade Clarity
	Primordial of Great Emptiness in Reddish Chaos Pneuma of the Supreme Jade Void	Lord of Numinous Treasure	Cavern of Mystery	Highest Clarity
	Primordial of Mystic Penetration into Dark Silence Pneuma of the Supreme Jade Void	Lord of Divine Treasure	Cavern of Divinity	Great Clarity

The meaning of *benwen* has now become clear. Liu Xiujing originally called it the "Origin of Scriptures" (*jing zhi benyuan* 經之本源) (P2256). In the phenomenal world, scriptures exist in the form of writings on silk or paper. However, their true form is not these scripts of the human world but writs of the celestial realm, which are crystallization of primordial pneuma in the air. It is thought that only talismanic characters are similar to "original writs." According to this view, a collection of talismans is the archetype of a Daoist scripture. It is believed that only a few people could decipher these celestial writs and transcribed them into earthly scripts. The Three Cavern scriptures were all considered to have been written in such celestial scripts. Yang Xi was a representative figure who transcribed the scripts of the Three Primordials and Eight Assemblies revealed by the Transcendent into a simplified type of Chinese character (*lishu* 隸書) (DZ1016, 2: 7b).

According to Daoist doctrine, the original writs and primordial pneuma are one and the same. From this argument that "script equals pneuma," an important Daoist theory of practice is derived. I will return to this question later, after I explore in the next section the aspect of scripture-worship.

The veneration of scriptures

The scriptures are the most important medium between Daoist adepts and celestial pneuma, and, what is more, they are containers of celestial pneuma. These ideas are enough to make them sacred objects of worship. It is noteworthy that Daoism established Dao, Scripture (*jing* 經), and Master (*shi* 師) as its own "Three Treasures" (*sanbao* 三寶), which are parallel to the Buddhist Three Treasures (Buddha 佛, Dharma 法, Sangha 僧).

Declarations of the Perfected records some interesting episodes about worshiping Daoist scriptures in the fourth century CE.

> Ma Lang and Ma Han venerated the scripture-treasure much more than they did their lord and father. They always kept two careful servants attending to the incense burner and cleaning [the house in which the scriptures were stored]. Every time when divine lights and numinous air appeared in the house, the wife of Ma Lang, who had the faculty of clairvoyance, said that Jade Maidens wearing green robes came and went in the air, just like flying birds. The Ma family became very rich, its assets worth millions, and all lived long lives. (DZ1016, 19: 13b–14a)

馬朗馬罕敬事經寶，有過君父．恒使有心奴子二人，常侍直香火，洒掃拂拭．每有神光靈炁，見於室宇，朗妻頗能通見云，數有青衣玉女，空中去來，狀如飛鳥．馬家遂致富盛，資產巨萬，年老命終．

Another example of venerating Daoist scriptures is seen in the case of the aunt of Zhou Ziliang 周子良 (497–516), who was a disciple of Tao Hongjing. Zhou's aunt practiced with the *Scripture of the Yellow Court* (*Huangting jing* 黃庭經) and the method of Three-to-One (*sanyi fa* 三一

法) and worshiped (*gongyang* 供養) the *Inner Biographies of Lady Wei* 魏夫人 and *Lord Su* 蘇君, the *Chart of the True Form of the Five Peaks*, the *Writs of the Three Sovereigns,* and the *Five Talismans of Numinous Treasure* (DZ302, 1: 11b). The *Inner Biography of Lady Wei* is a hagiography of Wei Huacun 魏華存 (251–334), who practiced with the *Scripture of the Yellow Court* and became the Perfected of Highest Clarity. The *Inner Biography of Lord Su* is a hagiography of the immortal of Center Peak (*zhongyue* 中嶽), Su Lin 蘇林, whose main practice was centered on the method of Three-to-One. These inner biographies, too, were treated as canonical scriptures as well as objects of veneration. *Gongyang* 供養 literally means "to give offering and care." In a Buddhist context, it usually means worshiping the Buddha with offerings of incense, lamps, flowers, and food. The meaning of "*gongyang*" in the fourth-to-sixth century Daoism does not seem to have been any different from this.

It is worth paying attention to the fact that talismans were also objects of veneration. In the history of Daoism, the worship of talismans and scriptures preceded that of divine images. This was witnessed by the Buddhist monk Falin 法琳 (572–640), who criticized Daoist worship of divine statues.

> Before the Liang and Chen periods [of the Southern Dynasties] and the Ji and Wei periods [of the Northern Dynasties], they only **placed scriptures in calabashes** and had no images of the Celestial Worthy...... The *Inner Biography of Tao Yinju* says that [Master Tao] built two shrines for Buddhism and Daoism on Mt. Mao and worshiped in the morning every other day. There were divine images in the Buddhist shrine, but no images in the Daoist shrine. (T52, 6: 535a)
> 考梁陳齊魏之前，唯以瓠盧成經本，無天尊形像．陶隱居內傳云，在茅山中立佛道二堂，隔日朝禮，佛堂有像，道堂無像．

This account testifies that divine statues of the Celestial Worthy of Primordial Beginning had been made since the sixth century. At the same time, it tells us that previously the object of worship in Daoism was scriptures themselves. The *Inner Biography of Tao Yinju* is a biography of Tao Hongjing. Tao restricted "true scriptures" (*zhenjing* 眞經) to "handwritten manuscripts of the Three Lords" (*sanjun shoushu* 三君手書). The Three Lords were Yang Xi, Xu Mi 許謐 and his son Xu Hui 許翽. He made great efforts to collect and store them in his "Tower of Luminous Numen" (*zhaoling tai* 昭靈臺). From the above accounts, we can surmise that Tao's storage was not a simple archiving, but a kind of sacred activity accompanied by worship. The above phrase "placed scriptures" was originally given as "made scriptures" (*cheng jingben* 成經本) in the text of the Goryeo Buddhist Canon, but other versions of the Song and Ming Buddhist Canon all have "placed scriptures [in a container]" (*cheng jingben* 盛經本). Judging from the context, "to place scriptures [in a container]" may be considered the correct form.

Chengjing, which means "to place a scripture [in a container]" or "to venerate a scripture," was indeed a technical term related to scripture-worship in Daoist liturgical texts of the fifth-to-sixth centuries. For example, the *Scripture of Original Deeds and Destiny* (DZ1114, *Taishang dongxuan lingbao benxing suyuan jing* 太上洞玄靈寶本行宿緣經) reads:

> Those who study Dao must always keep their clothes clean, burn incense in the separate oratory, install a high desk with incense burner, **venerate scriptures**, concentrate on meditation and visualize the Perfected, and practice breathing and stretching. (DZ1114, 6a)

> 夫學道，常淨潔衣服，別靖燒香，安高香座，盛經禮拜，精思存眞，吐納導養.

> A Daoist master who studies [Dao] in his worldly house should build a meditation chamber and perform a purification retreat, and when he installs a high desk and **venerates scriptures,** [he should] recite and visualize at the same time. The desk should be about 1.5 meters square, and its height should be the same. He should always burn incense and light lamps without cessation. (DZ1114, 14a–14b)

> 夫道士之於家學者，當建精舍清靜齋，及施高座盛經，并讀誦存思. 床方五尺，其高亦然，常燒香然燈不輟.

A "high desk" (*gaozuo* 高座) was usually installed for a lecturer or a divine statue, but here for venerating scriptures. "Burning incense" and "lighting lamps" are also activities for worshiping scriptures.

The *Genealogy of the Three Worthies of Highest Clarity* (DZ164, *Shangqing sanzun pulu* 上清三尊譜錄), which is attributed to *Jinming qizhen* 金明七眞, stipulates that this text is to be worshiped just like the Three Cavern scriptures. It includes instructions to venerate the scripture in an embroidered silk bag and to burn incense and worship every morning and evening (DZ164, 11b). It informs us that such worship was performed for the Three Cavern scriptures.

Because Daoist scriptures were objects of worship, the Master of Scriptures (*jingshi* 經師) rose in authority, and the relationship between a master and his disciples was reorganized around the transmission of scriptures. The Highest Clarity scriptures placed great importance on the relationship between a master and his disciples linked by a scripture. The term "disciple of scripture" (*jing dizi* 經弟子) was even created as a counterpart to the term "master of scripture" (*jingshi* 經師) (Kim 2011, 68).

Accordingly, the ritual of scripture transmission became one of the most important rituals in Daoism, with "venerating a scripture" as a central feature. Its archetype was created by Liu Xiujing. He determined the ritual process for transmitting Numinous Treasure scriptures and edited the *Ritual of Transmission for Numinous Treasure Scriptures* (DZ528, *Taishang dongxuan lingbao shouduyi* 太上洞玄靈寶授度儀). According to this work, prior to the transmission, five desks are installed in the five directions, with an incense burner on each. Among the five desks, the central desk is covered with red silk, on which the scriptures are placed, and green silk covers the scriptures. Liu explains that venerating the scripture with vermilion and green (*danqing* 丹青) silk replaces the ancient form of swearing an oath.

> The *Jade Instruction* says, 'Cut 1.5 meters of vermilion silk of the Southern Harmony, which is **red patterned silk, to make a cloth and spread it on the desk**. Then invoke the *True Writs of Five Chapters of the Numinous Treasure* and *Five Talismans*.'
>
> The *Jade Instruction* says, 'Cut 1.5 meters of silk of the Emerald Forest, which is **green patterned silk, to make a cloth and cover** the *Talismans* and the *True Writs*.'
>
> The *Jade Instruction* says, 'Let the *True Writs* and *Five Talismans* be placed between vermilion and green as a substitute for the oath of smearing blood [around the mouth] and cutting the hair. **The green is a substitute for the hair, and the vermilion for smearing animal blood around the mouth when taking an oath**. The Perfected does not harm one's mental virtue, and so he replaces them.' (DZ528, 1b–2a)
>
> 玉訣云，裂南和丹繒五尺，絳紋繒也，爲巾於案上，請靈寶五篇眞文及五符.玉訣云，割碧林之帛五尺，青紋繒也，爲巾以覆眞文符上. 玉訣云，令眞文.五符處丹青中間，以爲落髮歃血之盟也. 青以代髮，丹代歃血之盟誓. 眞人不傷神損德，故以代之爾.

The Daoist scripture-transmission ritual of both Southern and Northern dynasties followed this new tradition. As shown by the desk for venerating the scriptures being placed in the center of the platform, surrounded by four other desks, with purification by burning incense, venerating scriptures with vermillion and green silks was an important act in the transmission ritual of the Northern Zhou (*WSBY* 39: 2b, 40:1b).

A sixth century Daoist text of the Southern Dynasty, the *Jade Book of the Great Realm of Great High of the Cavern of the Perfected* (DZ1352, *Dongzhen taishang taixiao langshu* 洞眞太上太霄琅書), prescribed ten things in detail when preparing for the transmission of scriptures, including a scripture chest (*jingxiang* 經箱, approx. L40 × D30 × H20cm), a desk (*jingan* 經案, approx. L72 × D40 × H30), cases for [the scrolls of] scriptures (*jingguo* 經過), a cloth (*jingjin* 經巾, inside the scripture chest), a cloth for covering the scripture chest (*jingpa* 經帊), a veil-curtain (經帳, made of dark red cloth with a bamboo pole), and three high desks (*gaozuo* 高座) for veneration, recitation, and lecturing on the scripture (DZ 1352, 7: 3b–5b).

Such detailed prescriptions tell us of the solemnity of the ritual, which was restricted to qualified persons worthy of transmission. It was believed that supernatural powers would punish anyone who took Daoist scriptures without a proper transmission ritual. *Declarations of the Perfected* reports an episode about some people who stole a scripture for private practice.

> Wang Xing transcribed [the Highest Clarity scriptures] for Kong Mo (who was authorized to receive the scriptures) in advance and then secretly made copies of them, planning to practice [them himself] after returning to the East of the Jiang river. However, when he crossed the Zhe river first, he encountered a tornado and was shipwrecked. Only the *Scripture of the Yellow Court* could be saved. He blamed himself and remained on Mt. Shan, and started recitation sooner or later. But the mountain spirit set fire to his house. Again, he tried to recite the scripture on a platform in the open air, but was caught by a sudden shower, the ink on the paper became wet and blotted, and in the end, he could not finish the number [of recitations]. Wang repented deeply of his sin and severed worldly relationships. (DZ1016, 19: 11a)
>
> 王興先爲孔寫，輒復私繕一通，後將還東修學. 始濟浙江，便遇風淪漂. 唯有黃庭一篇得存. 興乃自加切責，仍住剡山，稍就讀誦，山靈即火燒其屋. 又於露壇研詠，俄頃驟雨，紙墨霑壞，遍數遂不得畢. 興深知罪譴，杜絕人倫.

As seen previously, the same source recorded an epiphany of magic lights in a room for venerating the scriptures. Such miraculous stories, in fact, are not unique to Daoism. Chinese Buddhism also has many similar testimonies, with Buddhist scriptures being worshiped just like the Buddha. The fifth-century Buddhist Canon, *The Monasteries of Luoyang* (Luoyang qielan ji 洛陽伽藍記) described the worship of scripture chest (*jinghan* 經函) in White Horse Temple 白馬寺, "People always burnt incense and worshiped the scripture chest. Sometimes it emitted bright light, illuminating the room. Therefore, monks and laypeople saluted and venerated it, just as they revered the real appearance [of the Buddha]" (T51, 4: 1014b). Certainly, Daoism and Buddhism vied with and imitated each other in producing such miraculous stories. These miraculous phenomena could be interpreted as auspicious signs (*ruixiang* 瑞祥 or *furui* 符瑞) that revealed Heaven's will in the context of Chinese traditions.

A famous example of a Daoist scripture presented to the emperor as an auspicious sign was the *Scripture of the Great Peace*. Its prototype, the *Scripture of the Great Peace Embracing the Primordial* (*Baoyuan taiping jing* 包元太平經), was presented many times as a token of Heaven's Mandate to the imperial court during the Han dynasty. During the reign of the emperor Chengdi 成帝 (r. BC33–BC7), Gan Zhongke 甘忠可 presented the scripture with prophecies that the destiny of the Han dynasty would decline without changes in the system (*Book of Han*, 3192). Jie Guang 解光 presented the scripture again during the reign of Aidi 哀帝 (r. BC7–BC1) (*Book of Han*, 340; *Book of Later Han*, 2299).

It has been pointed out that the emperor Wudi 太武帝 of the Northern Wei received a Daoist talisman and register (*fulu* 符籙) that functioned as auspicious signs to guarantee the legitimacy of the emperor (Seidel 1969b; 1983, *Book of Wei*, 94). Similar developments occurred in the fifth- to-sixth-century Southern dynasties. Tao Hongjing records instances in which some of the Highest Clarity scriptures and manuscripts of the Three Lords were presented to the emperors of the Liu Song 劉宋 and Southern Qi 南齊 dynasties. In 465, Lou Huiming 樓惠明 brought about twenty Highest Clarity scriptures to the capital in accordance with an imperial order to collect scriptures, and Shu Jizhen 戍季真 presented them to the emperor Jinghe 景和, while in 481 Dong Zhongmin 董仲民 presented the authentic handwritten manuscript of Yang Xi as an extraordinary wonder (*shenyi* 神異) to the emperor Gaodi 高帝 (DZ1016, 19: 15a–15b).

It is also known that during the Tang and Song period the imperial court strengthened the emperor's authority by performing the transmission ritual for Daoist scriptures. In 721, Xuanzong 玄宗 received Daoist scriptures from the Daoist master Sima Chengzhen 司馬承禎 (647–735) in order to promote the policy of revering Daoism and ensuring his power against political parties that had an affinity with Buddhism (*Old Book of Tang*, 5128). The emperor Wuzong 武宗, who is notorious for the persecution of Buddhism, received Daoist registers from the Daoist master Zhao Guizhen 趙歸真 (?–846) (*Old Book of Tang*, 585–586). The emperor Zhenzong 真宗 of the Northern Song manipulated the revelation of celestial scripts (*tianshu* 天書) and changed the name of the regnal era "Auspicious Token of Great Centrality" (*dazhong xiangfu* 大中祥符) in 1008 in an attempt to recover from his failure in the war with Liao 遼 (*Extended Continuation* 68, 1519–1520). In 1025, the Grand Empress Regnant, Zhangxian *huangtai hou* 章獻皇太后 (968–1033), performed a ritual for the transmission of the Highest Clarity scriptures, her model being the female Transcendent Wei Huacun (DZ304, 25: 3b–5a), and this event was not unrelated to ensuring her political power.

The power of Daoist scriptures originated in the belief that they are physically composed of celestial *qi* or pneuma and transmit the message of Heaven. Thus, a collection of Daoist scriptures, like the *Daoist Canon* or any kind of Daoist compendium, was believed to have the talismanic power of exorcism and blessing. This contributed to raising its commercial value.

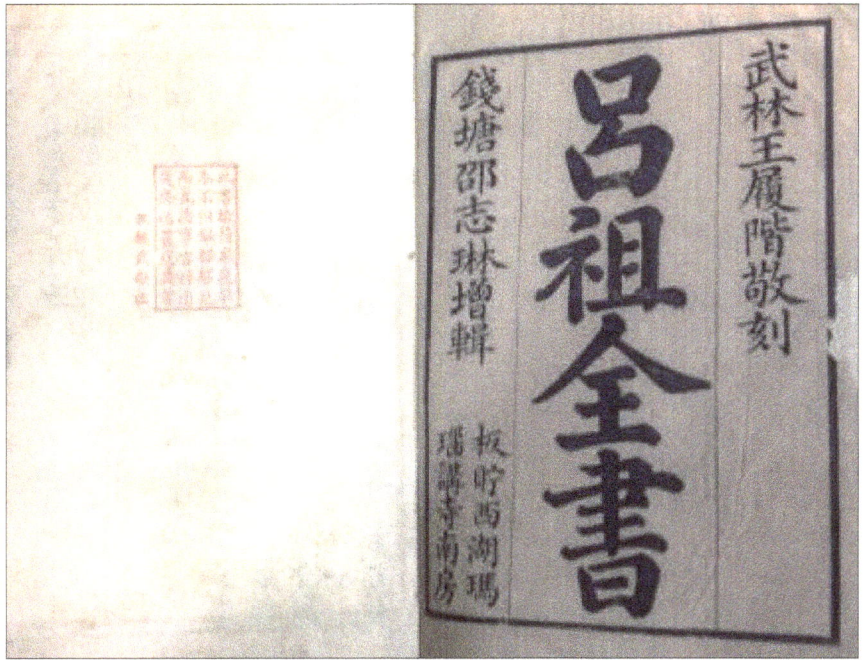

Figure 9.2 A seal on the *Compete Works of the Patriarch Lu*.

For example, the *Complete Collection of the Patriarch Luzu* (*Luzu quanshu* 呂祖全書), which was a collection of scriptures attributed to Lu Dongbin 呂洞賓 and printed during the Qing dynasty, has a vermilion seal on its front page that reads: "This book collection respectfully requests worship by the family [that possesses it]. It not only expels evil spirits and removes misfortune, but also makes everything auspicious, eliminates disasters and gives blessings. Its numinous effects are extraordinary. 此書敬請家庭供奉，不但驅邪解厄，而且諸事吉祥，消災降福，靈應異常." The owner of the seal, Wang Shengwu 汪繩武, was a famous Chinese merchant of the Qing period (Matsuura 2007, 174–218).

Scripture and practice

Let us return to the question of practice. We saw how the Three Cavern scriptures were explained as being composed of Three Pneumas, which are differentiated from the primordial *qi*. From this definition of "script = pneuma," there evolved the Daoist practice of reciting scripture to transform the ordinary body into a transcendent one. This is firmly grounded on Chinese ideas about the cosmic resonance of *qi*, according to which human beings and the myriad things exist within a relationship of mutual response. Daoism developed these ideas to an extreme level in both detail and scale.

The recitation of Daoist scriptures was not like chanting mantras without knowing their meaning. It was accompanied by a particular type of meditation, *cunsi* 存思, which literally means "to imagine and bring something into existence." It is often rendered as "visualization," but it assumes that one uses all five sensory faculties, not just the sense of sight but also hearing, smell, taste, and touch. Both visualization and recitation were regarded as indispensable for transforming one's *qi*. In practices involving Daoist scriptures, the adept visualizes the images of both corporeal and celestial gods so as to bring them into existence; at the same time, he/she recites the sounds of the letters so as to actualize the *qi* of the script and communicates with the celestial level of *qi*. Such sounds and images are stimuli to the cosmic primordial *qi*. In turn, the response of the *qi* transforms both the physical and the mental state of an adept into a transcendent state. In a description of this practice in the *Perfected Scripture of the Great Cavern* (*Dadong zhenjing* 大洞眞經), the Northern-Song Daoist master Chen Jingyuan 陳景元 (1025–1094) gives many hints regarding this way of thinking.

> [If] the subtle sound penetrates to the Nine [Heavens],
> And the true voice of chanting goes high,
> [Then] the pneuma of writs takes part in the mysterious [work] with the Jade Void,
> And the taste of glow unfolds with the Great Yang (*qi* of the sun).
> Moving lips to give utterance brings [the Goddess of] the Jade Blossom immediately;
> Reciting numinous verses makes the covenant with the [Lord of] Great High.
> Remain in stillness with arms folded! The Purple Chamber spontaneously appears in contemplation;
> Visualize what is indicated! Resonance will arise in accordance with the situation.
> That is the reason that seven generations of ancestors attain blessing,
> Receive their registers in the immortal palace,
> Transcend the dark demonic realm,
> And feast all together on the Vermilion Crest. (DZ 104: 1a–1b)
>
> 妙音九徹，眞聲高唱，文炁與玉虛參玄，霞味與太陽俱暢.
> 動脣發吐，則玉華立至；諷詠靈句，則携契太上.
> 靜止接拱，則紫房自觀；思念所期，則觸類感動.
> 所以七祖獲福，受籙仙宮，越從幽鬼，俱宴朱陵.

The "subtle sound" (*miaoyin* 妙音) and "true voice" (*zhensheng* 眞聲) of reciting scripture become stimuli to activate the "pneuma of writs" (*wenqi* 文炁) and bring a resonance from the pneuma of the Jade Void, where they originally belong, so as to take part in the cosmic work of Dao. The "taste of glow" (*xiawei* 霞味) is an analogy for a specific state of bodily fluids, such as saliva, which is the outcome of Daoist meditation on celestial bodies, such as the sun. It is telling that these inner liquids intensify the vital energy of the Daoist adept. By pronouncing the secret names given in the scripture, one can call upon the divine beings, the owners of the names, to be present in one's time and space; the recitation of the scripture results in a covenant to become a Transcendent.

As I have analyzed elsewhere (Kim 2007), Chen's writing places importance on the resonance of *qi* in the form of sound as well as image. When a Daoist adept visualizes the "Purple Chamber," which means the center of the cosmos and the inner space of the human brain at the same time, it appears spontaneously. The outcome of Daoist meditation is considered to be solid and effective, so that one can achieve salvation not only for oneself but also for seven generations of ancestors.

It is noteworthy that the Daoist scriptures are not simply objects for reading that convey some message or enlightenment. It is claimed that Daoist scriptures are a physically condensed or congealed state of cosmic *qi*, which should be carefully treated, worshiped, and practiced.

At the opposite pole of the belief that Daoist scriptures communicate with the realm of Dao, there is the belief that adepts are vulnerable to the test of demonic powers or celestial poisons. On account of this, Daoism developed many incantations and talismans to ward off evil spirits and ritual garments to wear when reciting scriptures. In the case of the *Perfected Scripture of the Great Cavern,* which is the ultimate text of medieval Daoism, incantation was necessary to eliminate the poisonous *qi* of the Nine Heavens and repel the tests of the Great Demon King, the Northern Thearch (*beidi damowang* 北帝大魔王) (DZ1360, 3a–3b). In this context, performing the recitation and visualization of Daoist scriptures requires special liturgical attire, including Daoist caps and robes. Without these, it is said that the celestial demons will invade one's spirit and distract the sounds of recitation, eventually bringing harm to the mind and body of the adept (DZ1138, WSBY43, 3a–3b).

Conclusion

The process of reading always purports to result in certain changes in the reader. However, the aim of reading Daoist scriptures is claimed to bring about not a change in one's mind, such as understanding and gaining a teaching, etc., but a transformation from a mortal to an immortal state of being. Therefore, this chapter has focused on understanding the relationship between Daoist scripture and practice. The Daoist view of the effect of practicing Daoist scriptures is grounded in a system of resonance of *qi*. On the basis of such thinking, pronouncing the sounds and visualizing the images in a scripture is regarded as a process of refining one's body with the cosmic *qi* of Daoist scriptures.

This chapter has highlighted how this Daoist view of scripture is closely related to its cosmology. The Daoist scripture is located in cosmological time after the beginning of the formation of Primordial Pneumas from Dao and before the division of Heaven and Earth. In Daoist cosmology, the scripts and writs were neither uttered nor created by any god, but emerge through the spontaneous concentration of pneumas, which is the operation of Dao itself.

Future research should give further consideration to Daoist imaginings about Original Writs and the archetype of Daoist scripture in relation to particular characteristics of the Chinese script. One is the aspect of pictogram or *xiangxing* 象形, which means literally "to represent the form." Another is *xingsheng* 形聲 or *xiangsheng* 象聲, which means "to represent the sound." Both indicate that Chinese characters were designed by copying images of what humans see and hear in the world. However, the Daoist view of the script is the reverse. According to the Daoist view, the letters and sounds of scriptures exist a priori, and they manifest themselves and make the forms and sounds of myriad things in the world.

References

Primary sources

DZ. Work number of *The Taoist Canon*. 2008. Edited by Kristofer Schipper and Franciscus Verellen. Chicago, IL. University of Chicago Press.

  DZ97. *Spontaneously Created Jade Characters and Esoteric Sounds of the Various Heavens* (*Taishang dongxuan lingbao zhutian neiyin ziran yuzi* 太上洞玄靈寶諸天內音自然玉字).

  DZ104. *Sounds and Meanings and Jade Instructions of the Perfected Scripture of the Great Cavern of Highest Clarity* (*Shangqing dadong zhenjing yujue yinyi* 上清大洞眞經玉訣音義).

  DZ164. *Genealogy of the Three Worthies of Highest Clarity* (*Shangqing sanzun pulu* 上清三尊譜錄).

  DZ302. *Record of Mr. Zhou's Communication with the Unseen World* (*Zhoushi mingtong ji* 周氏冥通記).

  DZ304. *Records of Mount Mao* (*Maoshan zhi* 茅山志).

  DZ528. *Ritual of Transmission for Numinous Treasure Scriptures* (*Taishang dongxuan lingbao shouduyi* 太上洞玄靈寶授度儀).

  DZ1016. *Declarations of the Perfected* (*Zhengao* 眞誥).

  DZ1032. *Cloud Bookcase with Seven Labels* (*Yunji qiqian* 雲笈七籤) (YJQQ).

DZ1114. *Scripture of Original Deeds and Destiny* (*Taishang dongxuan lingbao benxing suyuan jing* 太上洞玄靈寶本行宿緣經).

DZ1128. *Progression of Succession of Scriptures and Teachings in the Daoist School* (*Daomen jingfa xiangcheng cixu* 道門經法相承次序).

DZ1129. *Pivot of Meaning of the Daoist Teaching* (*Daojiao yishu* 道教義樞).

DZ1138. *Essentials of Supreme Secrets* (*Wushang biyao* 無上祕要) (*WSBY*).

DZ1352. *Jade Book of the Great Realm of Great High of the Cavern of the Perfected* (*Dongzhen taishang taixiao langshu* 洞眞太上太霄琅書).

DZ1360. *Scripture of Secret Names of a Hundred Gods and Incantations of the Highest Thearch among the Nine Heavens in Highest Clarity* (*Shangqing jiutian shangdi zhu baishen neiming jing* 上清九天上帝祝百神內名經).

DZ1389. *Jade Register of Eight Phosphors of the Golden Primordial of the Cavern of Perfection, the Lord of Great Dao the Most High of Highest Clarity* (*Shangqing gaosheng taishang dadaojun dongzhen jinyuan bajing yulu* 上清高聖太上大道君洞眞金元八景玉籙).

T. (Volume number of *Taishō shinshū daizōkyō* 大正新修大藏經).

T51. *Records of Temples in Luoyang* (*Luoyang qielan ji* 洛陽伽藍記).

T52. *Discourse on Differentiating the Right* (*Bianzheng lun* 辯正論).

Book of Han (*Hanshu* 漢書). Beijing 北京: Zhonghua shuju 中華書局.

Book of Later Han (*Houhan shu* 後漢書). Beijing: Zhonghua shuju.

Book of Wei (*Weishu* 魏書). Beijing: Zhonghua shuju.

Book of Sui (*Suishu* 隋書). Beijing: Zhonghua shuju.

Old Book of Tang (*Jiutang shu* 舊唐書). Beijing: Zhonghua shuju.

Extended Continuation of the Comprehensive Mirror to Aid in Government (*Xu zizhi tongjian changbian* 續資治通鑑長編). Beijing: Zhonghua shuju.

Ge Hong 葛洪. 1985. *Book of the Master Who Embraces Simplicity* (*Baopuzi* 抱朴子) (*Baopuzi neipian jiaoshi* 抱朴子內篇校釋). Collated by Wang Ming 王明. Beijing: Zhonghua shuju.

Secondary sources

Kamitsuka Yoshiko 神塚淑子. 2017. "Reihōkei ni okeru keiten shinseika no ronri: genshi kyūkei no 'kaigō dojin' setsu o megutte 靈寶經における經典神聖化の論理—元始舊經の「開劫度人」説をめぐって— [The Logic of the Sanctification of Scripture in the Numinous Treasure Scriptures: On Discourse about 'Opening Kalpas and Salvation' in the Original Scriptures of Primordial Beginning]." In *Dōkyō keiten no keisei to bukkyō* 道教經典の形成と佛教 [*Formation of Daoist Scriptures and Buddhism*], Nagoya daigaku shuppansha 名古屋大學出版社, 36-73 (originally published in 2005: *Nagoya daigaku bungakubu kenkyū ronshū, Tetsugaku* 名古屋大學文學部研究論集. 哲學 51: 71–94).

Kim, Jihyun 金志玹. 2006. "*Daidō shinkei* no jisshū ni okeru shintai: *Unkyū shichisen* shaku sanjūkyūshō kei o fumaete 《大洞眞經》の實修における

身體—《雲笈七籤》釋三十九章經を踏まえて [Body in Practicing the *Dadong zhenjing*: Based on the Jade Commentary]." *Tōhō Shūkyo* 東方宗教 107: 19–41.

Kim, Jihyun 金志玹. 2011. "Genshi to keishi: Dōkyō ni okeru atarashii shi no kannen to sono tenkai 玄師と經師 – 道教における新しい師の觀念とその展開 [Master of Mystery and Master of Scripture: New Concepts of Master in Daoism and Their Development]." In *Sankyō kōshō ronsō zokuhen* 三教交涉研究論叢續編, edited by Mugitani Kunio 麥谷邦夫, 57–97. Kyoto 京都: Kyōto daigaku jinbun kagaku kenkyūjo 京都大學人文科學研究所.

———. 2017. "Dogyo ūi chŏngjŏn hwa 道教의 正典化 [Daoist Canonization: With a Focus on Model Narratives and Ritualization]." *Han'guk sasang sahak* 韓國思想史學 [*History of Korean Thought*] 55: 205–245.

Kobayashi Masayoshi 小林正美. 2003. "Tōdai no dōkyō kyōdan to tenshi dō 唐代の道教教團と天師道." *Tōyō no shisō to shūkyō* 東洋の思想と宗教 20: 20–49.

Kusuyama Haruki 楠山春樹. 1979. *Rōshi densetsu no kenkyū* 老子傳說の研究. Tokyo 東京: Sōbunsha 創文社.

Matsuura Akira 松浦章. 2007. "Kenryū jidai no Nagasaki raikō Chūgoku shōnin: Ō Jōbu, Ō Chikuri, Tei Sekijō o chūshin ni 乾隆時代の長崎來航中國商人 – 汪繩武·汪竹里·程赤城を中心に." In *Edo jidai tōsen ni yoru nitchū bunka kōryū* 江戶時代唐船による日中文化交流, 174–218. Kyoto 京都: Shibunkaku 思文閣.

Mugitani Kunio 麥谷邦夫. 2005. "Dōkyō gisū to Nanbokuchō Zui shotō ki no dōkyō kyōrigaku 道教義樞と南北朝隋初唐期の道教教理學" In *Sankyō kōshō ronsō* 三教交涉論叢, 99–186. Kyoto: Kyōto daigaku jinbun kagaku kenkyūjo.

Nakajima Ryūzō 中島隆藏. 2004. *Unkyū shichisen no kisoteki kenkyū* 雲笈七籤の基礎的研究. Tokyo: Kenbun shuppan 研文出版.

Ōfuchi Ninji. 1979. "The Formation of the Taoist Canon." In Holmes Welch and Anna K. Seidel, eds., *Facets of Taoism: Essays in Chinese Religion*, 269–287. New Haven, CT: Yale University Press. https://doi.org/10.1017/s0395264900092817

Pregadio, Fabrizio, ed. 2008. *The Encyclopedia of Taoism*. 2 Volumes. London: Routledge.

Robinet, Isabelle. 1993. *Taoist Meditation: The Maoshan Tradition of Great Purity*. Albany: State University of New York Press.

Schipper, Kristofer. 1985. "Taoist Ordination Ranks in the Tunhuang Manuscripts." In *Religion und Philosophie in Ostasien*, edited by Kristofer Schipper, 127–148. Würzburg: Königshuasen and Neumann.

Schipper, Kristofer and Franciscus Verellen, eds. 2008. *The Taoist Canon*. 3 Volumes. Chicago, IL: University of Chicago Press.

Seidel, Anna. 1969a. *La divinisation de Lao tseu dans le Taoisme des Han*. Publications de l'École française d'Extrême-Orient. Volume 71. Paris: École française d'Extrême-Orient. https://doi.org/10.3406/ephe.1967.18418

Seidel, Anna. 1969b. "Image of Perfect Ruler in Early Taoist Messianism: Lao-tzu and Li Hung." *History of Religions* 9: 216–247. https://doi.org/10.1086/462605

———. 1983. "Imperial Treasure and Taoist Sacraments: Taoist Roots in the Apocrypha." In *Tantric and Taoist Studies in Honour of R. A. Stein*, volume 2, edited by Michel Strickmann, 291–371. Brussels: Institut Belge des Hautes Études Chinoises. https://doi.org/10.2307/601714

Wang, Chegwen. 2010. "The Revelation and Classification of Daoist Scriptures." In *Early Chinese Religion, Part Two: The Period of Division (220-589 AD)*, edited by John Lagerwey and Lü Pengzhi, 775–888. Leiden: Brill. https://doi.org/10.1163/ej.9789004175853.i-1564.98

Zürcher, Erik. 1980. "Buddhist Influence on Early Taoism: A Survey of Scriptural Evidence." *T'oung Pao* 66(1/3): 84–147. https://doi.org/10.1163/156853280x00039

— 10 —

Books as Sacred Beings

JAMES W. WATTS

Essays in this collection have shown some of the many ways that religious traditions teach their adherents how sacred texts can be embodied. Rachel McDermott describes how Sanskrit and Bengali Tantric traditions taught esoteric meditation to inscribe within one's own body the tantric map of the macrocosm that enthrones the goddess Kālī. Katharina Wilkens shows the aesthetic ideology at work in the teaching methods of madrassas that train students to memorize the Qur'an and then to drink the ink of its verses. Jihuyn Kim summarizes ancient Daoist beliefs that scriptures incarnate the universe's primordial energy that generated gods as well as the universe itself. These studies add evidence to the conclusions drawn by earlier research about how books get treated as beings in many religious traditions. The essays edited by Kristina Myrvold provided many more examples of treating books like people, especially by modeling on human funerals the disposal rituals for worn-out sacred texts among Sikhs (Myrvold 2010, 135), Jews (Schleicher 2010, 21-24), and some Hindus (Broo 2010, 96-102). Traditions of ritual, art and mysticism in Buddhism (Kinnard 1999, 114-175; Moerman 2010, 71), Judaism (Wolfson 2004, 223-224), and Christianity (Parmenter 2006 [2008],[1] 168-172) also merge books with human bodies and/or divine beings.

These excellent studies lead me here to consider the methodological implications for religious studies and for the broader humanities of this widespread human tendency to identify books with living bodies and beings. Why do we speak about books, people, and gods in similar ways?

---

[1] References to *Postscripts* are dated as follows: cover date [publication date].

James W. Watts is Professor in the Department of Religion at Syracuse University in Syracuse, New York, and a co-founder and Secretary-Treasurer of the Society for Comparative Research on Iconic and Performative Texts (SCRIPT).

What does this common rhetoric tell us about our typical assumptions about books, and about people?

Books as personal beings

The tendency to treat scriptures as sacred beings should draw our attention to the fact that books in general, not only sacred books, often get treated in one way or another as beings or persons, that is, as more than objects. This tendency is most obvious in our habit of talking about authors and their books as if they are one and the same thing. In the study of religion, we regularly say things like "Durkheim led me to understand ..." or "Eliade teaches us that ...," by which we mean that their books have shaped our thinking, though we never met these men ourselves. Equating books with people generates the common tendency to grant books agency like human beings. Everyday speech includes comments such as "this book touched me," "that book exerted a powerful influence," and even "this book changed my life." I have recently written about this common inversion of indexical significance about books (Watts 2012 [2017]). Here, I want to examine more closely the intuitive parallels between books and persons, between books and "beings," in order to clarify why some books get identified as sacred beings.

The human tendency to ascribe agency to objects has drawn theoretical analysis in recent decades. Bruno Latour's "actor-network-theory" is especially influential. Latour called attention to the agency of things in order to provide a more robust theory of social power than is possible by focusing on human social relationships alone. He argued that social power and hierarchies become enduring by incorporating the things (for example: land, weapons, media) whose agency makes possible greater social control. Latour, however, did not go so far as to claim that things exert precisely the same agency as humans:

> This, of course, does not mean that these participants 'determine' the action, that baskets 'cause' the fetching of provisions or that hammers 'impose' the hitting of the nail. [...] In addition to 'determining' and serving as a 'backdrop for human action,' things might authorize, allow, afford, encourage, permit, suggest, influence, block, render possible, forbid, and so on. (Latour 2005, 71–72)

Similarly, in the context of religious studies, S. Brent Plate (2015) has described the religious agency of common objects in religious practice.

As regards agency, however, books stand out from other common objects and artifacts. Books are an extreme case, because they are regularly accorded far more agency than are other things. Common language and even academic discourse routinely ascribe agency to books, or to authors through their books, in exactly the same way that they ascribe agency to human beings in statements like, "this book says" and "that book changed the discussion." While the agency of things is an innovative idea to modern thinkers (though less so to many forms of traditional and indigenous thought), the agency of books is taken for granted in modern discourse.

Books are ascribed agency like human beings because books resemble people in at least three ways. First, books like people invoke a sense of interiority. Books have contents like people have ideas. We speak of both as consisting of physical exteriors that contain immaterial ideas inside. Furthermore, in the case of both people and books, their ideas can be separated from one physical container and placed in another. Ideas can be passed from one person to another, and the ideas in a book, even its entire contents, can appear in many different volumes and may be translated into different languages. Common parlance therefore distinguishes books and other forms of recorded media from other kinds of objects because of their ability to "contain" immaterial "contents": ideas in books, songs on records, images on video recordings, software in computer hardware. Svensson (2020) describes this phenomenon as a "book-person blend." These artifacts of recorded media resemble human beings by physically incarnating the container metaphor (Lakoff and Johnson 2003, 29, 58, 148, 214) in a dichotomy of material container and immaterial contents.

The second resemblance between books and people, or at least between books and popular conceptions of people, derives directly from the first. Because a book's contents appear in different physical copies of that book, its ideas can survive the destruction of their physical container. Through recopying and reprinting, many books continue to exist through multiple reincarnations, which may well take different physical forms as scrolls and codices, and now as digital texts. As many people have observed, books offer the only demonstrable means of afterlife for authors, or at least for the authors' ideas. Reprints of old books are a routine expression of afterlife, a physical demonstration of a possibility that very many people hope for themselves. Many books live on after the destruction of their physical containers, just as many people hope to live on after their bodies die.

Indeed, the invention of computer technology has encouraged the pseudo-scientific hope that, someday, people's minds will be able to be uploaded to computers and downloaded into new bodies just like computer software (Kurtzweil 2005). The rise of computer technology has reinforced the tendency to think of human beings as a dichotomy of body (hardware) and mind (software), since software is written text that is conceived as disembodied. The mystical rhetoric of data "in the cloud" hides the fact that software must always be hosted on some kind of hardware and does not exist apart from it. The internet is built out of a large number of computer servers around the world connected by networks of fiber-optic cables. What is obscured by contemporary tech-rhetoric is exposed by ritualizing digital texts, which inevitably draws attention to their material forms, as rituals always do (Watts 2019, 71–81). Computer software is just another kind of written text. The recent tendency to think of minds as software is therefore another version of the common analogy between people and books.

The third resemblance between people and books involves the experience of encountering them. Many people report transformative encounters with particular persons, important places, or significant objects. Meeting a guru or visiting a shrine or seeing a famous image may provoke an experience of theophany—a transcendent experience of deity. Many people also say they experience such theophanies when encountering certain books, especially religious scriptures. They may say that reading this book "was a revelation to me." They may travel far to see ancient and rare books and spend a great deal of money to buy a first edition or an author's manuscript, just like others might go on a pilgrimage or buy a sacred relic.

Of course, other material objects and physical spaces also frequently get credited with inspiring theophanies: many sacred sites, divine images, and venerated relics are associated with such experiences. So books are hardly unique in being described as material mediators of transcendence. This resemblance between the function of books and some other objects, as well as with spaces and people, differs from the previous two precisely by emphasizing the book's physical nature. Like a theophany through a person, icon or place, the book that mediates a transcendent experience does so through an encounter with its material form.

These three common analogies between books and beings represent three different aspects of how books function. Specifically, they correspond to how religious communities ritualize three different dimensions of written texts.

The three dimensions of books as sacred beings

Academic and devotional study of sacred texts focuses mostly on the interpretation of their semantic dimension. This kind of interpretation gets ritualized in many ways, such as in sermons, lectures, and written commentaries. But before we can interpret the meaning of a written text, we have to convert the written signs into spoken or mental language. Religious communities also ritualize this expressive dimension[2] through

---

2 I have called this dimension "performative" in many of my previous publications, but that term creates confusion with performing rituals, which can involve all three

public readings, recitations, memorization, chanting and singing, artistic illustration, theater, and now television and film. But before we can read a text, we have to recognize its signs or its material form as a written text. Religious communities elaborate and decorate scriptures' iconic dimension—their scripts and type-faces, their page lay-outs, inks, parchment or paper, bindings or covers—to portray the value of their books. They also ritualize the material form of their scriptures by displaying them prominently in processions and in sanctuaries. Many books get ritualized frequently in one or two of these dimensions, but a distinctive characteristic of religious scriptures is that their communities ritualize them regularly in all three of these dimensions (Watts 2006 [2008]).

The correspondence between the three book/human analogies and the three dimensions in which religious communities regularly ritualize their scriptures highlights how communities use books for specific social functions. The correspondence shows that some typical religious beliefs get reinforced by the ritual practices of religious communities with their sacred books.

Souls and the semantic dimension

The semantic dimension of textual interpretation reinforces beliefs in a separable soul or spirit. In the first place, reading a novel to oneself produces a common out-of-body experience (though not as common as dreaming). This reading experience immerses people mentally in the novel's scenes and events, even in the minds of the novel's characters, to the point of forgetting their own bodies and surroundings. Reading expository prose gives the illusion of accessing the author's ideas directly. Modern books have been intentionally designed to facilitate such absent-mindedness by making the text so easy to read that readers have little conscious awareness of seeing the written signs at all (Plate 2010 [2012], 121). Reading thus produces an out-of-body experience that in other settings might be classified as mystical and religious. But in this case, these experiences are simply the expected result of manipulating an ordinary human artifact, a book. Modern technology has expanded the kinds of artifacts capable of producing this effect to include sound recordings and films. Recorded music and films act directly on the senses rather than through the reader's imagination and so more often prompt a bodily response than does reading books (Plate 2012 [2017], 97–102).

Ritualizing the act of literary (and musical and film) interpretation

---

textual dimension. "Performative" also evokes a broader range of theoretical implications (Velten 2012) and applications (Burrus in this volume). Therefore, I suggest calling it the "expressive dimension" instead to focus attention more narrowly on how people express texts mentally, orally, visually and dramatically.

in teaching, sermons, commentaries and critical reviews engages other interpreters and so recalls readers' attention to their own bodies and situations. But social acts of interpretation construct a triadic relationship between interpreter, audience, and "the text" which here becomes a completely disembodied construct—the memory of the experience produced by reading a particular book. Social acts of interpretation depend on the belief that the book you and I read is the same, even though we usually read from different copies. Whereas individual interpretation of the book in my hands does not require me to disassociate the book from its contents, social interpretation of a book's semantic dimension does require doing so. Thus reading a novel can create an out-of-body experience, and discussing the meaning of that novel reifies its contents as an immaterial text separate from both the book that contains it and the human body that reads it.

Let me give an example from the most popular novels of the twenty-first century. We frequently say things like "the Harry Potter books shaped the childhood of a generation." Such statements presuppose the existence of a singular immaterial text, the seven Harry Potter books, despite their embodiment in 450 million different copies. As in most semantic interpretation, this statement presupposes that all these copies are identical. Of course, that is not true. In the case of the Harry Potter novels, the text differed between the British and American editions because the publishers did not think Americans would understand British slang. Translations create much greater differences, and the Harry Potter books have been translated into 75 different languages, according to the publisher (Scholastic 2018). Then, there are the different formats in which readers have experienced the novels (hard-back, paper-back, e-book), different bindings and artwork, to say nothing of the millions of people who know the series only from seeing the Harry Potter films. Semantic interpretation traditionally pays attention to variations in the expressive dimension, that is, differences between books and their film adaptations and, sometimes, to translation differences, but usually ignores variations in the iconic dimension, such as the effects of format differences. Our imaginations meld all these different manifestations of the Harry Potter books into a single reality and then conflate them with their human author by saying, for example, that "J. K. Rowling taught a generation the magical power of love."

The fact that many readers have a vivid experience through the Harry Potter books and the films and have publicly praised and debated their meaning has also created a vivid social imaginary of the characters and settings depicted in the books, such as Hermione Granger and the Hogwarts School of Magic. Because of the text's widespread appeal, interpreters can then investigate it to understand its effects on the real world of readers, such as recent efforts to explain the younger generation's political views on the basis of the Harry Potter books (Gierzynski 2013; Emba 2017). When interpretation reaches this point, the disembodied text has become the basis for understanding real current events and for predicting future ones. In other words, it has become a means of divination.

So ritualizing the semantic dimension of a book in personal practice and, especially, in social rituals of interpretation promotes the experience of a disembodied text that can be treated as if it exists independently of its physical containers. Reading books provides a common out-of-body experience and a frequent example of the social influence of immaterial texts and their more-or-less authoritative interpreters. Books thus reinforce beliefs in the real existence of immaterial ideas apart from their material containers. The ubiquitous analogy between books and humans then strengthens belief in the possibility that human minds, spirits, or souls may also be separable from their physical bodies.

Resurrection and the expressive dimension

Let me turn now to the expressive or performative dimension. The act of expressing a text—reading it to oneself or aloud, singing or chanting it, memorizing it—turns visual signs into embodied language in people's ears, mouths and minds. These activities bring a text to life as language spoken and heard by human beings. Many religious traditions privilege this "living word" over physical books. That was true of early rabbinic Judaism's emphasis on the Oral Torah, of early Christianity's respect for the spoken Gospel, the continuing centrality of Qur'anic recitation in Islam, and the veneration of Vedas in oral transmission and recitation in Hinduism (Graham 1987, 67–77, 110–115). Yohan Yoo (2012 [2017]) has recently described the attention that Neo-Confucian teachers gave to reviving the voices of dead sages imaginatively through the experience of reading their works.

The experience of "reviving" written signs into mental and oral languages is so routine in modern times that it only elicits comment in exceptional circumstances. For example, reading the letters of deceased loved ones can bring their voices and appearance vividly to mind, prompting a surge of emotion. Modern media technology has now displaced written letters in many people's experience of the dead: photos and recordings preserve appearances and voices more effectively than writing. Another way in which the capacity of writing to resurrect voices attracts attention is through the decipherment and translation of the scripts of ancient "dead" languages. The stories and religious beliefs of the ancient Egyptians, for example, can now be heard again because of the capacity of writing to preserve them and of modern scholars to resurrect and translate them.

The unremarkably nature of most textual performances does not negate the observation that reading necessarily involves bringing texts to life as mental and spoken language. The prevalence of reading makes this experience of resurrection and reincarnation part of routine, everyday life. Writers hope for their work to be resurrected in this way, to have other people reincarnate their ideas in their own minds and words. The extreme cases of encountering dead loved ones in their writings or other recordings and of deciphering dead languages point out the powerful potential of this common experience. Reading and writing make the afterlife of texts part of the routine experiences of literate people.

Theophany and the iconic dimension

Ritualizing the third textual dimension, the iconic dimension of a book, opens the possibility of experiencing theophany by just seeing and holding the book. A book can function like an image or icon—indeed, it is an image and an icon. That is the case not only because the book takes a typical, and in some cases distinctive, visual and material form. Many religious traditions also decorate the bindings or covers of books with images. So the covers of a Gospel book may consist of a diptych depicting Christ crucified on one side and resurrected on the other—an icon like many others in a Greek Orthodox Church (Parmenter 2006 [2008], 167). Recently published research, including some by contributors to this volume, has highlighted how iconic books engage the human senses through the rituals of many religious traditions: David Ganz (2012 [2017]) has described the medieval manuscript evidence for manipulating Christian scriptures and prayer books, Katharina Wilkens (2012 [2017] and in this volume) has analyzed contemporary Muslim rituals of textual fumigation and ingestion, and Cathy Cantwell (2012 [2017]) has described Tibetan practices of ritual manipulation and textual ingestion.

Such experiences of iconic ritualization are not limited to religious contexts. Museums and libraries capitalize on our desire to see and, if possible, to touch books and other written texts that are especially beautiful, old, rare, or famous, or that were associated with famous people. Books function in museums like other valuable objects in their collections to attract visitors wishing to encounter them directly. People describe such unmediated experiences of books with words of amazement and awe, that is, with the language of theophany.

Secular books, like religious scriptures, can be deliberately constructed to facilitate such encounters. Publishers make popular books, even the

Harry Potter series, readily available in leather bindings and gilded pages so that the book's physical form can show its exceptional value to the buyer.[3] Modern artists, in turn, have found potent material in both books and the cultural ideals around books. They create book art to highlight and comment critically on book culture. As Brent Plate (2012 [2017]) has shown, contemporary book art draws attention to the role that aesthetics has always played in the cultural significance and ritual function of books. Dorina Parmenter (2012 [2017]) has observed that material books function in individual and social life with a degree of agency that resembles some other ritual objects. The agency of books, however, is explicitly acknowledged in ordinary discourse to a much greater degree than the agency of other objects, even art objects (Watts 2012 [2017]).

The appearance of a book therefore offers the possibility of a theophanic encounter with transcendence. Though other objects, such as relics and art, also offer that possibility, only books combine the possibility of theophany through encountering the physical book with the out-of-body and resurrection experiences that are part of reading its text. However, in the secular examples that I have highlighted here, the out-of-body, resurrection and theophanic experiences tend to arise from encountering different kinds of texts: novels and letters and rare books. That is because secular texts tend to be ritualized in only one or two dimensions.

A distinguishing characteristic of scriptures is that religious communities tend to ritualize them regularly in all three dimensions (Watts 2006 [2008]). It is therefore the ritualization of scriptures and other kinds of sacred texts that is most likely to generate all of these effects. People expect the possibility of a theophany when they pick up scriptures, they believe that reading them brings to life ancient divine teachings, and that doing so will transport their minds in time and space. These experiences are not unique to sacred texts, but they are uniquely concentrated in them. Because other stimuli for such experiences tend to be holy people or divine images, books can easily be perceived as sacred beings as well.

The implications of analyzing books as sacred beings for Religious Studies

Let me summarize the outcome of these considerations by saying that books in general, and sacred texts in particular, can physically incarnate metaphysical hopes. Hopes for an enduring soul or spirit, for resurrection

---

3 More rarely, authors themselves participate in the construction of elaborately iconic books. J. K. Rowling, for example, produced seven hand-written copies and also a leather-bound printed limited edition of *The Tales of Beedle the Bard*, a book that is itself referenced at key points in the plot of the seventh Harry Potter book (Cain 2016; Flood 2008).

or reincarnation, and for an encounter with the divine are frequent and wide-spread among human cultures and religions. The normal use of a common artifact, a book, provides people with versions of each of these experiences.

Experiences with books, of course, are not the only things that stimulate such ideas. Dreams are even more common experiences that reinforce such ideas and may be cultivated by being ritualized. Dreams have therefore attracted much attention from scholars of religious experience. The out-of-body experience produced by reading books is simply another, less recognized, prompt in the same directions.

But unlike dreams, books are physical objects, material artifacts deliberately constructed for particular uses. Yet, in addition to their pragmatic functions, the use of books reinforces certain religious aspirations. Interpreting books demonstrates the independence of immaterial ideas from their material containers. Reading books resurrects languages and ideas from mute signs. Seeing and holding books may provide an encounter with transcendence, even divinity, in material form. Though such spiritual aspirations gain support from other kinds of experiences as well, books are unique artifacts because they materially incarnate all three of these deeply felt hopes.

The religious effects of book experiences have several implications for the academic study of religion. Much discussion has focused recently on material aspects of religious practice, and also on the common tendency by devout people to deny the importance of material things. This tendency was called "dematerialization" by Birgit Meyer and Dick Houtman (2012, 8): "Dematerialization refers to a semiotic operation that downplays or overlooks (usually one's own) materiality, placing it in opposition to spirituality and establishing the antagonism between religion and things." The foregoing considerations show how books encourage such thinking, because books tend to dematerialize themselves in the reading experience of their readers.

That observation raises some questions for the academic study of religions: Does the experience of reading actually generate religious tendencies towards dematerialization? Has the rise of mass literacy been an important stimulus to the popularity of these religious beliefs? It is the case that encountering many books and the routine reading of texts is a common experience only in modern cultures of mass literacy. Such experiences used to be reserved for the scribal elite, though more people routinely encountered iconic inscriptions, whether they could read them or not.

It is tempting, therefore, to speculate about the effects of literacy and reading on the growth and spread of more transcendent and utopian forms of religious beliefs. Of course, examples evoke counter-examples: if we ask whether the famous antipathy of Protestants to material religious practices (emphasized by, among many others, Meyer and Houtman 2012, 9, 13) was a byproduct of their emphasis on Bible reading and expository preaching as the quintessential spiritual practices, we must also wonder why the centrality of textual interpretation in Jewish tradition did not lead to the same degree of dichotomization of body and spirit in religious practice. Such examples and counter-examples can be multiplied many times. It must therefore remain an open question as to whether books and other written texts merely represent human hopes by analogy, or whether their every-day use actually encourages people to hope for such experiences.

These observations about the religious impact of book practices have another consequence for religious studies. They bring the study of human beliefs in immaterial spirits, in incarnation and resurrection, and in theophanic experiences of transcendence firmly into the sphere of human interactions with human artifacts. Religious experience has engendered considerably controversy over whether and how it can be studied in an academically rigorous manner. However, in the case of books, there can be no question of inaccessible private experiences beyond the reach of public academic investigation. The study of book rituals can therefore serve to advance research on some fundamental issues in religious studies that often founder on the inaccessibility of religious experience to public study and discourse. Book rituals engage immateriality, incarnation and transcendence in the normal, and thoroughly human, uses of textual artifacts. Ritualizing books therefore makes these experiences readily available for scholarly analysis.

We equate books with human bodies and divine beings because we think of them as containers of ideas. Since it is obvious that those ideas can spread from any one material book to find their way both into other books and into human minds, we grant books agency like people and gods. Our experiences with books mirror our hopes for immaterial existence, for resurrection or reincarnation in other bodies, and for theophanic experiences of transcendence. What in other contexts would be described as religious experiences emerge here from the ordinary use of common artifacts: Books.

References

Broo, Måns. 2010. "Rites of Burial and Immersion: Hindu Ritual Practices on Disposing of Sacred Texts in Vrindavan." In *The Death of Sacred Texts: Ritual Disposal and Renovation of Texts in World Religions*, edited by K. Myrvold, 91–106. London: Ashgate. https://doi.org/10.4324/9781315615318

Cain, Sian. 2016. "Rare edition of JK Rowling's Beedle the Bard sells for £368,750." *The Guardian*. 13 December. https://www.theguardian.com/books/2016/dec/13/beedle-the-bard-jk-rowling-auction

Cantwell, Cathy. 2012 [2017]. "Seeing, Touching, Holding, and Swallowing Tibetan Buddhist Texts." *Postscripts* 8(1–2): 137–160. https://doi.org/10.1558/post.32531

Emba, Christine. 2017. "Millennials are turning to Harry Potter for meaning. That's a mistake." *Washington Post*. 24 July. http://wapo.st/2gY5LQr?tid=ss_mail&utm_term=.b53a7b06034a

Flood, Alison. 2008. "Rowling's Beedle the Bard revives Harry Potter midnight magic." *The Guardian*. 3 December. https://www.theguardian.com/books/2008/dec/03/harry-potter-beedle

Ganz, David. 2012 [2017]. "Touching Books, Touching Art: Tactile Dimensions of Sacred Books in the Medieval West." *Postscripts* 8.1–2: 81–114. https://doi.org/10.1558/post.32702

Gierzynski, Anthony. 2013. *Harry Potter and the Millennials: Research Methods and the Politics of the Muggle Generation*. Baltimore, MD: Johns Hopkins University Press.

Graham, William A. 1987. *Beyond the Written Word: Oral Aspects of Scripture in the History of Religion*. Cambridge: Cambridge University Press.

Kurtzweil, Ray. 2005. *The Singularity is Near: When Humans Transcend Biology*. London: Duckworth.

Kinnard, Jacob N. 1999. *Imaging Wisdom: Seeing and Knowing in the Art of Indian Buddhism*. Surrey: Curzon.

Lakoff, George and Mark Johnson. 2003. *Metaphors We Live By*. Revised edition. Chicago, IL: University of Chicago Press.

Latour, Bruno. 2005. *Reassembling the Social: An Introduction to Actor-Network-Theory*. Oxford: Oxford University Press. https://doi.org/10.1108/eoi.2008.27.3.307.2

Meyer, Birgit and Dick Houtman. 2012. "Introduction: Material Religion—How Things Matter." In *Things: Religion and the Question of Materiality*, edited by D. Houtman and B. Meyer, 1–23. New York: Fordham University Press. https://doi.org/10.5422/fordham/9780823239450.003.0001

Moerman, D. Max. 2010. "The Death of the Dharma: Buddhist Sutra Burials in Early Medieval Japan." In *The Death of Sacred Texts: Ritual Disposal and Renovation of Texts in World Religions*, edited by K. Myrvold, 71–90. London: Ashgate. https://doi.org/10.4324/9781315615318

Myrvold, Kristina. 2010. "Making the Scripture a Person: Reinventing Death Rituals of Guru Granth Sahib in Sikhism." In *The Death of Sacred Texts: Ritual*

Disposal and Renovation of Texts in World Religions, edited by K. Myrvold, 125–146. London: Ashgate. https://doi.org/10.4324/9781315615318

Parmenter, Dorina Miller. 2006 [2008]. "The Iconic Book: The Image of the Bible in Early Christian Rituals." *Postscripts* 2(2–3): 160–189. https://doi.org/10.1558/post.v2i2.160

———. 2012 [2017]. "How the Bible Feels: The Christian Bible as Effective and Affective Object." *Postscripts* 8(1–2): 27–38. https://doi.org/10.1558/post.32589

Plate, Brent S. 2010 [2012]. "Looking at Words: the Iconicity of the Page." *Postscripts* 6(1–3): 67–82.

———. 2015. *A History of Religion in 5½ Objects: Bringing the Spiritual to its Senses*. Boston, MA: Beacon.

———. 2012 [2017]. "What the Book Arts Can Teach Us About Sacred Texts: The Aesthetic Dimension of Scripture." *Postscripts* 8(1–2): 5–26. https://doi.org/10.1558/post.32516

———. 2017. *Religion and Film: Cinema and the Re-Creation of the World*. Second Edition. New York: Columbia University Press.

Schleicher, Marianne. 2010. "Accounts of a Dying Scroll: On Jewish Handling of Sacred Texts in Need of Restoration or Disposal." In *The Death of Sacred Texts: Ritual Disposal and Renovation of Texts in World Religions*, edited by K. Myrvold, 11–30. London: Ashgate. https://doi.org/10.4324/9781315615318

Scholastic. 2018. "Harry Potter Wizarding World." https://www.scholastic.com/kids/books/harry-potter/

Svensson, Jonas. 2020. "Ritualising Muslim Iconic Texts." In *The Oxford Handbook of Ritual and Theology*, edited by S. Balentine. Oxford: Oxford University Press.

Watts, James. 2006 [2008]. "The Three Dimensions of Scriptures." *Postscripts* 2(2–3): 135–159.

———. 2012 [2017]. "Scripture's Indexical Touch." *Postscripts* 8(1–2): 173–184.

———. 2019. *How and Why Books Matter: Essays on the Social Function of Iconic Texts*. Sheffield: Equinox.

Wilkens, Katharina. 2012 [2017]. "Infusions and Fumigations: Literacy Ideologies and Therapeutic Aspects of the Qur'an." *Postscripts* 8.1-2: 115–136. https://doi.org/10.1558/post.32508

Wolfson, Elliot R. 2004. "Iconicity of the Text: Reification of Torah and the Idolatrous Impulse of Zoharic Kabbalah." *Jewish Studies Quarterly* 11: 215–242. https://doi.org/10.1628/0944570043028437

Yoo, Yohan. 2012 [2017]. "Neo-Confucian Sensory Readings of Scriptures: The Reading Methods of Chu Hsi and Yi Hwang." *Postscripts* 8(1–2): 161–172. https://doi.org/10.1558/post.32267

Indices

AUTHOR INDEX

A

Abdullaah, Abu: 40, 47
Al-Munajjid, Muhammand Saalih: 40, 47
Allon, Mark: 100–102, 109
Althaus, Paul: 55, 63
An, Sanggyeong: 12–19, 23
Anderson, Brad: 4
Antonius: 85–87
Appadurai, Arjun: 97, 109
Appleton, Naomi: 104, 109
Assmann, Jan: 80, 81
Athanasius: 88, 95

B

Bainton, Roland H.: 55–56, 63
Balouch, Asif: 27, 33
Baums, Stefan: 97, 102–103, 109
Beal, Samuel: 104, 109
Bell, Catherine: 10, 23, 38, 47
Belting, Hans: 52, 63
Bennett, Jane: 44, 47, 96
Berglund, Jenny: 29–30, 33
Bielo, James S.: 38, 47, 59, 63
Black, Carolyn: 88, 95
Bloom, Rebecca: 112
Blunt, Katherine: 61, 63
Bowley, Graham: 42, 49
Boyle, Helen N.: 30, 33
Braarvig, Jens: 101, 109

Bradbury, Ray: 37, 50
Broo, Måns: 2, 6, 137, 148
Brooks, Douglas Renfrew: 69, 81
Brough, John: 100, 109
Brown, Bill: 84, 95
Brown, C. Mackenzie: 3, 6
Brown, Michelle P.: 53, 63
Brown, Robert L.: 104, 107, 109
Burrus, Virginia: 1, 5, 141

C

Cain, Sian: 37, 47, 145, 148
Calvin, John: 56–59, 63
Campany, Robert Ford: 97, 110
Cancik, Hubert: 25, 33
Cantwell, Cathy: 144, 148
Carr, Kevin Gray: 112
Castelli, Elizabeth A.: 88, 95
Chavannes, Édouard: 104, 110
Chen, Jingyuan: 130
Clivaz, Claire: 37, 47
Coburn, Thomas B.: 69, 81
Collins, Steven: 104, 110
Connolly, William E.: 44, 46, 47
Cox, Collett: 103, 110

D

Daly, Jim: 51, 53, 60, 62, 63–64
Davidson, Ronald M.: 68–69, 81
Deeg, Max: 107–108, 110
Dilley, Paul: 37, 47

Doran, Robert: 85, 95
Drewes, David: 98, 110
Drinkwater, Doug: 39, 47

E

Economist, The: 41, 47
Eickelman, Dale F.: 27, 33
Eisenstein, Elizabeth L.: 55, 64
Emba, Christine: 143, 148
Engelke, Matthew: 58–59, 61–62, 64

F

Falk, Harry: 100–102, 110
Flood, Alison: 37, 47, 145, 148
Flood, Gavin: 67–70, 80–81
Focus on the Family: 51, 53, 63
Foucher, Alfred: 104, 108, 111
Fussman, Gérard: 97, 111

G

Ganz, David: 53, 64, 144, 148
Ge, Hong: 116–117, 133
Germano, David: 98, 111
Gierzynski, Anthony: 143, 148
Glass, Andrew: 97, 109
Goudriaan, Teun: 69, 81
Graham, William A.: 2, 6, 28–29, 33, 38, 47, 54, 64, 143, 148
Gril, Denis: 26, 33
Gross, Steffen W.: 25, 33
Gu, Junghoe: 11–12, 15–16, 18, 23
Gupta, Sanjukta: 69, 81

H

Hamidović, David: 37, 47
Han, Jeongdeok: 18, 23
Hanks, Henry: 42, 47
Hardaker, Glenn: 30, 33
Hardy, Daniel W.: 56, 64
Harper, Katherine Anne: 69, 81
Harrison, Paul: 98–99, 109–112
Hartmann, Jens-Uwe: 98–99, 109–113
Haynes, Charles C.: 53, 64
Hefner, Robert W.: 27, 33
Heidegger, Martin: 84, 95

Heyman, George: 1, 6
Hill, Leslie: 92, 95
Holcombe, Madeline: 43, 48
Hornbacher, Annette: 26, 33
Hoskins, Janet: 44, 48
Houtman, Dick: 146–148
Humfress, Caroline: 52, 64
Hutchings, Tim: 38, 48

I

Ibn Adam, Muhammad: 49, 48
Ingram, Matthew: 37, 48
Islām, Kāzī Nazru: 78–79, 81

J

Jang, Inseong: 12, 16. 23
Joby, Christopher Richard: 56, 64
Johnson, Dominic: 91, 95
Johnson, Mark: 139, 148
Jones, Amelia: 90, 91, 95
Jones, Emily: 53, 60, 64
Jun, Ha Nul: 112

K

Kamitsuka Yoshiko: 115, 120, 133
Kapoor, Desh: 2, 6
Karashima, Seishi: 101–102, 110
Kaurin, Gregory S.: 56, 64
Keane, Webb: 26, 34, 48
Kermani, Navid: 25, 28–29, 34
Kieschnick, John: 97, 111
Kim, Jihyun: 6, 115, 125, 131, 133–134, 137
Kim, Yeongjin: 12–15, 19, 23
Kinnard, Jacob N.: 3, 6, 137, 148
Kobayashi Masayoshi: 115, 134
Koerner, Joseph Leo: 56, 65
Kripal, Jeffrey J.: 67, 82
Kugel, James L.: 16, 23
Kurtzweil, Ray: 139, 148
Kusuyama Haruki: 116, 134

L

Lakoff, George: 139, 148
Latour, Bruno: 44, 48, 138, 148

Author Index

Launay, Robert: 26–28, 30, 34
Le Miere, Jason: 43, 48
legitsadierob: 53, 60, 65
Lenz, Timothy: 100, 103–106, 111
Levenson, Eric: 40, 48
Levy, Gabrielle: 41, 48
Lewis, Todd: 105, 111
Li Rongxi: 104, 107–108, 112
Lietzmann, H.: 85, 96
Lim, Seungbeom: 12, 15, 20, 23
Lindsell, Harold: 57–58, 65
Lopez Jr., Donald S.: 112
Lopez, Donald S.: 108, 112
Lowden, John: 53, 65

M

Malley, Brian: 38, 48, 53, 57, 59, 65
Marty, Martin: 52, 55, 57–58, 65
Mathews, Thomas: 52, 65
Matsuda, Kazunobu: 101, 112
Matsuura Akira: 129, 134
McCann, Erin: 41, 48
McDermott, Rachel Fell: 4–5, 67, 70, 72, 74–78, 81–82, 137
McGann, Jerome: 37, 49
McGrath, Alister E.: 57, 65
Meyer, Birgit: 146–148
Michalski, Sergiusz: 56–57, 65
Moebus, Oliver: 27, 35
Moerman, Max D.: 2, 7, 137, 148
Mohr, Hubert: 25, 33
Mugitani Kunio: 122, 134
Myrvold, Kristina: 2, 6–7, 40, 50, 66, 137, 148–149

N

Najafizada, Enayat: 42, 49
Neelis, Jason: 5, 97, 99, 104, 112
Nemitz, Barbara: 86–87, 96
Nieber, Hanna: 32, 34
Nordland, Rod: 42, 49

O

O'Regan, Mark: 41, 49
Ōfuchi Ninji: 115, 134
Oh, Munseon : 17, 19–20, 23
Onasch, Konrad: 52, 65
Orlan: 92, 95
Orzech, Charles: 80, 82
Osteen, Joel: 61, 65
Oster, Marcy: 42, 49

P

Padoux, André: 69, 81
Paris, Helen: 91, 95
Park, Hyejeong: 12–15, 19, 23
Park, Jong-ik: 17, 20, 23
Parker, David: 38, 49
Parmenter, Dorina Miller: 2–4, 7, 38, 42, 49, 52–53, 65–66, 137, 144–145, 149
Patton, C. Kimberley: 19, 23
Peers, Glenn: 84, 93–94, 96
Perho, Irmeli: 25, 34
Peters, F. E.: 10, 23
Pierce, C. S.: 61
Plate, S. Brent Rodriguez: 43, 49, 138, 141, 144, 149
Posner, Menachem: 40, 49
Preda, Alex: 44, 49
Pregadio, Fabrizio: 118, 134
Promey, Sally M.: 25, 34

R

Rambelli, Fabio: 97, 112
Rāmprasād Sen: 72–74, 76–77
Rao, Padmanabha T.: 2, 7
Rawson, Philip: 71, 82
Richards, Erin: 60, 66
Robinet, Isabelle: 115, 134
Rodriguez, Salvador: 40, 49
Rotman, Andy: 97, 112
Rowling, J. K.: 142, 145, 148
Rubin, Alissa J.: 42, 49

S

Sabki, Aishah Ahmad: 30, 33
Salomon, Richard: 99–106, 109, 112
Samuel, Geoffrey: 69, 82
Savali, Kirsten West: 41, 49

Scheer, Monique: 29, 34
Schipper, Kristofer: 15–16, 24, 115, 117, 132, 134
Schleicher, Marianne: 2, 7, 137, 149
Schnieper, Annemarie: 52, 65
Scholastic: 142, 149
Schopen, Gregory: 97, 98, 113
Seidel, Anna: 116, 128, 134–135
Seo, Daeseok: 17, 24
Shaw, Sarah: 104, 109
Shinohara, Koichi: 105, 113
Siebers, Tobin: 84, 96
Sinopoli, Carla M.: 112
Skilling, Peter: 98, 113
Slouber, Michael: 69, 82
Smith, Jonathan Z.: 49
Smith, Wilfred Cantwell: 38, 49
Stargardt, Janice: 98, 113
Steiner, Shannon: 95, 96
Stephens, W. P.: 57, 66
Strauch, Ingo: 100–102, 110, 113
Strauss, Valerie: 51, 66
Strong, John: 98, 114
Stuart, John: 52, 66
Suit, Natalia K.: 3, 7, 25, 32, 34, 40, 46, 50
Supińska-Polit, Edyta: 86, 96
Svensson, Jonas: 26–27, 32, 34, 139, 149

T

Ter Borg, M. B.: 1, 7
Theodoret: 85
Tournier, Vincent: 106, 114
Trainor, Kevin: 98, 111, 114

V

Velten, Hans Rudolf: 1, 7, 141
Verellen, Franciscus: 15, 16, 24, 117, 132, 134

W

Waghorne, Joanne Punzo: 3
Walter, Christopher: 52, 53, 66
Wang, Chegwen: 115, 118, 120, 127, 129, 135
Ware III, Rudolph T.: 26, 28, 33, 34
Warr, Tracey: 86–87, 89, 91, 96
Watts, James W.: 1, 7, 10, 16, 18, 24, 38–39, 46, 50, 60–62, 66, 83–84, 96, 99, 138, 140–141, 145, 149
Weller, Sam: 37, 50
Westin, Jonathan: 43–46, 50
White, David Gordon: 68–69, 82
Wilke, Annette: 88–90, 95
Wilkens, Katharina: 4, 7, 25, 27, 30, 35, 137, 144, 149
Willis, Michael: 98, 113, 114
Wilson, Derek: 54, 66
Wimbush, Vincent L.: 16, 24, 96
Wolfson, Elliot R.: 2, 7, 137, 149
Woodroffe, Sir John.: 81, 82

Y

Yelle, Robert.: 26, 30, 35
Yi, Neunghwa: 12, 24
Yokota, Keiko: 112
Yoo, Yohan: 3, 17, 23–24, 98, 143, 149

Z

Zachman, Randall C.: 58, 66
Zadeh, Travis: 32, 35
Zaman, Muhammad Qasim: 27, 33
Zürcher, Erik: 115, 135

Subject Index

A

Abramović, Marina: 91, 95
actants: 46-46
aesthetics: 4, 25-27, 29, 84, 145
agency: 4, 6, 44, 44, 53, 138-139, 145, 147
Aisha: 27
Allah: 3, 30, 32
allegory: 57
amulets: 25, 100
analogy: 2, 131, 140, 143, 147
animist, animistic: 84
anjeungut: 12-14, 16, 18, 20
antaekgut: 13-14
anti-ritualism: 26
Arab, Arabic: 29-32
artifacts: 6, 97, 138, 139, 141, 146, 147
Athey, Ron: 91
aural: 28
austerities: 88
authority: 16, 17, 28, 31, 55, 125, 128
Avadāna: 100, 103-106, 108

B

Baumgarten, Alexander: 25
beauty: 29, 84, 87, 88, 90, 95
beings: 2-3, 9-10, 15-16, 18, 22-23, 46, 52, 54, 69, 70, 87, 97-99, 102, 104, 116-118, 120, 122, 131, 137-140, 143, 145, 147

belief: 1, 16, 32 58-61, 116, 128, 131, 141-144, 146-147
Bengal, Bengali: 4-5, 67-68, 71, 76-78
benwen: 117-118, 122
Bhagavad Gītā: 2-3
bhakti: 5, 67, 80-81
bhutki: 70
Bible: 2, 4, 39, 41-43, 45, 51-62, 147
biblicism: 59, 60, 62
Bodhisattva: 105-108
body, bodies: 1-6, 25-28, 32, 33, 52-53, 57, 61, 62, 67-81, 84-86, 89-93, 95, 97-99, 107, 129, 131-132, 137, 139, 141-143, 145-147
Book of Life: 52
Buddha: 2, 3, 5, 15-16, 22, 97-108, 123, 124, 127
Buddhism, Buddhist: 2, 4, 5, 15-17, 20, 68, 80, 97-108, 115, 117, 118, 123, 124, 127, 128, 137
Buñuel, Luis: 92-93
burning; burn: 2, 41-42, 79
byeonggut: 14, 19
Byzantine: 52, 56, 84, 93

C

cakra: 70-71, 74, 76-80
calligraphy: 25
Calvin, John: 56-59
Cang Jie: 120

canon, canonical: 1, 16, 54, 88, 102, 115–118, 127–128
Cartesian: 26
Catholic: 1, 27, 55, 56
chanting: 28–29, 79, 130, 141, 143
charisma: 1
chengjing: 123, 125
Chinese writing system: 115–116, 119, 123, 132
Christ: 3, 52–59, 144
Christianity, Christian: 2–5, 25–27, 38, 43, 46, 51–62, 83, 93, 137, 143, 144
cinnabar: 116; see talisman
codex: 40, 45–46, 54
commentaries: 38, 99, 102–103, 140, 142
concentration: 97
Confucianism; Confucian: 13, 15–16, 115, 143
contagion: 27
container: 6, 123–125, 139, 143, 146–147
copy: 39, 97
copying: 17, 98, 105, 132, 139
corporeal, corporeality: 26, 84, 130; see also body, bodies
cosmology: 11, 15, 20, 22, 23, 69, 132
cult of the book: 98
cunsi: 130

D

Daniel: 56
Dao: 116, 120, 123, 125, 131–132
Daoism; Daoist: 3, 6, 15–16, 115–132, 137
dematerialization: 54, 146
desecration: 39, 41–43, 46–47
devotion, devotional: 1, 5, 56, 67, 68, 72, 76, 78–80, 93, 97, 99, 140
Dharma: 3, 5, 20, 98–101, 105, 108, 123
digital texts, digitization: 4, 37–47, 146–147
disposal of texts: 2, 40, 137
divinization: 68–69, 80
dokgyeong: 9, 12
dreams: 75, 146

E

Eastern Orthodox Christianity: 54, 62, 144
education: 26–30, 32
Egyptians: 144
eikones: 84
embodiment: 10, 26, 30, 52, 67, 98–99, 142
emotion: 29, 92, 143
encounters: 94, 105–107, 140, 144–146
energy: 6, 70–71, 116, 131, 137
entextualization: 5, 68, 76–77, 79–80
esoteric: 5, 15, 67, 76–78, 80, 137
Esther: 53
Ethan's Story: 61
Eucharist: 57
Evangelical, Evangelicalism;: 4, 51, 53, 56, 59–60
experience: 6, 28–30, 60–61, 71–72, 75, 77, 140–147
expressive: 1, 3, 83, 140, 141, 142, 143

F

Falin: 124
Five Phases: 119, 121–122
Fundamentalists: 58
Funerary rituals: 2

G

Gandhāra, Gandhāran: 5, 97–114
Ge Hong: 116–117
gender: 31, 43
genizah: 100
gods: 2–4, 9–22, 52, 73, 122, 130, 137, 147
goddess: 3, 4–5, 67–81, 130, 137
golden elixir: 116; see talisman
Gongyang: 124
Gospel: 52–55, 60, 143–44
Guru Granth Sahib: 2
guru: 67–68, 76, 81, 140
gurudwara: 2
gut: 12–13, 18, 21
gyeonggaek: 9–10, 12–14, 17–20

Subject Index

H

hāfiz: 28
hagiographies: 5, 72, 83–95, 97, 106, 117
Harry Potter: 142–143, 145
healer, healing: 4, 11, 13, 19–20, 23, 30, 32, 52
hearers: see listeners
Hinduism, Hindu: 2–3, 26–27, 67–80, 137, 143
humiliation: 88
Hyecho: 108

I

icon: 51–52, 54, 56, 58, 62, 104, 108, 140, 144
iconic: 20, 27, 31–33, 51, 97
iconic dimension of books: 1–4, 38–41, 43, 45–47, 51–52, 59–62, 83–84, 99, 103–104, 107–108, 141–142, 144–146
iconoclasm: 54, 56–57
iconography, iconographic: 5, 52, 69, 80, 93, 106
identification: 1, 38, 101, 104
illumination: 25
images: 2–4, 19, 27, 52, 54, 56, 59, 78–79, 97–99, 104, 106, 108, 116, 124, 130–132, 139–140, 144–145
imagination: 132, 141–143
immortality: 91, 131, 143–144
index: 4, 51, 59–62, 138
innovation: 44, 101
inscription: 56, 68, 97, 99–100, 146
interiority: 6, 61, 139
internal, internalization: 4, 57, 76–77, 88
interpretation: 1, 10, 20, 23, 28–29, 38, 55, 57–58, 60, 67, 102, 117, 140–142, 147
Islam; Islamic: 4, 10, 25–35, 38, 40–41, 43, 46, 143

J

Jains: 99
Jātaka: 104–108
jing: 9, 115, 123
Jingyuan, Chen: 130
John of Damascus: 52
Jones, Terry: 41–42
Judaism: 2, 38, 40, 46, 137

K

Kabbalah: 2
Kali: 4, 67–82, 137
karma: 99, 102, 104, 107
Khan, Sadiq: 41
Korean shamanism: 3, 9–24
Kuṇḍalinī yoga: 68, 70–72, 75, 77, 80, 81

L

Lady of Purple Tenuity: 118, 121
Lady Wei: 124
Laozi: 116–117
legitimacy: 15, 39, 52, 59, 60, 62, 128
liberation: 71, 74, 97
limitations: 4, 43, 45–46
listener: 16, 28, 75
literacy: 4, 26–27, 29–33, 80, 146–147
liturgy; liturgical: 29, 53–54, 60, 117, 125, 131
Logos: 54
Long, Eddie: 42
Lord Su: 124
Lou Huiming: 128
Luther, Martin: 54–58
Luzu: 128–129

M

macrocosm: 5, 68–69, 71, 137
madrasas: 27, 30, 32
magic: 26, 31, 127, 142–143
Mahāyāna sūtras: 98
maṇḍala: 69
manifestations: 32, 52, 69, 107, 150
mantras: 3, 69, 75, 78, 79, 130
manuscripts: 17, 98–104, 108, 124, 128, 140, 144

material books: 1, 3–4, 6, 25, 29, 30–32, 37–39, 41, 43, 45–46, 58–60, 62, 139, 141, 143–147
material objects: 45, 51–58, 62, 86, 97–99, 140
material turn: 4, 26
materiality: 4, 25–26, 32, 41, 46, 83, 85, 146
materialization; materialize: 10–11, 16–20, 22–23
Mecca: 29
media: 4, 64, 84–85, 93, 99, 108, 115–116, 138–140, 143
   digital: 39, 44,
   social: 51, 61
mediation: 1, 2, 5, 84, 91, 93, 94
mediator: 13, 52, 59–60, 140
medicine: 25, 30–33
memorization: 1, 4, 12, 17–18, 27–30, 32–33, 80, 137, 141, 143
memory: 80, 142
Messer, Ralph: 42
metaphor: 4, 57, 139
microcosm: 5, 68–69
mind: 26–27, 30, 75–78, 131, 139–141, 143–145, 147
modernization, modernity: 17, 26, 30
Mohammed: 4, 27
monstrosity: 87
mortality: 88, 91, 131
mukti: 70
Murak, Teresa: 86–87
muṣḥaf: 25–28, 32–33, 40
myths: 52, 117, 119

N

narratives: 5, 29, 56, 83, 93, 99–100, 102–108
New Testament: 54
Nicephorus: 52

O

oath: 39–41, 43, 45, 126
Obama, Barack: 41–42

oral, orally: 1, 17, 26, 28, 55, 58, 99, 103, 108, 115, 143
original writs: 116–118, 120, 132
otherworldly: 14, 91

P

Pāli: 97–99, 101, 104, 106
Pane, Gina: 87–88
paper banners: 3, 11–12, 14, 18, 19–20, 22
paper figures: 10, 11–12, 14, 18, 19–20, 22–23
Perfection of Wisdom sūtra: 3, 97, 101–102
performance art: 5, 83–95
performative: 1, 5, 10, 38, 60, 83–85, 92–95, 97, 99, 103–104, 140–141, 143
pilgrim: 5, 93, 95
pilgrimage: 5, 29, 76–77, 94, 108, 140
pneuma: 116, 120–123, 128–132
portrait: 51–52, 60, 90–91
power: 9–10, 14–17, 19–20, 22, 30, 39, 43, 52–56, 60, 62, 68–72, 76, 78, 80, 84, 87, 91, 116, 121–122, 127–128, 131, 138, 142, 144
Prajñāpāramitā: see Perfection of Wisdom sūtra
Prātimokṣa: 102
previous births: 99, 105, 107–108
proclamation: 10, 14, 19, 56
protest: 39, 41–43, 47
Protestants: 4, 51–66, 147
Puranas: 3, 69
purification: 5, 14, 40, 69, 125–126
purity: 14, 33, 40, 68
Pūrvayoga : 100, 103–106, 108

Q

qi: 6, 116, 120, 122, 128–132
quasi-objects: 44
Qur'an; Qur'anic: 2, 4, 6, 25–35

R

Rāmprasād Sen: 72–74, 76–77

Subject Index

re-enactments: 84, 104, 107
readers: 5, 16, 37, 55, 59, 75, 87, 131, 141–143, 146
rebirth: see reincarnations
recitation: 3, 9–22, 25, 29, 32, 38, 97, 104, 115, 126–127, 130–131, 141, 143
reincarnations: 6, 91, 99, 104, 106–108, 139, 144, 146, 147
relic: 2, 5, 84, 97–101, 105, 107–108, 140, 145
religious commodities: 97
religious communities: 59, 69, 97, 140–141, 145
repetition: 16, 26, 29, 75, 79, 91
resurrection: 6, 55, 143–147
reveal, revelation: 2, 15, 19, 27, 52, 55, 57–58, 69, 116–118, 120, 123, 127–128
rhetoric: 1, 3, 4, 38, 51, 53, 59, 138–140
ritualization: 1–4, 10–11, 20, 22–23, 38, 40, 43, 67, 83, 97, 140–147
ruqya: 31

S

sacraments; sacramental: 53–54, 56–57, 62
sacred: 10, 57, 60
  beings: 1, 3 17, 38, 48, 53–54, 62, 67, 69, 99, 104, 116, 138
  books/texts: 1–6, 10–11, 16, 19, 22–23, 26–30, 33, 36–46, 52–53, 58, 60, 62, 71, 123–124, 137, 140–141, 145–146
  geography: 69, 93, 105
  images: 28
  knowledge: 13
sacrifice: 2, 57, 79, 80, 108
saint: 5, 83–96
Sainte Orlan: 91
Saints' Lives: 83–96
Śakti: 73–74
Sangha: 123
Sanskrit: 67, 69, 76, 101, 104–105, 137
scriptures:
  definitions: 38–39, 60, 115, 145

ritualizing: 1–4, 11, 17, 38, 60, 145
scripturality: 26
scrolls: 42, 45, 46, 99–101, 103–104, 106, 108, 126, 139
sculptures: 89, 99
Second Council of Nicaea: 52
secularization: 4, 26, 30, 59
semantic: 1, 4, 20, 26–27, 29–31, 38–39, 46, 60, 83–84, 99, 101, 104, 140–143
senses: 74, 78, 92, 130, 141, 144
sensual: 25–26, 28, 29
seolwi-seolgyeong: 9–24
seolwi: 10–11, 19–21
sexual rites: 68
shamanistic rituals: 3, 9, 11, 22
shamans: 9–24
shi: 118, 123
Shizheng, Pan: 120
signs: 26, 62, 127–128, 140–141, 143, 146
Sikhs: 2, 137
silsila: 28
Simeon the Stylite: 85–87, 92–94
singing: 1, 38, 72, 79, 83, 141, 143
Śiva: 69–71, 73–75, 79
social engagement: 41, 43
somatic: 27, 29, 31–33
sonic: 27–29, 32
souls: 141, 143
spirit: 57, 131, 141, 143, 146–147
spirits: 13, 56, 127
  evil: 9–12, 14–20, 22–23, 116, 129, 131
spiritual: 3, 5, 30, 67, 69–71, 74, 77–79, 146–147
stūpas: 2, 98–101, 107–108
subjects, subjectivity: 19, 44, 69, 80
superstition: 30
suṣumnā: 70
Śyāmā Saṅgīt: 72–73, 78
symbol, symbolism: 3, 16, 19, 39, 42, 55, 57, 80, 88, 97
Syncletica: 88–90

T

Taharah: 40
talismans, talismanic: 15, 41–43, 47, 116–117, 119, 123–124, 126, 129, 131
Tantra: 67–81
testimonial: 51, 60
theophany: 6, 140, 144–145
thingly: 5, 84–85, 93–95
Three Caverns: 116–117, 122
Three Powers: 116, 121–122
Torah: 2, 6, 40, 42, 143
transcendence: 2–3, 6, 22, 57, 129–130, 140, 145–147
translations: 32, 43–46, 59, 142–143
transubstantiation: 57
Trump, Donald: 41

U

Upanisadic: 69

V

values: 44–46, 60–62, 91, 97
Vedas, Vedic: 68, 143
veneration: 3, 54, 79, 98, 111, 116, 123–124, 126, 143
Vinaya: 102
visual: 1, 5, 20, 43, 54, 56, 59–60, 71, 83–85, 92–95, 97–100, 102, 104, 106–108, 141, 143–144
visualization: 17, 19–20, 22, 125, 130–132

W

Wenming, Song: 117, 121
Wilke, Hannah: 88–90
women: 31, 89–90

X

Xiujing, Liu: 116–117, 121–122, 125

Y

Yang Xi: 123–124, 128
Yin and Yang: 118–119, 122

Z

Zadamitra: 105
Ziliang, Zhou: 123
Zwingli, Ulrich: 56–57, 59

www.ingramcontent.com/pod-product-compliance
Lightning Source LLC
Chambersburg PA
CBHW042117300426
44117CB00020B/2970